I0414814

The Red-Green Axis 2.0:
An Existential Threat
to America and the World

THE RED-GREEN AXIS 2.0

An Existential Threat
to America and the World

By

JAMES SIMPSON

Center for Security Policy Press

This book may be reproduced, distributed and
transmitted for personal and non-commercial use.
Contact the Center for Security Policy
for bulk order information.

For more information about this book, visit
SECUREFREEDOM.ORG

The Red-Green Axis 2.0:
An Existential Threat to America and the World
is published in the United States
by the Center for Security Policy Press,
a division of the Center for Security Policy.

ISBN 9781070931401

The Center for Security Policy
Washington, D.C.
Phone: 202-835-9077
Email: info@SecureFreedom.org
For more information, visit SecureFreedom.org

Inner design by Bravura Books

CONTENTS

FOREWORD

The original edition of *The Red-Green Axis: Refugees, Immigration and the Agenda to Erase America*, published by the Center for Security Policy Press in July 2015, provided a detailed and carefully documented examination of the networks of hard-left foundations, government agencies and non-profit organizations involved in the immigration and refugee resettlement business. And "business" it is—a big and massively funded business, at that.

As author James Simpson revealed in that monograph—including through a series of charts and graphs packed with data—this network has enabled massive numbers of third-world immigrants to be able to enter and reside in the United States, in the process impacting the nation's demographics, laws, national character, and the very foundational principles on which our Republic was established. Among these waves of newcomers have been many from Muslim countries with a tradition of sharia-supremacism who have no inclination to assimilate but every incentive to take advantage of America's generous system of welfare benefits. Some, particularly from among Somali expatriate communities, have even turned America into a wellspring for jihadism, with some of its recruits becoming suicide bombers overseas.

The Center is pleased now to present Jim Simpson's follow-on study, *The Red-Green Axis 2.0: An Existential Threat to America and the World*. This monograph explores the identity and ambitions of the forces behind these networks. He describes them as the "Red" and the "Green"—two factions that are joined temporarily in a mutually opportunistic alliance to overwhelm, corrupt, and collapse our system.

The "Red" part of this unlikely and unholy alliance are the communists, Marxists, and socialists who not only increasingly define the left in America but have, for all intents and purposes, taken over the Democratic Party. The "Green" (a color that holds particular symbolism in Islam) refers to the forces of the global Islamic Jihad, whose U.S. vanguard is the Muslim Brotherhood and its political umbrella group, the U.S. Council of Muslim Organizations (USCMO).

The Red-Green Axis is strategic, as well as opportunistic. It takes advantage of and melds the cultural factors, strengths, and tactics of both of its core ideological elements. For example, as Simpson notes, "...The Council on American Islamic Relations (CAIR) now supports Black Lives Matter (BLM) and participates in its protests. The American Civil Liberties Union (ACLU) and the Southern Poverty Law Center (SPLC) also work with BLM, CAIR, and open borders groups."

The evolving Red-Green axis' impact on the fabric of American life has been, as intended, nothing less than devastating. Government budgets, facilities and personnel at every level are overwhelmed—financially, in the courts and schools, at our hospitals and clinics, and on the streets where local law enforcement struggles to cope with the onslaught of criminality, including the wave of unfamiliar sharia crimes like domestic abuse, Female Genital Mutilation, and honor killings.

As if these manifestations of the Red-Green agenda were not sufficiently ominous, they are generally accompanied by rhetorical attacks aimed at silencing and suppressing—if not actually *destroying*—anyone who opposes that agenda. Defamatory charges of "Islamophobia," "racism," and "bigotry" are typically leveled by self-appointed arbiters for the purpose of obscuring their assaults on the founding vision and core institutions of our constitutional republic.

We know where such behavior takes us. Freedom of speech here in the United States is increasingly facing the sorts of compulsions to self-censorship and even outright restrictions on expression now operating in Europe—where speaking truth about migrants or sharia can land a citizen in court, or even jail. This coercive program is very much choreographed among the Red-Green players, who seem ever more brazen in their supremacist programs, exhibiting overtly antisemitic, communist, and globalist proclivities and otherwise working for the destruction of the Westphalian nation-state system and of Western civilization overall.

In this new volume, investigative reporter, public speaker, and freedom-fighter Jim Simpson delves deeply into such phenomena. He identifies the key players and their goals, their allies, and the funders that are behind the existential threat posed to the very fabric of our American society by barely vetted, poorly managed and largely unchecked volumes of immigration—especially in the absence of any requirement that its beneficiaries assimilate and be self-sufficient.

With the publication of *The Red-Green Axis 2.0: An Existential Threat to America and the World*, the Center hopes that everyday American citizens will become better informed and ultimately more engaged in the civic processes of our nation. If so, there will likely be more responsible leadership at every governmental level—from the local to the state and federal—as elected officials are obliged to address *and counter* the forces deeply inimical to the character of this Judeo-Christian-based constitutional Republic that are working hand-in-glove, day-in-and-day-out to suborn, subvert and destroy the America we know and love.

Frank J. Gaffney, Jr.
Executive Chairman
Center for Security Policy
May 4, 2019

INTRODUCTION

The Red-Green Axis is a collusion between the Democratic Party, American Communists, Socialists and other brands of "progressives", *i.e.,* the Red, and the forces of the Islamic jihad, the Green—so named because the color green carries much symbolism in Islam, and most Muslim nations feature green in flags, emblems, and other identifiers. Its collective goal is to alter and undermine our national character, traditions, and laws so much that it can overthrow our Constitutional republican form of government without firing a shot.

The alliance allows each to take advantage of the tactics, strategies, and cultural features of the other, and mobilizes a vastly larger number of people. For example, the Council on American-Islamic Relations (CAIR) now supports Black Lives Matter (BLM) and participates in its protests. The American Civil Liberties Union (ACLU) and the Southern Poverty Law Center (SPLC) also work with BLM, CAIR, and open borders groups.

Immigration is one of the Red-Green Axis's most effective tools. Under the banner of "compassion," it advocates for open borders and endless waves of refugees, asylum seekers, and other third-world immigrants to stress government budgets at all levels, overburden communities with medical, language, crime, welfare, and other burdens, while rhetorically and sometimes physically attacking those who object, calling opponents "racists," "bigots," "xenophobes," and the latest innovation, "Islamophobes."

None of the Axis claims has any basis in reality. There are, and always will be racists, bigots, etc., but they are usually not the ones being targeted. The Left's purpose is to vilify, marginalize and ultimately destroy anyone who challenges *any aspect* of its agenda, and it focuses its venom primarily on such people and groups. Since the election of President Trump in 2016, the violent left, represented by groups like Antifa as well as openly antisemitic and socialist elements of the Democratic Party (dominated by the Democratic Socialists of America-DSA), has become the increasingly ugly public face of the Axis.

It is fair to say that immigration is among the top issues threatening America today. Following the election of Donald Trump, the Left revealed the true magnitude of its interest in this issue with the unprecedented tidal wave of opposition it has erected to block all aspects of the Trump immigration agenda. It is unprecedented and truly frightening in its flagrant defiance of a duly elected president and utter disregard for our nation's laws and Constitution—especially from blatantly partisan jurists and political leaders. They have literally fomented a constitutional crisis.

This crisis is much further along in Europe and is a canary in the coal mine that we ignore at our mortal peril. Hungarian Prime Minister Viktor Orbán summarized it well in a 2016 speech, quoted in part below:

> Europe is not free. Because freedom begins with speaking the truth. Today in Europe it is forbidden to speak the truth. Even if it is made of silk, a muzzle is a muzzle. It is forbidden to say that those arriving are not refugees, but that Europe is threatened by migration. It is forbidden to say that tens of millions are ready to set out in our direction. It is forbidden to say that immigration brings crime and terror to our countries. It is forbidden to point out that the masses arriving from other civilizations endanger our way of life, our culture, our customs and our Christian traditions. It is forbidden to point out that those who arrived earlier have already built up their own new, separate world for themselves, with its own laws and ideals, which is forcing apart the thousand-year-old structure of Europe. It is forbidden to point out that this is not an accidental and unintentional chain of consequences, but a preplanned and orchestrated operation; a mass of people directed towards us. It is forbidden to say that in Brussels they are concocting schemes to transport foreigners here as quickly as possible and to settle them here among us. It is forbidden to point out that the purpose of settling people here is to reshape the religious and cultural landscape of Europe, and to reengineer its ethnic foundations—thereby eliminating the last barrier to internationalism: the nation-states. It is forbidden to say that Brussels is now stealthily devouring more and more slices of our national sovereignty, and that in Brussels many are now making a plan for a United States of Europe—for which no one has ever given authorization.[1]

In pursuing an open borders agenda, the leftwing true believers' towering arrogance is only matched, or perhaps exceeded, by their ignorance. For they seem not to be aware that the fifty-plus year effort to overwhelm our nation with populations indifferent or hostile to the concepts, institutions, and legal framework that have made our country the greatest in the world, is a strategy pursued by their fellow leftists to undermine and ultimately destroy it. America is the last hope against a worldwide movement bent on totalitarian control. If successful, they will throw the world into an economic and societal cataclysm worse than any in history, and most of them won't survive.

When I sat down to write the first edition of The Red-Green Axis, my charge was to produce a 2,500-word report detailing the refugee resettlement program, its funding, and agenda. But that was nowhere near enough to describe the depth, breadth, and sheer complexity of this multi-agency goliath and its pernicious agenda. When I finally finished, the piece was ten times that size.

Even that wasn't enough, and over the few years since, more and more has been revealed. This has been a slow process. To catalog the issues immigrants and refugees create is overwhelming, even though the evidence is right before our eyes. For example, accurate data on individuals we allow to immigrate is obscured once they are here. Media and government seek to hide, rather than expose immigration status when these people commit crimes. It doesn't jibe with the "diversity is our strength" mantra. They have to really distinguish themselves with some heinous act to warrant mention.

Here's one who did—but even then, it wasn't the media that uncovered the truth. On Halloween day in 2017, we were treated to the spectacle of Uzbek immigrant Sayfullo Saipov murdering eight and wounding twelve people by running them down with a truck on the walkway bordering New York City's West Side Highway. The next morning, President Trump tweeted that Saipov was a Diversity Visa lottery winner. Trump also correctly identified Democratic New York Senator Chuck Schumer as a co-sponsor of the 1990 Immigration Act, which codified the Diversity Visa and many other bad additions to immigration law.

Saipov was inspired by Islamic State (IS) guidance to use vehicles as weapons in imitation of the 2016 Nice, France, Bastille Day attack, where a Tunisian truck driver mowed down pedestrians, murdering 86, including 10 children, and injuring another 458.[2] Saipov said he wanted to kill as many people as possible. He asked to hang an IS flag in his hospital room.[3] But without the Trump tweet, it would have been a while before the truth about this migrant surfaced. [Note: the more familiar acronym ISIS, *i.e.,* Islamic State in Iraq and al-Sham, changed its name to simply Islamic State in June 2014 to mark its expansion beyond its original territory of origin; it has been IS ever since.]

Under President Trump's administration, information has been more forthcoming. During the Obama administration, it was practically impossible to learn the immigration status of foreigners who committed crimes or acts of terrorism. Refugee agencies and media relentlessly claimed that "no refugee has ever been involved in terrorism." In the last few years we have had a number of notable examples of terrorist refugees, so then they said "no one has ever been killed by a refugee." That is false, but the short casualty list wasn't for lack of trying. Here are some of the more notable refugee attacks in the past few years:

- November 2012, Abdullatif Ali Aldosary — murdered fellow employee, bombed Asocial security office;[4]
- April 2013, Dzhokhar and Tamerlan Tsarnaev — Boston Marathon Bombers, killed four and wounded hundreds;
- November 2016, Abdul Razak Ali Artan — launched car and knife attack at Ohio State University, wounding 11. Killed by police;[5]
- September 2016, Ahmad Khan Rahami — injured 31 in bombings in New York and New Jersey;[6]
- September 2016, Dahir Adan — 9 injured in Minnesota mall knife attack; Adan shot by off-duty policeman.[7]

Many more refugees have attempted to commit terrorist acts but were caught first. The Heritage Foundation compiled a meticulous list of FBI-confirmed post-9/11 terror plots and attacks, now numbering 104. [8] Following the election of President Trump, news blackouts on refugee terrorism were lifted. Federal law enforcement officials revealed that 300 refugees were the subject of terrorism investigations, as part of a larger group of 1,000 that were under suspicion.[9]

This second edition of the Red-Green Axis delves deeply into the immigration/refugee resettlement issue to catalog not only the breadth and depth of the program and its supporters, but to expose the massive problems and cultural changes that have been created, I believe deliberately, as the key element in the Axis agenda to erase America as we know it.

DIVERSITY IS NOT OUR STRENGTH

"The problem with Ireland? It's 'Too Irish'"—Michael Walsh

T hat introductory quote sums up in one sentence the views of leftwing elites toward Western nations. To paraphrase, "The problem with America? It's too White." This rhetorical attack on traditional America is now a regular feature in the media, in protests by Antifa, Black Lives Matter, and other hard Left groups, and on college campuses. Many colleges now require training for teachers and students on "White Privilege," a concept created and promoted in the late 1960s by a member of the most hard-core branch of the Communist Party USA.[10] On December 24, 2016, Drexel University professor George Chiccariello tweeted, "All I Want for Christmas is White Genocide."[11]

This is the logical endpoint to the "Diversity is Our Strength," narrative that has become a cause célèbre and tiresome slogan among the liberal establishment. But is diversity really our strength? Anyone who has to deal with our increasingly "diverse" society up close knows it isn't. It is a major weakness. In fact, it is creating major crises as wave after wave of third-world immigrants flood American communities nationwide. Even setting aside the toxic cultural differences among the many diverse populations, the day-to-day problems of dealing with them are overwhelming our institutions and state and local government budgets.

There are now over 400 languages spoken in the U.S.[12] Courts, first responders, teachers and the community must deal with languages from every corner of the globe, including many unknown languages like Kirundi (from Burundi), Dzonkha (from Bhutan), Cushitic (spoken in parts of Kenya, Tanzania, and the Sudan), Amharic (from Ethiopia), and other heretofore unknown dialects.[13] Some of the Central American illegal alien minors resettled throughout the United States under the Unaccompanied Alien Children (UAC) program speak heretofore unknown remote highland village dialects.

The Department of Labor now offers instructions for filing labor complaints in ten languages: Spanish, Chinese, Korean, Polish, Tagalog, Thai, Russian, Vietnamese, Haitian Creole and Somali.[14] What happens when those speaking the other 390 languages want to complain? They can make a legitimate case that DOL is violating their civil rights. At the same time, the need to provide signs in multiple languages mocks the legal requirement for those seeking citizenship to speak English.

K-12 English Language Learner (ELL) public school programs are overwhelmed as education budgets explode to handle the influx. For example, following is a list of languages spoken by students in Portland,

Oregon public schools: Akan, Albanian, Amharic, Arabic, Bengali, Bosnian, Bulgarian, Burmese, Cambodian, Canjobal, Cantonese, Cebuano, Chamorro, Chuukese, Creole, Czech, Danish, Dinka, Dutch, non-standard English, Ewe, Farsi, Fijian, Filipino, French, Fulbe, German, Guatemalan, Hebrew, Hindi, Hmong, Island Carib, Italian, Japanese, Kannada, Karen, Khmer, Kinyarwanda, Kirundi, Korean, Kurdish, Lao, Lingala, Mandarin, Marshallese, Mayan, Mien, Nepali, Oromo, Palauan, Pashto, Persian, Pohnpeian, Portuguese, Romanian, Russian, Saho, Sango, Spanish, Somali, Sonsoroles, Swahili, Tagalog, Tamil, Telugu, Thai, Tibetan, Tigrinya, Tonga, Turkish, Ukrainian, Urdu, Vietnamese, Visayan and more—over 85 languages in all.[15]

English language learner classes frequently have no instructors knowledgeable on the numerous languages. Some school districts are being sued for not providing needed instruction to such students. For example, ACLU sued the state of California for not adequately providing such instruction. The Obama administration Justice Department joined the suit despite the fact that the federal government is largely to blame for this mess.[16]

Table 1 provides a list of a few school districts showing the size of their ELL programs and the number of languages spoken by students trying to learn English:

Table 1

English Language Learners in K-12 U.S. Public Schools				
	Languages Spoken	% Student Body	# Students ELL	Total
Amarillo, TX	75	15.2%	5,041	33,066
Anchorage, AK	99	13.0%	6,200	47,692
Buffalo, NY	84	10.5%	3,895	37,000
Chicago, IL	99	18.7%	67,664	361,314
Denver, CO	124	37.0%	33,650	87,398
Des Moines, IA	100	20.6%	6,800	32,500
Federal Way, WA	120	30.9%	7,141	23,075
Lewiston, ME	35	28.1%	1,547	5,503
Lincoln, NE	125	7.5%	3,000	40,000
Manchester, NH	76	11.2%	1,968	17,500
Minneapolis, MN	90	21.6%	7,800	36,093
Nashville, TN	120	29.8%	25,300	85,000
Omaha, NE	76	14.0%	7,000	50,000
Philadelphia, PA	100	10.6%	13,800	130,000
Portland, ME	58	24.8%	1,719	6,940
Portland, OR	85	7.8%	3,798	48,459
Sioux Falls, SD	90	9.8%	2,350	24,000
Worchester, MA	80	34.4%	8,717	25,306
U.S. Overall	>400	9%	4,813,693	53,700,000
Sources: State and local public education records, research studies and news stories				

Costs of managing these diverse languages and the number of students needing ELL have skyrocketed. For example, in 2001, approximately 5,000 Somalis and other refugee immigrants migrated from Georgia to Lewiston, MN, following the discovery that Maine was the most generous welfare state in the nation. As a result, Lewiston's ELL budget has increased 4,000 percent since the year 2000.[17] In FY 2017, Lewiston's ELL budget was $3,204,795, or $2,130 per student, increasing the total cost for ELL students by 18 percent over the basic cost ($11,899) for students in Lewiston schools.[18,19]

But that only captures part of the cost. ELL students also are enrolled in special needs and free lunch programs. For example, in Portland, Oregon, 17.8 percent of ELL students were also identified to have special needs during the 2015-2017 school years.[20] Fewer than 1 percent were identified as gifted and talented, while fewer than half of all Portland ELL students made progress in learning English during that period.[21]

In Minneapolis, Minnesota, 93 percent of ELL students qualify for its free or reduced cost lunch program, and 13.6 percent qualify for special education.[22] According to a 2015 report, in Holyoke, Massachusetts, where 29.2 percent of the student body requires ELL, 95.9 percent come from low income households and 33.6 percent need special education. In the state of Massachusetts, 80.5 percent of ELLs live in low-income households and 25.1 percent require special ed.[23] Throughout the U.S., 14.7 percent of the ELL population requires special ed.[24]

In 2014, former Lynn, Massachusetts mayor Judith Flanagan Kennedy summed up the problem:

> This year, I have had to increase my school department budget 9.3 percent and have had to cut all of my other city budgets between 2 percent and 5 percent to make up for the influx of the unaccompanied children and the surge.[25]

> It's gotten to the point where the school system is overwhelmed, our health department is overwhelmed, the city's budget is being ... altered [to] accommodate all of these admissions. ... The way this is going, Lynn looks like a microcosm of the United States, in that we have been filled to capacity and we can't take any more without having the people who are already here suffer.[26]

It has only gotten worse since.

The significant barriers to learning created by so many different languages heavily impacts school ratings. Former Manchester, New Hampshire, Mayor Ted Gatsas complained that 82 different languages are spoken at Central High, a school of 2,200 pupils. English illiteracy among immigrants is killing Manchester's public school ratings.

This is borne out by ratings for the state's schools. Manchester's West High School is rated lowest in the state, and the other three Manchester high schools rank near the bottom.[27] Students complain that classrooms smell. Similarly, Manchester's four middle schools rate in the bottom 11, with Southside Middle School dead last in the state.[28] Among New Hampshire's 231 elementary schools, Manchester hosts 6 of the 10 worst, according to rating website Schooldigger.com.[29]

The increasingly diverse student population creates conflict as students from widely differing cultures are forced together in overcrowded schools where the usual stresses of striving for an education are multiplied. Add to that the health, language, and other issues they bring, and you have a recipe for chaos.

Such problems are being swept under the rug by both school administrators and the media, but a few examples have made national news. As reported on March 13, 2018:

> MINNEAPOLIS — Safety concerns arise as violence continues to escalate at Southwest High School. On top of an already failing administration, Southwest High School staff are struggling to maintain peace between students. Last Friday, March 2, multiple fights broke out during the school's second lunch period. Despite attempts to sweep the issue under the rug and downplay the violence, persistent students and parents forced the administration to address the situation.[30]

Finally, Muslim immigrants are being told by their leaders *not to assimilate*. These are very explicit instructions and have been repeated publicly by numerous, high profile Islamic leaders in the U.S. Linda Sarsour, the hard-core leftist, sharia-adherent Muslim who has gained fame and notoriety for her deliberately inflammatory language, said in a public forum on July 1, 2017:

> Our number one and top priority is to protect and defend our community. It is not to assimilate and to please any other people in authority. Our obligation is to our young people, is to our women, to make sure our women are protected in our community, and our top priority, even higher than all those priorities, is to please Allah and only Allah ...[31]

Brigitte Gabriel of Act for America and Ayaan Hirsi Ali have spoken out bravely against the virulent aspects of Islamic law (called sharia), such as the barbaric practice of Female Genital Mutilation (FGM). In response, Linda Sarsour tweeted about them, as follows:[32]

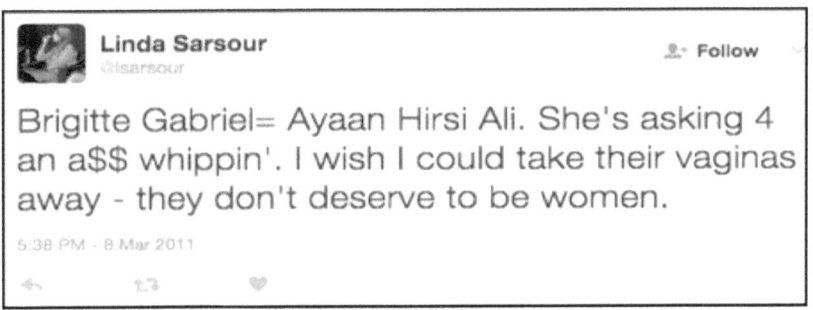

Ali, a Somali native and former member of the Dutch Parliament, lost her friend and colleague, Theo Van Gogh, who was murdered by a Muslim in broad daylight on the street in Amsterdam. He and Ali had co-produced a film describing the treatment of women in Islam. A death threat addressed to Ali was pinned to Van Gogh's chest with a knife.

At a 2017 U.S. Senate hearing, Ali stated, "Islam is part religion, and part a political-military doctrine, the part that is a political doctrine contains a worldview, a system of laws and a moral code that is totally incompatible with our constitution, our laws, and our way of life."[33]

Diversity is clearly *not* our strength, but our PC culture is afraid to articulate that indisputable fact for fear of being labeled "bigot." As usual, by misrepresenting "diversity" as a good thing, and aggressively smearing anyone who objects, the Left has manipulated language to advance its agenda.

Ironically, in one way they are correct, because diversity very much *is the Left's strength*. Whenever the Left talks about "our," "us," or "we," they want us to think it applies universally, when in fact it applies only to them and is destructive for the rest of us. But if we don't adopt the language nonetheless, we will be pilloried as "racists," "bigots," "xenophobes," etc.

Diversity will slowly give the Left the one-party state it seeks if it isn't stopped. *Diversity is indeed their strength*. And it is so because *Demographics is Destiny*.

Demographics Is Destiny

America is being undermined by a tidal wave of immigration. Federal agencies collaborate with multinational entities and thousands of liberal organizations to bring in people from all over the world under a universe of immigration programs, while so-called "Volunteer Agencies" (VOLAGs), and hundreds of small tax-exempt organizations, are remunerated handsomely with taxpayer dollars to resettle and assist refugees, asylum seekers and other similar groups. It has turned into a multi-billion-dollar industry.

The Left, represented politically by the Democratic Party, and its establishment enablers in the business community and GOP have engaged in a long term project to change America by changing its people. The Left seeks power above all else, and while we all debate the wisdom of this or that policy, and businesses benefit from cheap foreign labor—both legal and illegal—the Left has gradually been importing enough people to permanently change voting demographics in its favor.

It is indisputable that this is the primary goal of open-borders policies and the reason the Left is so fanatically fighting President Trump on all aspects of immigration. Immediately following the 2018 election, members of Democracy Alliance—a secretive group of billionaire leftist funders, including George Soros and Tom Steyer—met in Washington, DC to discuss how demographic changes impacted the 2018 election in their favor and what they must do to capitalize on them for 2020.[34] But this was not the first time. Prior to the 2008 election, Democrat insiders John Podesta, Andrew Stern, and Anna Burger wrote a secret memo to these same billionaire leftists. As stated in the memo (emphasis theirs):

> **Ensure that Demographics is Destiny**. An "emerging progressive majority'" is a realistic possibility in terms of demographic and voting patterns. But it is incomplete in terms of organizing and political work. Women, communities of color, and highly educated professionals are core parts of the progressive coalition. Nationally, and in key battleground states, their influence is growing. Latinos and young voters are quickly solidifying in this coalition as well. But many of these voters are new to the process. All of these groups--in addition to working class voters and independents picked up in 2006-- will require significant long-term engagement in order to keep them reliably on our side.[35]

This goal was publicly repeated in a 2009 speech by Socialist labor leader Eliseo Medina, one of the most influential open-borders advocates in the U.S. Assuming the oft-repeated low-ball estimate of about 12 million illegals in the U.S., Medina said:

> We in the last election had the largest turnout of Latino voters in our history. And everything tells us these voters fully intend on becoming engaged into elections in the future... Number one: if we are to expect this electorate to win, the progressive community needs to solidly be on the side of immigrants. Let us solidify and expand the progressive coalition for the future... Number two, we reform the immigration laws, it puts 12 million on the path to citizenship and eventually voters. Can you imagine if we have even the same ratio [as Obama got] two out of three, if we had 8 million new voters that care about our

issues and would be voting, we would create a governing coalition for the long-term, not just for an election cycle.[36]

Consider that we now know the illegal population exceeds 20 million and could be as high as 30 million or more.[37] That translates to 14-20 million new Democrats. But this agenda precedes Medina by decades. Every year since the 1980s, the U.S. government allows approximately 1 million immigrants to become legal permanent residents (LPR) in the United States. In FY 2017, the latest data available, we imported 1,127,167.[38] And while advocates will say we need these people to supplement a shrinking labor force, in 2016 only about 12 percent of LPRs immigrated for employment reasons. Most of the others arrive under family reunification programs, and this is typical [39] For the most part we are *not* importing people for employment reasons. A *sane* legal immigration policy would allow in only those needed to cover shortfalls in critical employment fields, approximately 150,000 annually at present.

Additionally, among those obtaining permanent resident status are people from countries very unfriendly to the U.S. About 150,000 emigrate annually from Muslim majority countries. About 180,000 emigrated in FY 2016, President Obama's last year in office. An even greater number emigrate from communist countries; on average, about 220,000 a year. Of these, the most significant is the People's Republic of China. About 76,000 Chinese nationals receive LPR status annually, and this has been true since at least 2008. From the communist and Muslim nations, then, the U.S. is receiving about 400,000 legal immigrants per year.* Given the conditions in many of those nations, you can be confident that some do represent a threat of terrorism, espionage, sabotage, influence operations or all of the above.

California, for example, has become a haven for Chinese espionage. Many of the Chinese nationals awarded immigrant and non-immigrant visas have actually turned out to be spies. In one case, Chinese intelligence officers working out of China's San Francisco Consulate bussed in between 6,000 and 8,000 Chinese students in California on J-Visas (for scholars, professors and exchange visitors) to disrupt an anti-Chinese government rally in San Francisco held by members of the Chinese Falun Gong religious group, Tibetan, and Uighur dissidents and others.[40]

The Chinese communists have been infiltrating spies into the U.S. for fifty years. Currently, there are approximately 25,000 Chinese spies in the

---

* The estimates for Muslim and Communist countries were derived from "Table 3. Persons Obtaining Lawful Permanent Resident Status by Region and Country of Birth: Fiscal Years 2008 to 2017," *Department of Homeland Security*, October 2, 2018, accessed November 10, 2018, https://www.dhs.gov/immigration-statistics/yearbook/2017/table3. The Muslim majority nations list was taken from 48 named member countries of the 56 nation Organization for Islamic Cooperation that have Muslim majority populations. Not all listed OIC nations are Muslim majority.

U.S.; 5,000 of these came in after 2012 as students, businessmen, or immigrants. According to national defense expert Bill Gertz, another 18,000 Americans of various ethnic groups including Chinese have been recruited by Chinese intelligence. So, we're looking at the possibility for over 40,000 Chinese espionage agents and spies in the U.S.[41]

The annual influx of 76,000 Chinese provides a large pool of recruits for specific operations, like the San Francisco protest or for other nefarious purposes. While many may come here for legitimate reasons, Chinese intelligence knows who they are and where they are, and can be called on at any time, whether they like it or not. U.S.-based Chinese intelligence operatives threaten to retaliate against relatives still in China if they don't comply.[42]

It boggles the mind that U.S. legislators and bureaucrats overseeing immigration and national security policy are so utterly ignorant about Communism and Communist tactics that they would allow enemy nations a virtual open door to the U.S. Or perhaps they do understand and let them in anyway, which is even scarier. With all the demands for open borders and "compassion" toward illegal aliens, migrants and legal immigrants, one never asks why China and Russia don't share this compassion. Why don't these open border advocates ever demand China and Russia open their borders, since so many are openly sympathetic to communism and communist causes? If communist countries create such a paradise, why not?

So, we are getting over 1 million legal immigrants per year, with an unquantifiable number of bad actors among them. And those are the *legal* ones. It has been estimated that when illegals are included, President Obama's policies may have boosted total immigration during his last year in office to as high as 1.8 million.[43] We all witnessed the Obama administration's unconstitutional encouragement to illegal aliens through his Deferred Action for Childhood Arrivals (DACA) and Deferred Action for Parents of Arrivals (DAPA) programs. DAPA was ended by court order, but DACA remains in place.

Obama even violated federal law by granting $310 million in taxpayer money to the Vera Institute of Justice to assist illegal minors battling extradition. While illegals can get representation in court, they cannot get federal money to help their cases.[44] The Vera Institute is a non-profit that focuses on criminal justice issues. Its 2016 revenues claimed $69 million, of which $59.2 million were government grants.[45] The Institute has received $6.5 million from George Soros Open Society foundations and $16.8 million from the Ford Foundation since 2000.[46] Both foundations are central to the open borders agenda.

Candidate Donald Trump promised to end DACA his first day in office, and his pledges on this and other immigration issues was one of the primary reasons he won the 2016 election. President Trump did take action on DACA in September of 2017, suspending the program and ordering Congress to find a legislative solution by March of 2018. He did not, however, begin to deport DACA enrollees, and indicated that he would like to find a solution for them. With hostile court actions and a Congress unwilling to act, the program remains in place.

Enforcement on the border, however, increased almost immediately with the appointment of Senator Jeff Sessions (R-AL) as Attorney General. In 2016, Obama's last year in office, Customs and Border Protection apprehended 563,204 illegal aliens along the Southwest border. In the months before the election, border apprehensions skyrocketed as illegals attempted to slip in ahead of the elections. In the months following the election however, apprehensions plummeted. This is dramatically illustrated in Chart 1 below. Between October 2016 and April 2017, apprehensions declined 76 percent as fewer attempted to cross the border.

Chart 1

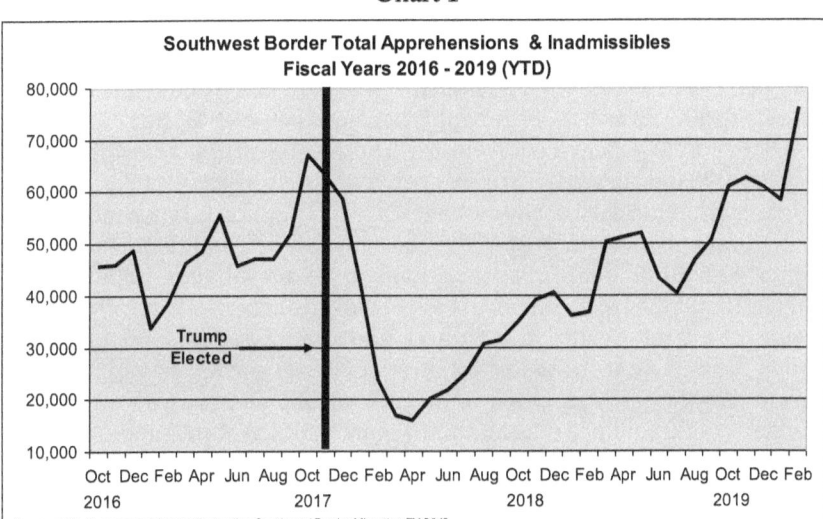

During the rest of FY 2017, however, border crossings slowly rose again as it became apparent that illegal immigration was not going to be impeded by the Trump administration, despite its best efforts. The Left's blanket "resistance," with repeated lawsuits by open borders organizations accommodated by blocks on Trump border policies from leftwing activist judges, Democratic governors declaring sanctuary states and removing National Guard troops from the border, have brought border crossings to record levels as of this writing. The Department of Homeland Security expects 100,000 in March 2019.[47] That is the equivalent of two US cities. DHS has projected 1 million illegal alien apprehensions for the year. Because of catch and release, most of these will not go home.

As the result of partisan judicial intervention, overcrowded holding facilities and a defiant bureaucracy still seeded with many Obama holdovers, the Trump administration has been forced to continue Obama administration "catch and release" policies. [48] Illegal aliens are being transported by air and bus from facilities along the border to undisclosed locations within the U.S, accompanied by personnel from the Department of Health and Human Services, which oversees the Unaccompanied Alien Children (UAC) program. [49] So this burgeoning, secretive open-borders agenda is being facilitated by the federal government with your tax dollars, and has been for years.

Illegal Alien Population

And those are the ones we caught. The Border Patrol claims its apprehension rate from 2012 to 2018 has averaged 75.8 percent.[50] It is impossible to know, really. Other sources claim the apprehension rate could be 30 percent or lower. But giving them the benefit of the doubt and applying that rate to all Southwest Border apprehensions between FY 2012 and 2018, over 820,000 illegals avoided capture. Thus, using DHS's own statistics, at least 100,000 illegal border crossers per year sneak in successfully.

As mentioned earlier, the current illegal population is much more likely to be 20-30 million or more, not the absurdly low "official" estimate of 12.1 million. [51] In 2005, Bear Stearns estimated the illegal alien population at roughly 20 million based on telltale evidence like increases in remittances to foreign countries, school enrollments and use of social services among border states.[52] A recent report by three Ivy League scholars estimates the current illegal alien population in the U.S. at 22.1 million, with an upward boundary of 30 million.[53] Recall that Obama's DHS was printing 34 million green cards and work permits to accommodate his "executive amnesty."[54] Why would they need that many?

With numbers like these, it is apparent why the Left puts so much emphasis on immigration, and especially amnesty for illegals. DACA recipients total about 800,000, and they are a subset of a much larger group of aliens, some illegal, some children of illegals, whom the media has dubbed "DREAMers." The acronym is short for the **D**evelopment, **R**elief, and **E**ducation for **A**lien **M**inors (DREAM) Act. It is longstanding legislation that has already been passed in some form by certain states. It provides, among other things, in-state tuition for resident illegals, who then compete with resident students for openings at public universities and colleges.

Federal legislation, which includes amnesty, has been proposed repeatedly since 2001, but has not passed yet. This larger "DREAMer" population has been estimated to be as high as 3.6 million but given the absurd underestimates of illegal aliens bandied about for so long, it could be much larger than that.[55]

Given amnesty, this population is enough to swing votes throughout the nation. When families that would become eligible for legalization through family reunification once the DREAMer group received amnesty, the number would swell to four or five times that amount—enough to create a one-party nation in the U.S. for the foreseeable future. It is easy to see why. A 2014 report by the Center for Immigration Studies found that 62.5 percent of immigrant citizens vote Democratic, while only 24.6 percent vote Republican. The rest were independent or unknown.[56]

In the 2018 midterm elections, 69 percent of Latinos voted Democrat.[57] Vast demographic changes have occurred throughout our nation as a direct result of this wave of legal and illegal immigration. The 2018 election showed many Republicans in previously safe seats winning by razor-thin margins.

For example, deep red Texas is unlikely to remain so for long. Table 2 shows the radical demographic changes that have occurred in the Lone Star State since 1980. Texas is now a minority majority state. The Hispanic population has increased over 300 percent since 1980, and currently exceeds that of whites, who were 65.7 percent of the population in 1980 but now comprise only 40.3 percent of the population.

Table 2

Texas Population 1980 to 2018					
	White	Hispanic	Black	Other	Total
1980	9,350,297	2,985,824	1,692,562	200,508	14,229,191
%Total	65.7%	21.0%	11.9%	1.4%	100.0%
1990	10,291,680	4,339,905	1,976,360	378,565	16,986,510
%Total	60.6%	25.5%	11.6%	2.2%	100.0%
2000	11,074,716	6,669,666	2,364,255	743,183	20,851,820
% Total	53.1%	32.0%	11.3%	3.6%	100.0%
2018	11,826,470	12,181,167	3,348,098	2,010,744	29,366,479
% Total	40.3%	41.5%	11.4%	6.8%	100.0%
Source: Texas Department of State Health Services, Texas Population 1980 - 2018					

The only things keeping Texas red are 1) low turnout among Hispanics and other minorities, and 2) a large proportion of illegal aliens, only some of whom attempt to vote. The "other" category almost quadrupled since 2000. Under President Obama, Texas surpassed California as the largest refugee resettlement state, which was no doubt deliberate, but many more categories of minority whose immigration status is not specified, make up the "other" numbers.

Democrats have been engaged in a full-throated effort to register low-turnout minorities and immigrants in Texas for years, and even try to register non-citizens, including pre-checking the U.S. Citizen box on voter registrations and urging non-citizens to vote.[58]

California's rapid descent into third-world status is also explained by Table 3. The white population has actually declined as increasing taxes, regulation, and the massive increase in illegal aliens and their associated costs, have driven them out in a dramatic example of "white flight." Whites now comprise only 37 percent of the total population.

Table 3

California Population 1980 to 2017					
	White	Hispanic	Black	Other	Total
1980	15,763,992	4,544,331	1,783,810	1,575,769	23,667,902
%Total	66.6%	19.2%	7.5%	6.7%	100.0%
1990	17,029,126	7,687,938	2,092,446	2,950,511	29,760,021
%Total	57.2%	25.8%	7.0%	9.9%	100.0%
2000	15,816,790	10,966,556	2,181,926	4,906,376	33,871,648
%Total	46.7%	32.4%	6.4%	14.5%	100.0%
2017	14,616,636	15,477,306	2,164,239	7,278,472	39,536,653
%Total	37.0%	39.1%	5.5%	18.4%	100.0%
Sources: CensusScope; Population by Race 1980-2000; Census FactFinder; Hispanic or Latino Origin by Race; 2010 - 2017					

The state currently faces an unrecoverable combined state and local debt of $1.3 trillion.[59] The illegal alien population literally mires the state in intractable problems which the liberal political establishment meets with ever more deficit spending.

Despite these facts, California Governor Jerry Brown has made it worse by declaring California a sanctuary state, and signed numerous bills protecting illegal aliens, including violent felons, from being removed by Immigration and Customs Enforcement (ICE). He called opponents of his actions, "low-life politicians."[60]

It was not always so. When the Vietnam War ended, some 130,000 Vietnamese refugees were granted asylum in the U.S. by then President Gerald Ford, then Governor Jerry Brown—yes, the same one—vigorously opposed Vietnamese refugees coming to his state. Why?

Brown said he had too many Hispanics already, too many on welfare, and too much unemployment. "There is something a little strange about saying, 'Let's bring in 500,000 more people' when we can't take care of the 1 million [Californians] out of work," he said.[61]

Brown even tried to prevent aircraft carrying Vietnamese refugees from landing at Travis Air Force base. According to an NPR report, "they didn't want these people."[62]

Brown was joined in this protest by his then Secretary of Health and Welfare, Mario Obledo. Obledo co-founded the Mexican American Legal Defense and Education Fund (MALDEF), one of the most virulent open borders organizations. In 1998 Obledo said, "California is going to be a Hispanic state and anyone who doesn't like it should leave. If they [whites] don't like Mexicans, they ought to go back to Europe."[63]

And they call the rest of us "racists."

Many other prominent Democrats supported Brown and Obledo, including Joe Biden, who tried to stall refugee legislation in Congress. Liberal New York representative Elizabeth Holtzman said that "some of her constituents felt that the same assistance and compassion was not being shown to the elderly, unemployed and poor in this country."[64]

Why did Democrats so adamantly oppose refugee resettlement then? Because *those* refugees were fleeing communism. And whether Democrats thought the Vietnamese—many of whom fought alongside U.S. forces in the Vietnam War—would be more likely to vote Republican, or if they were just turned off by the notion of anyone fleeing one of their beloved socialist states, is unknown. When Joe Biden finally did support refugee resettlement legislation in 1980, it was when the emphasis on saving victims of communism was no longer part of the goal.

UCLA Professor Marcelo Suárez-Orozco has said, "Where L.A. goes is where the rest of the state goes and where the rest of the country goes. We announce, demographically speaking, the future for the rest of the country."[65]

He is right. These demographic changes are occurring all over the nation as shown below, and will guarantee that "demographics is destiny," if nothing changes. The Left will get its "permanent progressive majority" and the U.S. will become the last domino to fall in the international socialists' quest for world domination. It will throw our nation and the world into a depth of darkness from which it may never return.

Table 4

U.S. Population 1980 to 2017					
	White	Hispanic	Black	Other	Total
1980	180,256,103	14,608,673	26,104,285	5,576,744	226,545,805
%Total	79.6%	6.4%	11.5%	2.5%	100.0%
1990	188,128,296	22,354,059	29,216,293	9,011,225	248,709,873
%Total	75.6%	9.0%	11.7%	3.6%	100.0%
2000	194,552,774	35,305,818	33,947,837	17,615,477	281,421,906
%Total	69.1%	12.5%	12.1%	6.3%	100.0%
2017	197,285,202	58,846,134	40,129,593	29,458,249	325,719,178
%Total	60.6%	18.1%	12.3%	9.0%	100.0%
Sources: CensusScope; Population by Race 1980-2000; Census FactFinder; Hispanic or Latino Origin by Race; 2010 - 2017					

Migrant Caravans

The migrant caravans of 2018 and 2019 are further evidence of the Left's intention to swamp the border with illegals, creating crisis after crisis. The caravans were not spontaneous. They were highly organized and assisted by multiple agencies of the United Nations and numerous leftwing illegal alien advocacy groups. These included two related Chicago-based organizations, Pueblo Sin Fronteras (People Without Borders), a project of La Familia Latina Unida (The United Latin Family), and Centro Sin Fronteras Community Services Network, which provides funding.[66] Reportedly, there are at least 100 Pueblo Sin Fronteras workers embedded with the caravan.[67]

Emma Lozano, founder of both Centro and Pueblo, is a leftwing radical and ironically a pastor at the Lincoln United Methodist Church in Chicago. She fights deportation of illegals, and wants Illinois to become, "an Immigrant Freedom Zone." She makes her open-borders agenda plain, "We need to change America, we are all America."[68]

Lozano has been assisted by La Familia Latina Unida founder Elvira Arellano, an illegal alien who advocates for her fellow illegals. She was deported in 1997 but quickly returned. She was arrested again in 2002 for using a false social security number.[69] She faced possible deportation but avoided it through the personal intervention of then Chicago Rep. Luis Gutierres and community pressure.[70]

Both Lozano and Arellano work with another radical illegal alien advocacy group, the League of United Latin American Citizens (LULAC).[71] Additional help was provided by the CARA Family Detention Project, which offers pro-bono legal help to illegals, and the Popular Assembly of Migrant Families, a Mexico-based group that organizes caravans.[72] Reportedly, CARA has been coordinating caravan efforts with Pueblo Sin Fronteras from bases in the U.S.[73]

Unsurprisingly, Centro Sin Fronteras receives donations from leftwing foundations, some of which get government funding. The Catholic Legal Immigration Network (CLINIC), which receives funding from government, works closely with CARA Family Detention Project, and distributes much of its grant money to Catholic Charities and other organizations specifically to assist immigrants in becoming citizens and push for amnesty.[74] CLINIC has received at least $2.2 million from Soros Open Society foundations since 2002. The Ford Foundation, probably the largest supporter of open borders, has provided $2.9 million since 2011.[75]

Centro also received over $1.5 million from the Illinois Coalition for Immigrant and Refugee Rights (ICIRR) between 2010 and 2012.[76] ICIRR in turn gets 80 percent of its funding from the state of Illinois. From 2015 to 2017 ICIRR received $15.3 million from the Illinois Department of Human Services and other government sources, according to IRS returns.[77] Some of the state money likely came from the federal government's Refugee and

Entrant Assistance State Administered programs, one of numerous HHS grant programs for refugees and illegal aliens. During those same years, the Illinois DHS received $24.6 million through this program.[78]

In an example of the Byzantine nature of the open borders agenda supported by your tax dollars, ICIRR distributed between $11,000 and $246,000 in government grant money to each of 59 separate organizations for "Immigrant and Refugee Rights" in 2017 alone.[79] And the Left does not distinguish between true immigrants and illegal aliens. How much of this money is now being spent to assist the caravans? ICIRR's 2018 spending is not yet public, but it would not be surprising to see donations to Centro Sin Fronteras and other related organizations included. According to its 2015 tax return, ICIRR also "provides comprehensive services to assist Illinois' more that 325,000 legal permanent residents become U.S. citizens."[80]

The National Immigration Forum has provided at least $60,000 to Centro Sin Fronteras. NIF describes itself as a "conservative" pro-immigrant organization, but gets its funding, $5.5 million in 2016, from the radical Left, including the Soros Open Society Foundations.

Another extreme Left organization helping out is the National Lawyers Guild, labeled a Communist front by Congress decades ago when such things mattered to Congress. It is a subsidiary of the International Association of Democratic Lawyers, founded as a Soviet propaganda front.[81] NLG has brought volunteer attorneys to help caravan migrants with their asylum applications.[82]

NLG is heavily involved in the open borders movement through its National Immigration Project, and gets ample funding from George Soros and other notorious open border funders. The Ford Foundation has probably done more to destroy the sanctity of our borders than any other and has provided at least $1.3 million to NLG since 2002.[83] The NLG partners with many open borders groups, for example CASA de Maryland, an influential Maryland-based tax-exempt that helps illegals avoid capture.

The media reported with great fanfare on the mass of caravan migrants, estimated at anywhere between 4,000 and 12,000, walking doggedly on the 1,000 plus mile journey to the border. But left unreported was the fact that the caravan trekkers made most of the trip by bus. Journalist and filmmaker Ami Horowitz reported directly from Mexico, where he was embedded with the migrants. Horowitz said that the migrants walked some of the way, but that, "They had chartered these, almost luxury tour busses, just dozens of them..."[84]

Horowitz said that what struck him most was the degree of organization and dollars involved. "[The busses] didn't come from nothing, this isn't manna from Heaven. This was highly organized, chartered, and that's how they got this caravan... 1,000 miles across Mexico," he said. Horowitz estimated just the cost of providing water to the caravan it almost $1 million.

He added that the Mexican government did not want the caravan in Mexico, so it was always under police escort.

Horowitz also revealed another major source of assistance: the United Nations. Horowitz said there were "numerous" UN organizations on the ground in Mexico, but the most prominent were the UN High Commissioner for Refugees (UNHCR) and the United Nations International Children's Emergency Fund (UNICEF). These organizations provided "an incredible degree of services," including mobile hospitals, children's' services and more. They also trained migrants how to speak to the press using words that would inspire sympathy and gave PowerPoint presentations explaining what to tell border agents in order to apply for asylum.[85]

In a phone interview, the UNHCR representative admitted that the UNHCR had been involved in the caravan from the beginning and acknowledged that part of its purpose was to "poke Trump in the eye." Horowitz said that the goal of all the groups involved was to "Degrade U.S. security... degrade U.S. sovereignty and to create this manufactured crisis, which they did in order to push the agenda."[86]

In 2016, the latest year for which data is currently available, the UNHCR received 38.2 percent of its operating budget from the U.S. government, and is State's largest multilateral partner.[87] UNICEF received 24.6 percent of its budget from the U.S. government.[88] In both cases, the U.S. provides far more funding than any other nation. So, while thumbing their noses at us and deliberately using the caravans to threaten U.S. sovereignty, we taxpayers were paying them to do so.

Horowitz estimated the caravans to be comprised of about 90 percent men. Women and children were present, but they were a small minority, no doubt included to boost the sympathy factor. When caravan males tried to storm the San Ysidro border crossing in late November 2018, the Border Patrol turned them back with tear gas. The presence of women and children caused an outcry in the media. But, in a scene reminiscent of recent border clashes between Israelis and Palestinians, none reported that the men thrust women and children forward as human shields, while they pelted the Border Patrol with rocks.[89]

Every single migrant interviewed by Horowitz said that they joined the caravan for economic reasons. Not one cited danger or violence at home. The caravans were organized to challenge the Trump administration's border policies and were designed to bring the issue front and center in time for the election.

The migrant caravans are also complicating an already difficult job for border agencies. Preoccupied with those attempting to cross, they cannot simultaneously protect the more remote areas of the border, leaving many opportunities for drug smugglers and terrorists to enter the U.S.

The Red-Green Axis is openly assisting the caravan. In December of 2018, CAIR announced it intends to amass activists in San Diego to support the caravans:

> **December 10**, representatives of chapters of the Council on American-Islamic Relations (CAIR), the nation's largest Muslim civil rights and advocacy organization, will join hundreds of other faith leaders from around the nation at a solidarity action for asylum seekers at the U.S.-Mexico border in San Diego as part of the "Love Knows No Borders: A Moral Call for Migrant Justice" mobilization, **organized by the American Friends Service Committee (AFSC).**[90] [Emphasis theirs.]

The AFSC is a nominally Quaker group with ties to the Communist Party USA and its Soviet overseers going back to the 1920s. AFSC has also formed an alliance with MEChA, the radical Latino group whose goal is to retake portions of the Southwest sold by Mexico to the U.S. in 1848.[91]

Even without the caravans, however, the Southwest border apprehension statistics cited earlier show that at least 10-12,000 are coming to the border every week separately. We are being overwhelmed. DHS Secretary Kirstjen Nielsen has estimated that in 2019 we will face 1 million illegal aliens crossing the border.[92] It is nothing less than an invasion, and as with Europe, one manufactured by our enemies in the radical Left.

In fact, there is strong evidence that the mass migration to Europe from Syria, the Middle East, and Africa was instigated by Russia. An explosive report, co-authored by Russia expert J.R. Nyquist and Romanian author and physician Dr. Anca-Maria Cernea, describes how the mass exodus from Syria was turbocharged in 2015 when Russian aircraft deliberately bombed civilian areas on the pretext that they were attacking the Islamic State. Few fled the areas actually controlled by IS because the terrorists sealed them in.[93]

The mass migration to Europe was comprised primarily of economic migrants, *not Syrian refugees*. About 80 percent came from Africa and other Middle East nations.[94] At least two thirds were young, military-age males and 90 percent of those under 18 were males.[95] As we have seen since, these migrants have stressed welfare systems and spread violent crime and terrorism throughout Western Europe.

Russia and most Eastern European nations sealed their borders, facilitating the flow into the West. German leader Angela Merkel, a former East German Communist, flung open the gates.[96] Leftwing non-profit groups swept in to help. The entire migrant crisis appears to have been stage-managed by our enemies and today Western Europe is on its knees, a goal long sought by Russia.

Aliens not Immigrants

Democrats conspicuously advocate for endless immigration and they do not discriminate between legal and illegal immigrants. In fact, by manipulating language they now lump them all into the same category. This was the strategy behind cultivating the term "undocumented immigrants."

The Department of Homeland Security defines "alien" as "Any person not a citizen or national of the United States."[97] Illegals are not immigrants at all. They are aliens. Dictionary.com describes an alien as anyone "residing under a government or in a country other than that of one's birth without having or obtaining the status of citizenship there."[98] In other words, even those here legally who have not established citizenship are aliens. Given that illegals cannot establish citizenship, they are aliens by definition, and because they have entered the United States illegally, or have overstayed their visa, which is also illegal, they are *illegal aliens*, and should not be referred to in any other way.Consider how the Left manipulates language. "Undocumented Immigrant" is only one example, but let's dissect it. "Undocumented" does not define the alien's legal status at all. Presumably, someone who arrives in the U.S. illegally either has no documents, *i.e.,* is "undocumented," his documents are fraudulent., or he is actually carrying identification documents from his home country. "Undocumented" is merely a *description*. It is not a legally useful term, and it will not even hold true in many cases. Because he is in the country illegally, he is an *illegal alien*.

Having established the term "undocumented immigrant" in the public mind, however, the Left then drops the term "undocumented," and now simply refers to illegal aliens as "immigrants." This provides a pretext (the Left doesn't need a reason, just an excuse) to vilify anyone who opposes illegal aliens as being "opposed to immigrants." And once again, illegal immigration opponents become "racists," "xenophobes," or "bigots."

The Left claims that such people, "don't want immigrants here because they don't look like us." The truth is that opponents of illegal immigration don't want them here because the United States is a nation of laws and if you condone illegal entry to the U.S. and award such lawbreakers with citizenship or even just legal residence, you not only punish those who immigrate legally, but undermine the foundations of our Republic and reward criminal behavior. There are also many other pressing and practical reasons to adamantly oppose illegal immigration.

Costs

Illegal aliens impose heavy costs on schools and welfare. A 2017 study by the Federation for American Immigration Reform (FAIR) found that illegals and their offspring impose a net cost after taxes of $115.9 billion per year in welfare costs.[99] The Center for Immigration Studies has found that 63 percent of non-citizen households utilize welfare programs compared with 35 percent of American households.[100]

Furthermore, over 70 percent of English Language Learners in public schools are Hispanics, many of whom are illegal or were born of illegals.[101] The cost of ELL has yet to be calculated nationwide but is substantial. The Federation for American Immigration Reform produced a 2018 study finding that students with limited English proficiency cost, on average, $1,365 more than non-LEP students annually.[102] Applied to the 4.8 million ESL students now in K-12 schools nationwide, the cost would be $6.6 billion annually. A big slice of that cost can be attributed to illegals.

Finally, one in five U.S. births today are to immigrants, and illegal aliens are responsible for about 38 percent of these, based on a study by the Center for Immigration Studies. It found that in 2014, illegal aliens accounted for approximately 297,000 of the 791,000 immigrant births in the U.S. Immigrants, legal and illegal, also accounted for 24 percent of taxpayer-funded births, and almost half of those (11 percent) were illegal aliens. The combined cost for these births is an estimated $5.3 billion, of which illegals account for $2.4 billion.[103]

Diseases

Illegals import epidemics and exotic diseases. There are immediate consequences that can be literally life threatening. It is reported that *one-third* of the caravan migrants in Tijuana as of this writing are being treated for health issues, including tuberculosis, HIV/AIDS and chicken pox. Many have lice and other skin issues.[104] But this is not unusual. Illegal aliens have been bringing serious illnesses with them for years, with serious and sometimes fatal consequences for Americans.

The first large flood of illegal alien minors in 2014 likely caused the unprecedented nationwide enterovirus outbreak that was responsible for at least 6 child deaths and 45 cases of paralysis. At least six Chicago area hospitals stopped admitting patients under 18 due to the huge number of cases that overwhelmed their capabilities. Children's Hospital Colorado saw some 3,600 patients in one month, 10 percent of whom needed ventilators or other methods to keep them breathing.[105] Little information of value was forthcoming from the Obama administration. The CDC essentially created a news blackout. Most information came from reports in local media. While enterovirus cases were rare in the U.S. prior to 2014, they are relatively common in Central America.

In 2018 there was another outbreak of a disease with polio-like characteristics that had spread across 22 states as of this writing.[106] Ninety percent of the 122 cases have been in children who are 4 years old on average. The symptoms are similar to those 2014 enterovirus cases that resulted in paralysis, but the actual disease remains a mystery.The deadly

Chagas disease, formerly limited largely to Central and South America, is now spreading to the U.S., with an estimated 300,167 cases nationwide, including 40,000 pregnant women.[107] Northern Virginia has been described as "ground zero" for the disease. While most cases of Chagas were contracted by Latin American immigrants before they arrived in the U.S., its vector, the kissing bug, has been identified in at least 28 states.[108] Approximately 50 percent carry the Trypanosoma cruzi parasite responsible for the disease.[109] In addition to the direct threat of the disease and its high treatment costs, our blood supply is threatened by donor infected blood.[110]

Crime

Anecdotes abound regarding illegal alien crime. Almost daily we hear about innocent people killed in a hit-and-run accident, murdered, or brutally raped by illegals. Kate Steinle's death has become a national symbol for the outrageous acts committed by illegals in the U.S. Comprehensive statistics on illegal alien crime have been difficult to come by, although this has improved with President Trump's *Executive Order on Enhancing Public Safety in the Interior of the United States.* Federal law enforcement is now required to collect data and report it quarterly. ICE has reported that in FY 2018 alone, its officers arrested a total of 7,378 criminal aliens who were either charged with or already convicted of homicide or sexual assault. Of these, 387 were charged with homicide and 1,641 had already been convicted of homicide. Another 1,610 were charged with sexual assault and 3,740 had already been convicted of it. In total, ICE-arrested criminal aliens were charged with and/or convicted of 542,798 crimes. A total of 314,910 of these were serious crimes, excluding immigration violations, motor vehicle charges like drunk driving, and other miscellaneous charges. Sixty-six percent of all aliens arrested by ICE have prior criminal convictions. A large proportion are illegal. All are deportable. Table 5, reproduced from the ICE report, lists all the crimes and convictions.[111]

Table 5

Criminal Charge Category	Criminal Charges	Criminal Convictions	Total Offenses
Traffic Offenses - DUI	26,100	54,630	80,730
Dangerous Drugs	21,476	55,109	76,585
Traffic Offenses	30,594	45,610	76,204
Immigration	11,917	51,249	63,166
Assault	20,766	29,987	50,753
Obstructing Judiciary, Congress, Legislature, Etc.	11,189	11,863	23,052
Larceny	5,295	15,045	20,340
General Crimes	8,415	10,973	19,388
Obstructing the Police	5,754	10,155	15,909
Fraudulent Activities	4,201	8,661	12,862
Burglary	2,829	9,834	12,663
Weapon Offenses	3,672	8,094	11,766
Public Peace	4,029	7,236	11,265
Invasion of Privacy	2,255	5,090	7,345
Sex Offenses (Not Involving Assault or Commercialized Sex)	1,913	4,975	6,888
Stolen Vehicle	1,693	4,568	6,261
Family Offenses	2,465	3,526	5,991
Robbery	1,139	4,423	5,562
Sexual Assault	1,610	3,740	5,350
Forgery	1,632	3,526	5,158
Damage Property	1,872	2,597	4,469
Stolen Property	1,335	3,127	4,462
Liquor	1,995	2,290	4,285
Flight / Escape	1,090	2,264	3,354
Kidnapping	791	1,294	2,085
Homicide	387	1,641	2,028
Health / Safety	522	1,242	1,764
Commercialized Sexual Offenses	729	1,010	1,739
Threat	583	791	1,374

Notes: Immigration crimes include "illegal entry," "illegal reentry," "false claim to U.S. citizenship," and "alien smuggling." "Obstructing Judiciary & Congress & Legislature & Etc.," refers to several related offenses including, but not limited to: Perjury; Contempt; Obstructing Justice; Misconduct; Parole and Probation Violations; and Failure to Appear. "General Crimes" include the following National Crime Information Center (NCIC) charges: Conspiracy, Crimes Against Person, Licensing Violation, Money Laundering, Morals - Decency Crimes, Property Crimes, Public Order Crimes, Racketeer Influenced and Corrupt Organizations Act (RICO), and Structuring.

The first quarterly report for Fiscal Year 2018 under President Trump's executive order found that the 38,132 known or suspected criminal aliens incarcerated by the Bureau of Prisons comprised 21 percent of the total BOP population at the end of 2017. Sixty-two percent of these, 23,642, were illegal aliens, and the status of many others had yet to be determined. A large proportion, 46 percent, were incarcerated for drug trafficking. Other offenses included production and distribution of child pornography, trafficking, racketeering, kidnapping, murder, larceny, terrorism, bribery, extortion, rape, and other offenses.[112] The Texas Department of Public Safety recently published a study of criminal alien crime in Texas, including illegal alien crime.[113] Table 6 compiles data from this report, showing the lifetime criminal histories of illegal aliens arrested in Texas over the study period.

Table 6

Criminal Histories of Texas Illegal Aliens Arrested June 2011 to November 2018		
	Arrests	Convictions
Assault	57,082	25,098
Burlary	18,332	9,598
Drugs	65,518	34,501
Homicide	2,941	1,599
Kidnapping	1,019	422
Robbery	5,893	3,543
Theft	31,014	14,661
Sex Offenses	12,847	7,226
Weapons	8,188	3,579
Other	300,867	136,631
Total	503,701	236,858

The Government Accountability Office (GAO) has published three studies titled Criminal Alien Statistics, in 2005, 2011 and 2018.[114] From the most recent report, GAO provided the author with unpublished data on SCAAP illegal alien convicts in Arizona, California, Florida New York and Texas state prisons in FY 2015. The State Criminal Alien Assistance Program (SCAAP) reimburses states for illegal aliens incarcerated in state facilities. Table 7 shows the data covering selected violent crime:

Table 7

	Total	Homicide		Drugs		Sex Offenses		Assault	
		% Total	# Crimes	% Total	# Crimes	% Total	# Crimes	% Total	# Crimes
	SCAAP Illegal Aliens imprisoned in FY 2015 for Selected Violent Crimes								
Arizona	6,325	6%	381	47%	2,992	9%	591	7%	417
California	18,589	28%	5,288	5%	908	24%	4,497	13%	2,395
Florida	6,253	23%	1,419	14%	890	22%	1,399	5%	323
New York	3,375	33%	1,106	10%	345	16%	545	9%	308
Texas	9,596	10%	999	16%	1,531	23%	2,212	13%	1,262
Total	44,137	21%	9,193	15%	6,666	21%	9,244	11%	4,705

Source: GAO unpublished SCAAP conviction data provided to author upon request

The numbers reflect those incarcerated in 2015, but they may have been convicted earlier. The table describes 9,193 people who died at the hands of illegal aliens. That is 9,193 Kate Steinles. That is 9,193 mothers, fathers, sisters, brothers, and children, who will never see or be seen by their families again. Remember that next time you are accused of being unsympathetic towards illegal aliens.

The five states included in this study house 64 percent of all incarcerated SCAAP illegal aliens. Note that for these states, homicides were 21 percent of all crimes committed by illegals. If that rate were applied to the illegal aliens incarcerated in all states, that would equate to over 14,000 deaths at the hands of illegals.

When these statistics do surface, the open-borders lobby quickly jumps in, claiming that illegal aliens commit fewer crimes than Americans do. It is a straw man argument of course. If there were strong border controls, none of these crimes would have been committed. Those 14,000 bereaved families could have lived their lives without the crushing grief of losing a loved one. Ask them if they care whether or not illegal aliens murder more people than American citizens.

But it is a false argument anyway. Table 8 compares the total number of individuals incarcerated compared to criminal aliens incarcerated for specified crimes as of December 2018. For example, criminal aliens committed 18.5 percent of kidnappings, 17.9 percent of all sex crimes, 16.7 percent of child molestations and 12.5 percent of homicides. Criminal aliens commit crimes wildly out of proportion to their numbers in the population, and many of these are illegal aliens. A 2010 study by the Arizona Prosecuting Attorneys' Advisory Council found that "While an exact determination cannot be made of how many foreign nationals in custody are undocumented aliens, it is likely that a high percentage of them are."[115]

Table 8

Arizona Incarceration Statistics December 2018			
		AZ Corrections	
Charge	Total	Aliens	% Total
Assault	5,604	316	5.6%
Kidnapping	1,344	248	18.5%
Homicide/Murder	3,875	483	12.5%
Rape & Other Sex Offenses	3,436	616	17.9%
Child Molestation	1,772	296	16.7%
Drug Posession/Sales	8,560	1,110	13.0%
Other	17,346	362	2.1%
Total	41,937	3,431	7.6%
Source: Arizona Dept. of Corrections; Corrections at a Glance, 12/18			

It has gotten much worse since then. A recent study by veteran researcher John Lott confirms this overall impression, finding that the illegal alien crime rate in Arizona is double that of legal AZ residents.[116] So there is no crisis at the border? Tell that to the kidnap, rape, and murder victims.

GAO has also estimated the costs for housing illegal aliens in federal and state prisons to total around $2.3 billion per year.[117]

Finally, North Carolinians For Immigration Reform and Enforcement, (www.NCFire.info), compiles child rape/sexual assault charges against illegal aliens in North Carolina. In the past five years, 1,527 illegal aliens have been arrested for a total of 6,824 sex crimes against children. That is an average of 4.5 violations per individual.

On October 29, 2015, the author attended an Immigration Law forum put on by Georgetown School of Law and the Migration Policy Institute. Many of the usual suspects performed in a fawning open-borders propaganda show for law students. In a panel discussion, Marielena Hincapié of the National Immigration Law Center bewailed the fact that an illegal alien dad was not going to be able to share Christmas with his young son because he was incarcerated for violating immigration laws. What would Ms. Hincapié say to *the thousands* of mothers, fathers, sisters, brothers, children, who will *never see their deceased beloved ever again* because organizations like hers prevented our nation from protecting itself against the very people she is trying to help?

Another panelist said those opposing illegal immigration and refugee resettlement did so because "they don't look like us." Of course. So, we're all "bigots" for getting upset about mass murder, welfare fraud, drugs, and other criminality, as well as job theft, welfare burdens, language barriers, and more. The list of legitimate grievances is endless. But that kind of arrogant, presumptuous slander is the go-to response for these people, because when the facts are presented, they don't have an argument.

Sanctuary city and state policies are not helping. They are literally safe hideouts for criminals and terrorists who are sometimes even aided and abetted by people in positions of responsibility. In November 2018, Luis Rodrigo Perez, an illegal alien, allegedly murdered three people in New Jersey. ICE had tried to deport him in 2017 following an arrest for domestic violence in 'sanctuary' Middlesex County, New Jersey. But the County released Perez without alerting ICE. Three are dead as the result.[118]

In April 2018, a Newton, Mass, district judge apparently colluded with the prosecutor and defense attorney to assist an illegal alien wanted on drug and other charges, to flee the courthouse to avoid an ICE officer waiting to detain him. This is apparently not the first time in Newton. In 2017 another judge reduced bail from $100,000 to $2,500 for an illegal alien charged with raping a Boston College student. He paid and fled. In this case, however, a grand jury has been empanelled by Boston's US Attorney to investigate the judge and others involved.[119]

Sanctuary Cities. Source: Center for Immigration Studies; using Immigration and Customs Enforcement Data

And then there is the case of Mollie Tibbets, a 20-year old Iowan girl who was knifed to death by Cristhian Bahena-Rivera, an illegal alien from Mexico, who had chased her down while she was jogging. The presiding judge in the case awarded $5,000 to Bahena-Rivera for his defense. Citizens were so outraged, a letter-writing campaign demanded the judge stop using taxpayer money to pay for his defense.[120] Iowa is buried in sanctuary cities, as is apparent from the map above. None of these unconscionable crimes would have been committed if our borders were secure as they should be. Politicians on both sides of the aisle share responsibility, and their continued refusal to secure the border guarantees more of the same for the American people.According to official data, 8.3 million illegal aliens, approximately 73 percent of the claimed U.S. total in 2012, were from El Salvador, Guatemala, Honduras, and Mexico.[121] This is almost 60 percent of the 14.5 million U.S. residents born in those four countries.[122]Between 2007 and 2016, 1,545.183 criminal aliens were removed from the U.S.[123] Of these, 1,435,918 or 92.9 percent, came from those same four countries.[124] During the same period, 1,934,726 individuals born in El Salvador, Guatemala, Honduras and Mexico became legal permanent residents (LPR) in the U.S., which represents 18.1 percent of the 10.7 million LPRs admitted. [125] So, while these people represent 18 percent of those establishing residence in the U.S. legally, they comprise 93 percent of those getting thrown out. The GAO found that 91 percent of the approximately 39,500 criminal aliens currently in federal prisons are citizens of Colombia, Dominican Republic, El Salvador, Guatemala, Honduras or Mexico. [126] Clearly these populations are problematic. In February 2019, President Trump reluctantly signed a compromise border security bill in order to avoid another government shutdown, even though it provided only a fraction of the funding he sought for a complete barrier on our southern border with Mexico. As always, the Democrats and establishment Republicans sought to obstruct Trump's determination to secure this country from the crisis-level flood of illegals storming the U.S.-Mexico border. On 15 February 2019, Trump declared a National Emergency Concerning the Southern Border of the United States (Proclamation 9844).[127] That declaration allowed the President legally to access other funds, already appropriated by Congress but not yet allocated or spent, to construct a proper barrier along the U.S. southern border that would make it as difficult as possible for illegals to penetrate areas until now unsecured.

What will it take to make America safe again?

WHERE IT ALL BEGAN

O ver the past 50 years, the UN has devoted extensive resources to promoting population control. Educated Westerners listened and today this demographic is reproducing barely at replacement rates. We all thought this was the point. But now the UN is promoting what it calls "replacement migration." [128] Because Western populations are reaching retirement age in large numbers without similar numbers of new births, and because the UN now says the workforce cannot sustain itself without help, our population must be supplemented with those who never got the memo about containing population growth.

So, after exhorting us to limit family size through abortion and birth control, the UN now wants to backfill our declining populations with newcomers from countries where abortion and birth control are not practiced and often illegal. This is the kind of insanity that occupies the minds of the UN globalists.

But there is a method to their madness: *it is the Left's goal to build a "permanent progressive majority"* ruling class. The open borders agenda is the perfect vehicle. Millions of needy poor migrants become bought-and-paid-for leftwing voters. Refugees can become citizens and vote within five years. Illegal aliens may eventually vote either through amnesty, vote fraud or in some cases even local laws that allow non-citizens to vote.

Meanwhile, the flood of immigration by people who do not share our beliefs and values slowly dilutes American culture, causing us to abandon longstanding traditions and also threatens the rule of law. The multiple problems these populations import inspires calls from the Left for still more government to solve the manufactured crisis.

The more exotic and incompatible the immigrant population, the better. The Left always seeks to introduce chaos and disorganization, because disoriented masses are easy to rule. The threat posed by jihadis and our nation's other enemies does not concern the Left. The way some of them see it, such a threat only serves to edge American society closer to anarchy and collapse.

The Left envisions its cherished dictatorship of the proletariat rising like a phoenix from the ashes. Europe has pursued this goal for years and much more aggressively, and with the mass migration instigated by the Syrian civil war, Europe is now tottering on the brink of total collapse. The Left seeks to have that happen here.

UN History and Its Relevance

Since its 1945 founding, the UN has engaged in an almost non-stop effort to obstruct, criticize, and undermine U.S. policy, despite receiving more financial support from the U.S. than any other nation. There is a reason for this.

The UN Charter was drafted by Soviet agent-of-influence Alger Hiss, one of the most notorious traitors in American history.[129] Hiss's was appointed secretary-general to the 1945 UN Charter organizing conference.[130] TIME magazine noted at the time, "As secretary-general, managing the agenda, [Hiss] will have a lot to say behind the scenes about who gets the breaks."[131] He did.

Hiss had a lot of help from other notorious Soviet spies, including Harry Dexter White, Lauchlin Currie, and Lawrence Duggan,[132] and a long list of prominent American officials who had attempted to create its predecessor, the League of Nations. Communist Party leader Earl Browder stated, "American Communists worked energetically and tirelessly to lay the foundations for the United Nations ..."[133]

During the initial Dumbarton Oaks organizing conference in 1944, Hiss worked alongside Stalin's deputy, Vyacheslav Molotov.[134] Hiss guided UN discussions at the 1945 Yalta Conference, where he was instrumental in convincing President Roosevelt to give the Soviet Union three votes to America's one.[135] The votes were for the USSR, Belarus, and Ukraine, all part of the USSR, and the USSR created missions for each. It was compared to giving America extra votes for Texas and California.[136] Hiss traveled to the USSR immediately after Yalta, where the Soviets congratulated him for his work.[137] Nobody ever questioned it.

From its founding to the present day, every single UN Secretary-General has been a socialist or Communist. Antonio Guterrez, Secretary-General since 2017, was formerly UN High Commissioner for Refugees (UNHCR). He is a lifelong Socialist, former president of the Socialist International (1999-2005), and former prime minister of Portugal.[138]

The Soviets always considered the UN an instrument of Soviet foreign policy—"a forum for spreading Soviet views."[139] This has not changed in the post-Soviet era. The second most important post in the original UN Charter was Under-Secretary-General for Political and Security Council Affairs, which oversaw international security (military) and peace issues. Edward Stettinius, then U.S. Secretary of State and Ambassador to the United Nations, agreed to allow the Soviet Union to control this critical post. Instead of demanding that post for the U.S., American negotiators accepted the largely administrative post of Assistant Secretary-General for the Administrative and Financial Services.[140] The Deep State existed even then.

From 1945 until 1992, the Under-Secretary-General for Political and Security Council Affairs position was held by 14 different individuals, all

Communists and all but one from the Soviet Union.[141] Since 1992 it has been held by representatives of Russia, Great Britain, Nigeria, and the U.S.

The U.S. obtained UN support for the Korean War only because the USSR had quit to protest the UN refusal to throw out Nationalist China and allow Communist China to join.[142] In 1971, they got their way. Communist China was voted in and Nationalist China out. UN delegates smiled and danced in the aisles.[143]

At the aforementioned immigration forum attended by the author, then-UNHCR Guterres called fears of terrorists hiding among refugees from Syria, "stupid."[144] Two weeks later, two terrorists who posed as Syrian refugees to reach Europe with the migrants, participated in the mass-murder of 130 people in Paris, France.[145] As UNHCR, Guterres advocated resettlement of 130,000 Syrians to Western nations. The quota given his home country of Portugal: 23.[146] Guterres' successor, current UNHCR Filippo Grandi, wanted to resettle 400,000 Syrians.[147] Hillary Clinton advocated America receive 65,000 of these during her presidential campaign.[148] America dodged a bullet temporarily with her defeat.

The outlines of the open borders agenda were framed in the Vancouver Plan of Action at the 1976 UN Conference on Human Settlements, held in Vancouver, British Columbia.[149] The Plan makes no mention of refugees or immigrants. But that fact is totally irrelevant. As we have shown, the UN is entirely socialist and globalist in intention and design and seeks to see the entire world unified under UN control.So, it is irrelevant whether we are talking about migrants or home country populations. The UN envisions redistributing not only wealth, but land, resources, and populations worldwide, not as a matter of individual choice, but of UN crafted policy. As it states in the document, "Human settlement policies can be powerful tools for the more equitable distribution of income and opportunities."[150]

Note in the following proposals that it is the government deciding where and how everyone in the country lives.:

A.1 National Settlement Policy:
- *All countries should establish as a matter of urgency a national policy on human settlements, embodying the distribution of population, and related economic and social activities, over the national territory.*

A.2 Human Settlements and Development:
- *A national policy for human settlements and the environment should be an integral part of any national economic and social development policy.*

A.4 More Equitable Distribution:
- *Human settlements policies should aim to improve the condition of human settlements particularly by promoting a more equitable distribution of the benefits of development among regions; and by*

*making such benefits and public services equally accessible to all
groups.[151]*

A.4 describes how resources are distributed among "regions," not states
or nations, which is another indication of the UN mindset: globalist
governance. The settlement provisions did pay back-handed lip service to the
notion of national sovereignty and property rights. For example, Settlement
policies and Strategies Preamble point 3 states, "The ideologies of States are
reflected in their human settlement policies. These being powerful
instruments for change, they must not be used to dispossess people from
their homes and their land, or to entrench privilege and exploitation."[152]

That is exactly what the UN intends to do, however, because the UN and
its communist brethren worldwide see the U.S. as a poster child for
entrenched "privilege and exploitation." Point 1 in the preamble to the land
section[153] makes clear the UN body's utter contempt for property rights.
Point 2 emphasizes that land *must* be controlled by government:

1. *Land, because of its unique nature and the crucial role it plays in
   human settlements, cannot be treated as an ordinary asset,
   controlled by individuals and subject to the pressures and
   inefficiencies of the market. Private land ownership is also a principal
   instrument of accumulation and concentration of wealth and
   therefore contributes to social injustice; if unchecked, it may become
   a major obstacle in the planning and implementation of development
   schemes. Social justice, urban renewal and development, the
   provision of decent dwellings-and healthy conditions for the people
   can only be achieved if land is used in the interests of society as a
   whole.*

2. *Instead, the pattern of land use should be determined by the long-
   term interests of the community, especially since decisions on
   location of activities and therefore of specific land uses have a long-
   lasting effect on the pattern and structure of human settlements.
   Land is also a primary element of the natural and man-made
   environment and a crucial link in an often delicate balance. Public
   control of land use is therefore indispensable to its protection as an
   asset and the achievement of the long-term objectives of human
   settlement policies and strategies.*

The UN justified these measures based on expectations about
population growth, various environmental policies, and of course "social
justice." These three concerns later morphed into the three "pillars" of the
UN Agenda 21's "sustainability" concept: environment, economy, and social
equity. It is merely socialism repackaged but explains why the UN has now

invented yet another oppressed class in need of resettlement: climate refugees.[154]Forty years later, the UN stated explicitly that these concepts apply to "migrants," including refugees. In a September 2016 summit at the UN, then-U.S. President Obama signed the *New York Declaration for Refugees and Migrants*, which would begin the process of developing a *Global Compact for Safe, Orderly and Regular Migration.* [155] The Compact declared that "migrants, regardless of status; all are rights holders."[156] National laws be damned, they all have "rights," that must be fully protected. There are many other pernicious aspects of this new proposal, but here are two particularly dangerous provisions:

OBJECTIVE 17: Eliminate all forms of discrimination and promote evidence-based public discourse to shape perceptions of migration.

This advocates enacting hate crime laws that will outlaw any kind of speech or action critical of migrants or the UN migration agenda. The effort to stifle speech with blasphemy laws and other restrictions has been an ongoing effort by the Organization of Islamic Cooperation, a confederation of 56 Muslim nations and the Palestinian Authority. It is the second largest intergovernmental organization in the world, next to the UN. The criminalization of speech in the Migrant Compact is certainly part of OIC's effort. This entire book would likely be outlawed—facts be damned. If you criticize the open borders agenda, it can only be because you are a bigot.

In November 2018, Europe of Nations and Freedom (ENF) party members of the European Parliament held a press conference to discuss the Compact on Migration. Parliament member Marcel de Graaff, a member of the Dutch Party for Freedom, warned what the Compact would mean:

> The participating countries are set to sign this agreement. And although this joint agreement isn't binding, it's still meant to be the legal framework on which the participating countries commit themselves to build new legislation. One basic element of this new agreement is the extension of the definition of hate speech. The agreement want [*sic*] to criminalize migration speech. ***Criticism of migration will become a criminal offense, and media outlets... that give room to criticism of migration can be shut down. The compact for migration is legalization of mass migration.*** (Emphasis added.) It's declaring migration as a human right. So in fact, it will become impossible to criticize Ms. [German Chancellor Angela] Merkel's "welcome migrants" politics, without being at risk to be jailed for hate speech.[157]

Despite its claim that the Compact is "nonbinding," the UN is aggressively promoting this policy, pressuring signatory countries to censor any speech that sheds a negative light on Islam or the mass immigration that has occurred over the last few years. In a recent debate in the German Bundestag, Chancellor Angela Merkel said that the Compact will, in fact, be binding. It will also require signatory nations to abide by other odious UN programs, like Agenda 2030.[158]

The UN has already begun flexing its muscle. For example, the "UN Committee on the Elimination of Racial Discrimination" has demanded Norway become more aggressive in its prosecution of "haters." One best-selling Norwegian writer, Hege Storhaug, published a 2015 best-selling book now translated into English, titled *Islam: Europe Invaded, America Warned*.[159] Storhaug and her book have been reported to the UN, ironically by a liberal group that includes gays, and the UN has been asked to seek her prosecution.[160] Storhaug became educated to the nature of Islam through Pakistani Muslim friends of hers, who warned her about allowing Islam to establish itself in Norway. She has been reporting and writing on the issue since 1992 and has lived in an undisclosed location under police protection for 11 years.

OBJECTIVE 19: Create conditions for migrants and diasporas to fully contribute to sustainable development in all countries.

Objective 19 is yet another example of rhetorical gymnastics, this time used to justify support for Agenda 2030, the updated version of Agenda 21. The following description proposal should send chills down your spine:

> Integrate migration into development planning and sectoral policies at local, national, regional and global levels, taking into consideration relevant existing policy guidelines and recommendations, such as the GMG Handbook on Mainstreaming Migration into Development Planning, in order to strengthen policy coherence and effectiveness of development cooperation.

This anticipates the explicit inclusion of the open borders agenda in the settlements policies first articulated at the 1976 Conference. The GMG Handbook is put out by the Global Migration Group (GMG), an interagency organization that includes the UN's International Organization for Migration (OIM), international labor, the World Bank, the World Health Organization, UNHCR and 11 other UN agencies, so it is not a trivial effort.

Agenda 21 has advanced in the U.S. to a great degree because socialist "sustainability" concepts were early on insinuated into the American Planning Association's (APA) guidelines used almost universally by planning and zoning boards. Now we will see the demands of migrants incorporated into official state, regional, and local planning concepts.

In a taste of what is to come, Minneapolis in late 2018 passed a zoning law abolishing single family zoning to facilitate multi-family housing in suburban neighborhoods. As you might know, Minneapolis is ground zero for Somali refugee resettlement. The rationale is straight out of the UN:

> In Minneapolis, the decision came as part of a sweeping plan to propel the city into the future by addressing issues like

housing, racial equity and climate change. The plan, called Minneapolis 2040, drew thousands of public comments, "Don't Bulldoze Our Neighborhoods" yard signs and a last-minute lawsuit, but ultimately passed on a 12-1 vote.[161]

Expect to see more of this popping up in cities around the nation, unless they are somehow recaptured by patriotic American leaders who understand the ramifications. This is one place where local activism to stop this agenda could have an impact.

The Trump administration bailed out of the Global Compact and its corollary, the *Global Compact on Refugees*. Numerous other countries are following Trump's lead. But with a change in leadership, the U.S. could shortly see itself suffering under these UN edicts. President Obama would have signed it, as would Hillary and most, if not all, other Democrats.

While they cheerfully sign on to all these proposals, Communist countries completely ignore the UN because the UN agenda is not meant for them, and no one ever calls them on it. Think of Russia, China, or Cuba resettling 10,000 Somali Muslims or 65,000 Syrians. Think again. Only Western-style governments, and especially America, have escaped the grip of communism so far, so only the West is targeted *because the West is the target.*

The 1980 Refugee Act

The current domestic refugee resettlement program, formally called the U.S. Refugee Admissions Program (USRAP), was created with passage of now-deceased Senator Ted Kennedy's Refugee Act of 1980. The bill's impetus was aided by the massive Vietnamese "Boat People" seagoing diaspora ongoing at the time; however, Kennedy's bill was almost certainly inspired at least in part by the UN Human Settlements agenda.

A decade earlier, Kennedy—also the architect of the 1965 Immigration and Nationalities Act, urged on Congress by leaders of the California Communist Party[162]—echoed what would become the UN's rationale, saying, "All nations are under obligation to eliminate ignorance, poverty, inequality and injustice."[163] And much like the 1965 Act, Kennedy sought to broaden the base of future refugees by creating a "non need-based policy that was not specifically designed for people from communist regimes in Eastern Europe or repressive governments in the Middle East, as it was in the past."[164]

So now they could deemphasize those troublesome anti-communist refugees, almost certain to vote Republican once they became citizens, and rig the system to produce New Democrats, which was what motivated Teddy Kennedy to also push for the 1965 Immigration and Nationalities Act. But as usual the "compassion" cover story ruled the day. The bill passed the U.S. Senate with a unanimous vote on March 17, 1980.[165]

U.S. Support of the UN

Under the heading "never give a sucker an even break," the United States pays the lion's share of both the UN budget, as well as that of the UN High Commissioner for Refugees (UNHCR). As shown by the latest UN statistics in Table 9 below, the U.S. has provided $7.4 billion, almost 40 percent of the UNHCR budget since 2010. 2016 UNHCR contributions from our largest adversaries, China and Russia, were a paltry $2.8 million and $2.0 million respectively, a combined total of 0.02 percent of the budget. The combined contributions from the Gulf states of Saudi Arabia, Qatar and the United Arab Emirates totaled $19.2 million in 2016 (0.5 percent of the UNHCR budget). You'd think they could have done more, given the Syrian refugee crisis.[166]

Table 9

UN Budget: Selected Programs ($ Billions)								
	Total	2016	2015	2014	2013	2012	2011	2010
UN Peacekeeping Operations	$55.5	$8.9	$8.8	$7.9	$7.3	$7.5	$7.6	$7.6
United Nations administration	$33.3	$5.7	$5.6	$5.1	$4.3	$4.2	$4.4	$4.0
UNHCR	**$20.0**	**$4.0**	**$3.3**	**$3.3**	**$3.0**	**$2.3**	**$2.2**	**$1.9**
All Others	$201.1	$30.2	$30.4	$30.0	$27.9	$28.7	$27.4	$26.4
Total	$309.9	$48.8	$48.1	$46.4	$42.5	$42.8	$41.5	$39.8
U.S. Contribution to U.N.	$53.1	$9.7	$9.9	$10.7	$7.7	$5.4	$4.6	$5.0
Percent of total U.N. budget	17%	20%	21%	23%	18%	13%	11%	13%
U.S. Contribution to UNHCR	$7.4	$1.5	$1.4	$1.3	$1.0	$0.8	$0.7	$0.7
Percent of UNHCR budget	37%	38%	41%	38%	35%	34%	32%	38%

Source: Agency Revenue by Government Donor; United Nations System Chief Executives Board for Coordination

In 2016, the U.S. contributed $9.7 billion, or about 20 percent of the overall UN budget of $48.8 billion. The 2016 chart below illustrates how this contribution also dwarfs that of all other nations. Russia and China, arguably those nations that benefit the most from UN meddling, contributed a combined total of $1.9 billion, or less than 4 percent of the total UN budget.

Chart 2

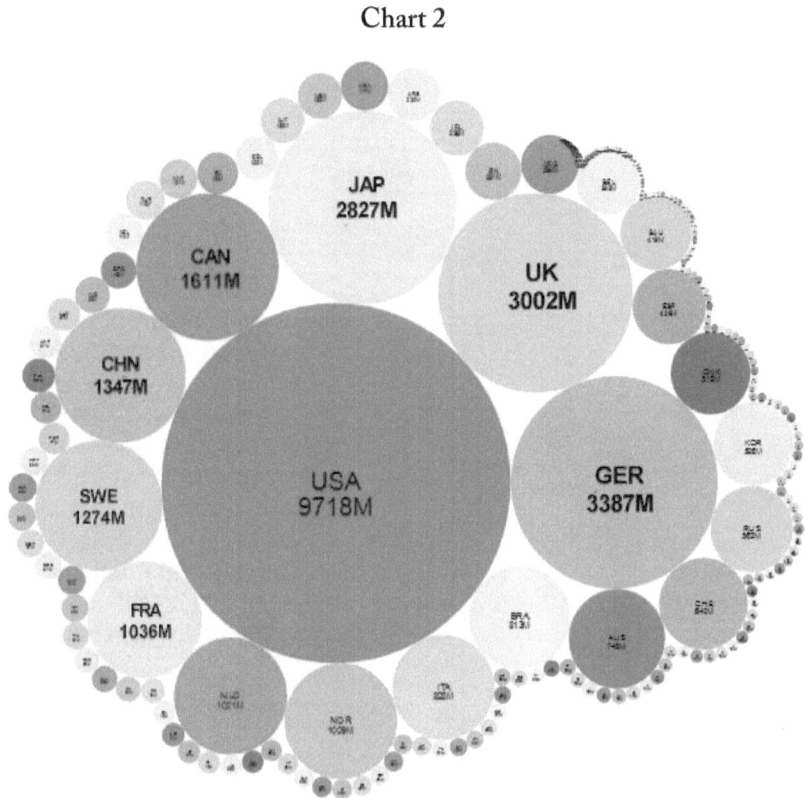

Source: Total Revenue by Government Donor; United Nations System Chief Executives Board for Coordination. https://www.unsceb.org/content/FS-D00-02.

Only Westerners take UN pontificating seriously and only Western nations implement the UN's destructive policies at home. Unfortunately, the American Left treats UN edicts as gospel and the most fertile opportunities are found in the open borders movement.

The entire illegal alien/refugee/asylum agenda must be viewed as a UN-inspired plan aimed at the West, especially America, to *erase borders and dilute Western culture through mass immigration from the world's failed nations.* The goal is to gradually turn America into a minority majority nation, with third-world minorities that do not share our culture, our Judeo-Christian heritage, or interest in a society based on constitutional principles and the rule of law, but who will instead ignorantly vote to elect Americans who promise endless benefits without understanding that in reality these politicians have committed themselves to the destruction of America as we know it.

As traditional American society is gradually eliminated, our political power goes with it. And neither the Left nor Muslim activists are worried about controlling these new, heavily government-dependent populations. While many are fleeing the consequences of socialist policies, they nonetheless bring with them the socialist mindset that presumes the only difference between America and their failed nations is that America can afford it.

Islamic Influence at the UN

The Organization of Islamic Cooperation (OIC)[167] is a close partner with the UN and exercises disproportionate influence over UN policy.[168] Its goal is to seed America and other Western countries with devout, faithful Muslim populations which will not assimilate but instead attempt to dominate through stealthy, but aggressive, imposition of Islamic Law (sharia), thereby steadily degrading the non-Islamic societal character of those countries. Under President Obama, Muslim immigration and refugee resettlement numbers skyrocketed.

THE REFUGEE PROGRAM

The U.S. Refugee Admission Program (USRAP) is administered by three separate federal agencies: the State Department Bureau of Population, Refugees and Migration (PRM), the Department of Health and Human Services' Office of Refugee Resettlement (ORR), and the Department of Homeland Security's U.S. Citizenship and Immigration Service (USCIS).

Additionally, the Department of Justice adjudicates some, but not all, asylum cases through its Executive Office for Immigration Review (EOIR). The Department of Agriculture provides grants to refugee farmers, while the Department of Education offers grants for English Language Learners (ELL) and civics education. There are likely grant programs in other agencies as well. But the primary resettlement agencies are PRM, ORR, and USCIS.

Organizational Chart for the State Department, Bureau of Population, Refugees and Migration (PRM)

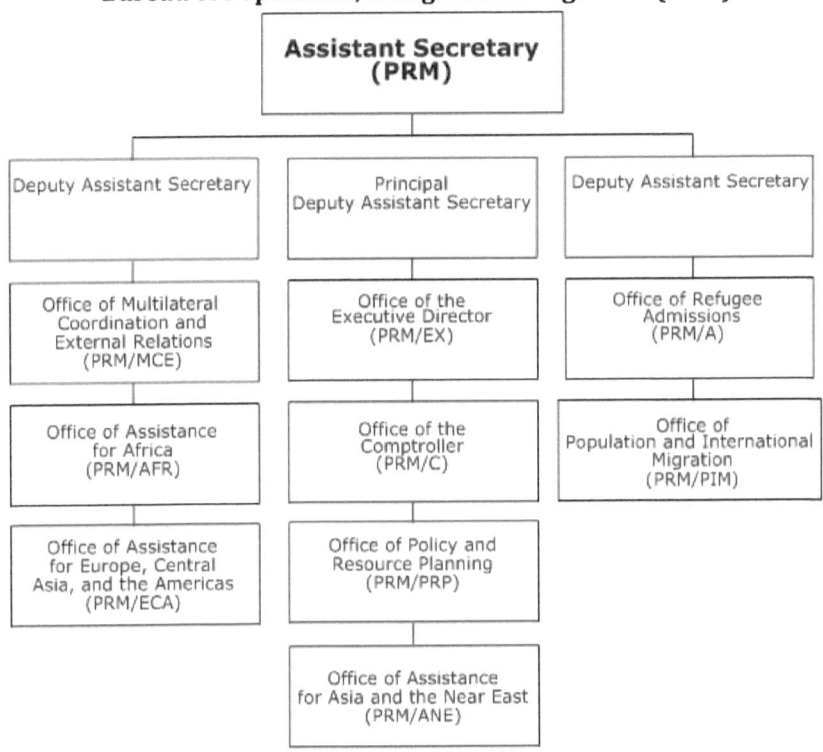

The State Department's Reception and Placement Program is managed by PRM, which oversees nine public and private Resettlement Support Centers (RSC) across the globe. These centers select refugees—usually from a list of those within refugee camps supplied by the United Nations High Commissioner for Refugees (UNHCR). PRM then assigns selected refugees to nine private contractors called Voluntary Agencies (VOLAGS), which meet weekly to decide where the refugees will be resettled in the United States. The International Office of Migration (IOM), a UN agency, coordinates with the RSCs and the VOLAGs to bring refugees to the U.S. [169] VOLAGs are provided State Department seed grants of $2,125 per-head to resettle refugees.[170] VOLAGs are allowed to pocket about 45 percent of this and use the rest to pay initial resettlement costs.

The Health and Human Service Department's Office of Refugee Resettlement (ORR) provides most funding for refugee resettlement programs over and above the seed money provided by PRM. ORR also offers numerous grants for refugee social services, business startups and other funding ostensibly to help qualified refugee populations get established in the U.S.

Refugee Vetting

Both the USCIS and Customs and Border Protection (CBP) vet refugees. Under President Obama, the vetting process was excessively lax, despite the existential threat of terrorism.[171] But under President Trump's "extreme vetting", the refugee flow has been reduced substantially.

The refugee industry continually parrots the line that refugees are thoroughly vetted. USCIS officers do interview refugees, but they also rely on multiple agency databases. In many cases, no real records exist, so as former FBI Director James Comey said, "We can query our databases until the cows come home," but if there are no records, you get no results.[172]

A.J. Irwin is a former special agent and ICE regional director who oversaw all Joint Terrorism Task Force investigations for the U.S. Central Region. In a public television forum Irwin was even more blunt. He stated of the vetting process:

> "[W]hen we send refugee officers over there to interview people, they have a mission and their mission is not to detect fraud or identify terrorists, it's to process these people and get 'em into the system... They don't spend a lot of time talking to them. They get their basic information; they see if they meet the basic requirements, do they have credible fear, what it's based on, and then they move on to the next person. So, this process is very rapid, and the mission again is more service, it's not enforcement, it's not detection of fraud or national security.[173]

The Obama administration knowingly and routinely allowed illegal aliens falsely claiming asylum to remain in the United States. 174 A September 2016 DHS Inspector General report found that 1,982 aliens from countries known for immigration fraud or terror-links who were scheduled for deportation were instead granted citizenship using false identities because fingerprint records were missing.[175]

Systemic Fraud

The entire refugee resettlement program has systemic fraud, creating both national security and crime risks, in addition to the many other problems created by unassimilable third world populations. Refugee advocates claim the vetting process is airtight, but U.S. security officials say exactly the opposite. An internal Immigrations, Customs, and Enforcement (ICE) memo states:

> [The] refugee program is particularly vulnerable to fraud due to loose evidentiary requirements where at times the testimony of an applicant alone is sufficient for approval. As a result, a range of bad actors, who use manufactured histories, biographies and other false statements, as well as produce and submit fictitious supporting documentation, have exploited this program...[176]

The memo goes on to say that "the immigration system is a constant target for exploitation" by terrorists.

Former U.S. Senate candidate and Temple University law professor, Jan Ting, served as an assistant commissioner of the Immigration and Naturalization Services (INS) under President H.W. Bush. When asked if it were true that 90 percent of percent of refugee and asylee applications were fraudulent, he said, "95 percent."[177]

Mary Doetsch, a retired 25-year veteran of the State Department who served as refugee coordinator over Africa, Cuba, Europe, Russia, and the Middle East, for eight years, said incidents of fraud are legion:

I had first-hand knowledge of country conditions and political realities, and I saw and read hundreds of fraudulent refugee claims. Disturbingly, the majority of refugee claims are ultimately approved, despite serious questions regarding the applicants' reliability and truthfulness, often based solely on their testimony.[178]

She concludes:

> Despite claims that refugees are subject to the most intense scrutiny prior to resettlement into the United States, the bottom line is that in countries with ill-functioning governments or where no reliable data exists, it is virtually impossible to vet refugee candidates.[179]

The refugee resettlement program is broken down into three categories. From USCIS:

- **Priority 1 (P-1)**: Cases that are identified and referred to the program by the United Nations High Commissioner for Refugees (UNHCR), a United States Embassy, or a designated non-governmental organization (NGO).

- **Priority 2 (P-2)**: Groups of special humanitarian concern identified by the U.S. refugee program.

- **Priority 3 (P-3)**: Family reunification cases (spouses, unmarried children under 21, and parents of persons lawfully admitted to the United States as refugees or asylees or permanent residents (green card holders) or U.S. citizens who previously had refugee or asylum status)

The P-3 program for Africa had to be shut down for four years because it was discovered through DNA testing that over 80 percent of those claiming familial relationships were false. Between October 1, 2004 and 2008, when the program was suspended, 36,000 Africans—mostly from Somalia—resettled in the U.S. through the P-3 program. That means 28,000 or more could have committed fraud to get here.[180] The program restarted again in 2012. Not a single person was prosecuted or sent back.

Most U.S. Somalis originally arrived as refugees, asylum seekers, or through P-3 family reunification. Many now take months-long trips back to Somalia, making a mockery of the entire resettlement program, as it is based on refugees' claimed "credible fear" that returning home would put them in mortal danger. But the stupidity doesn't end there. Minneapolis actually grants rent relief because Somalis complained about the financial burden of overdue rent upon their return.[181]

Further complicating matters, refugees are exempt from the Trump administration's travel ban, even though many come from travel ban countries where reliable vetting is extremely difficult if not impossible.

Retired ICE Associate Legal Advisor, Charles Thaddeus Fillinger, published a scathing review of the program, and pointed specifically to USCIS failure to deal with those fraud refugees still in the U.S.:

This year marks the passing of a full decade since the greatest refugee fraud crisis in modern times. The overseas P-3 refugee "family reunification" program was suspended in 2008 following revelations of shocking fraud levels... *Left unresolved was the issue of thousands of fraudulent refugees who were admitted to the United States before the suspension* (emphasis added). In contravention of clear principle, solid evidence, and direct experience, U.S. Citizenship and Immigration Services (USCIS) continued to use the wrong screening strategy to process the pre-suspension P-3 caseload. USCIS disbursed domestic immigration benefits to fraudulent refugees without in-person interviews for many benefits, without required DNA tests for any benefits, and without administrative fraud checks for older cases. A Niagara of overseas refugee fraud was met with a dribble of domestic defense. This was staggering irresponsibility, possibly the biggest blunder in immigration history. Yesterday's fraudulent refugees became today's green card holders, international travelers using refugee travel documents, and U.S. citizens.[182]

Fillinger goes on to cite all the costs and hardships these fraudulent refugees are likely to impose, including terrorism, trafficking women and children, and excessive welfare use. And rather than clean up its act, he says that USCIS proposed a plan to destroy all records of this failed system, virtually guaranteeing it would start again. Fillinger says the domestic P-3 screening program needs to be every bit as rigorous as it now is overseas.

People willing to commit document fraud to gain citizenship are often willing to commit other crimes once resettled to the U.S. Nationwide, welfare, food stamp, and other forms of fraud have become commonplace among both individuals and businesses run by refugees and illegal aliens.

In Minneapolis, Minnesota, approximately $100 million is being stolen annually under the state's Child Care Assistance Program (CCAP), where crooked child care providers have been systematically overbilling the state for services they don't perform. Millions in cash stuffed in suitcases depart the Minneapolis airport for Somalia, where some of that money may be financing terrorism.[183]

State Department of Health Services employees have stonewalled the state legislature, ignoring requests for information on the scandal and an inspector general report has been withheld from the public. With the November 2018 election of hard Leftist Muslim Keith Ellison as state attorney general, along with newly-elected Democratic Governor Tim Walz, the investigation is likely to be shelved, or at least stymied.

Food stamp fraud conducted by refugees and other immigrants has become a nationwide phenomenon, with major scandals in Alabama, Connecticut, Florida, Maine, New York, Missouri, Ohio, Oregon, Rhode Island and elsewhere. [184] A 2018 study on SNAP (food stamp) fraud by the Government Accountability Institute found:

- Multiple criminal cases involving millions in fraudulently obtained Supplemental Nutrition Assistance Program (SNAP) dollars funding terrorism, domestically and overseas going all the way back to 1985
- A Florida flea market operation netted $13 million by charging a fee to as many as 41,000 customers who sought illegally to receive cash using SNAP cards
- Vendors provide cash, drugs, weapons, prostitution, and more

- From 2012-14, nearly 36,000 stores, approximately 11.8 percent of all SNAP retailers, mostly small convenience stores, engaged in trafficking fraud each year
- Illegal aliens routinely obtain food stamps despite being ineligible for them[185]

In some cases, this criminal activity is overlooked and even sanctioned by the U.S. government. Illegal aliens routinely engage in identity theft in applying for various benefits. DACA beneficiaries use fraudulent or stolen identities to apply for jobs. One analysis found, for example, that:

> ... many if not most DACA applicants who held regular jobs had committed the crime of perjury, by providing their employers with a stolen or fake Social Security number (SSN) for tax reporting purposes. The Social Security Administration (SSA) has estimated that three out of every four illegal aliens possess an SSN that belongs to somebody else.[186]

The Obama administration dropped the requirement for DACA recipients to provide an SSN if they had not officially received one for themselves, publicly stating that it would not enforce violations of "some federal law in an employment relationship." [187] The administration then suspended the practice of informing employers when Social Security numbers did not match the names of those it had on file, a potentially devastating consequence for the citizen whose SSN was being fraudulently used.

The IRS went even further, encouraging illegal aliens who filed taxes to use stolen SSNs. An internal IRS document tells employees to describe the identity theft as "borrowing." Illegal aliens have received billions in tax refunds, while innocent Americans whose IDs they've stolen, face charges of tax fraud and underreporting income due to the illegal filings. They have to spend months submitting documents to prove their innocence, even though *the IRS may know who the identity theft is.*

IRS employees were forbidden from reporting to Americans when their identities had been stolen. One IRS source for this report said:

> "And we see it every day—eight hours a day—you see this over and over and over and over again... And I know where the person lives, where they work... I see all of that and I'm not allowed to say anything. I'm not allowed to tell them. I talk to mothers who get [IRS] letters [about under-reported income] for their newborn babies. I talk to widows calling about [IRS letters claiming under-reported income for] their dead spouse, and there's nothing I can do. I know who stole their identity, but I can't say 'Look, I'm sorry, but your baby's Social Security

number is being used in the Bronx, New York, by this person that lives at this address."[188]

Successive Treasury Inspector General for Tax Administration (TIGTA) reports found:[189]

- 1.2 million undocumented workers cited income earned with another person's Social Security number when they filed their tax returns in 2007.
- Individual Taxpayer Identification Numbers (which illegals use to pay taxes) did not match SSNs included on W-2 forms 91 percent of the time.
- Some illegals use multiple ITINs and submit multiple tax returns, which has resulted in multiple tax refunds.

In nine years of TIGTA audits, it found that 1.3 million illegal aliens received $14.2 billion in child tax credit refunds.[190]

The Center for Immigration Studies (CIS) reported, "Americans who are the victims of DACA identity theft were left with destroyed credit, arrest records attached to their names, unpaid tax liabilities, and corrupted medical records; while the DACA recipients walked away scot-free from multiple felonies — forgery, Social Security fraud, perjury on I-9 forms, and identity theft."[191]

The CIS report suggested that victims of these crimes should be compensated and the open borders lobby should share the penalties with illegal aliens who commit them:

> Providing justice for the victims of DACA applicants would require the establishment of what might be called the DACA Victims' Restitution Fund (DVRF). The DVRF would be funded by a fine paid by each DACA recipient who used an unlawfully obtained Social Security number for any purpose before obtaining DACA status. The fine might be $3,000 for the unlawful use of one number and $5,000 for the unlawful use of two or more Social Security numbers...

> If DACA applicants and/or their parents, who could afford to pay a coyote to traffic their children into the United States, don't have the money to pay the fines, the U.S. Chamber, Mark Zuckerberg's Fwd.US, religious organizations, employers, politicians, sanctuary cities, and others who support DACA can help applicants cover their fines rather than simply insisting that they be granted amnesty from their felonies while leaving their American victims holding the bag.[192]

Don't hold your breath.

When violations of law are ignored by government, law becomes meaningless and arbitrary. This is one of the Red-Green Axis's most diabolical agendas in its effort to deconstruct our Republic.

Refugee Resettlement Budget

Table 10 below provides official budget estimates for the refugee resettlement program. Included in this table are the cost of Overseas Contingency Operations (OCO) for migration and refugee assistance. While not part of the domestic resettlement program, that cost is included here to get a total picture of the U.S. commitment to refugees worldwide. The OCO budget includes some of the funding provided to the UNHCR. It also funds the aforementioned International Organization for Migration.

Table 10

Refugee Resettlement Program Budgets ($ Millions)						
	FY 2015	FY 2016	FY 2017	FY 2018	FY 2019[1]	FY 2020[2]
DoS - Bureau of Populattion Refugees & Migration (PRM)						
Migration & Refugee Assistance Enduring Programs	$931.9	$938.9	$929.8	$934.8	$934.8	$365.1
Refugee Admissions	$394.2	$462.7	$496.0	$251.3	$251.3	$365.1
Percent Change Enduring Programs	NA	0.7%	-1.0%	0.5%	0.0%	-60.9%
Overseas Contingency Operations	$2,127.1	$2,127.1	$2,486.2	$2,431.2	$2,431.2	$0.0
SUBTOTAL PRM	$3,059.0	$3,066.0	$3,416.0	$3,366.0	$3,366.0	$365.1
Percent Change	NA	0.2%	11.4%	-1.5%	0.0%	-89.2%
DHS - U.S. Citizenship and Immigration Service (USCIS)	$32.3	$50.0	$67.8	$64.1	$50.0	$50
Percent Change	NA	54.8%	36.6%	-5.5%	-22.0%	0.0%
HHS - Office of Refugee Resettlement (ORR)						
Unaccompanied Alien Children	$948.0	$892.4	$1,414.6	$1,569.6	$1,303.2	$1,303.0
Refugees, Asylees & Others	$611.9	$788.7	$726.7	$481.9	$602.0	$501.0
SUBTOTAL ORR	$1,559.9	$1,681.1	$2,141.3	$2,051.4	$1,905.2	$1,804.0
Percent Change	NA	7.8%	27.4%	-4.2%	-7.1%	-5.3%
TOTAL	$4,651.2	$4,797.1	$5,625.1	$5,481.5	$5,321.2	$2,219.1
Percent Change	NA	3.1%	17.3%	-2.6%	-2.9%	-58.3%

[1] Estimates based on 2019 Continuing Resolution
[2] President's 2020 Budget Proposal
Sources: Report to Congress, Proposed Refugee Admissions FYs 2016, 2017, 2018; 2019;
    HHS Office of Refugee Resettlement and State PRM 2020 budget proposals & prior budgets
    HHS Administration for Children and Families FY 2018-19 Operating Plans
    Congressional Research Service Refugee Admissions and Resettlement Policy

The 2020 President's Budget shows a drastic reduction based on zeroing out the Overseas Contingency Operations function (OCO) and much of the Enduring Programs, leaving only the Refugee Admissions budget, which actually increases from its low of 2018 and 2019. These changes do not reflect an actual reduction in the budget, however, but rather result from shifting OCO out of the PRM budget into a new International Humanitarian Assistance (IHA) budget. The IHA now will receive $2.4 billion that would have gone into PRM's OCO budget.

The Trump administration has wisely advocated assisting refugees in or near their home countries. This is the most compassionate way to handle refugees because almost all would prefer to return home once it is safe to do so, and we can provide much more help to refugees in place. It costs twelve times more to resettle one refugee to the U.S. than to help that refugee in place.[193] Prior to the 2020 budget proposal, the OCO account paid for this and other things. Now it will be covered by the new IHA budget, which will get additional funding from other accounts, for a proposed total of $6.0 billion. Much of this will go to the UNHCR.

Finally, another thing to notice is that regarding domestic resettlement, the largest single expense is for the Unaccompanied Alien Children (UAC) program, under the Health and Human Services' Office of Refugee Resettlement. In other words, the greatest domestic expenditure in the refugee program goes to resettle illegal aliens *who are not refugees.*

The Refugee Resettlement Program Is Not the Refugee Resettlement Program

Every September, just prior to the start of the new fiscal year on October 1, the President sets the maximum number of refugees to be admitted in the upcoming fiscal year, (the refugee cap). For fiscal year 2018, the Trump administration proposed a refugee cap of 45,000, slightly under its 2017 cap of 50,000, which outgoing President Obama had initially set at 110,000. Between 2000 and the 2016, the caps averaged about 75,000, so the Trump administration is least working toward reducing the numbers of refugees America takes in each year. The cap for FY 2019 is 30,000. Reducing those caps was a battle royale according to administration sources and President Trump should get credit for it.

But those who enter the U.S. as official "refugees" are only a tiny component of the total admitted to the U.S. through the multifaceted programs administered under the term "refugee resettlement." As with much else about this program, its true dimensions are hidden from the general public—only available to those willing to dive into numerous publications and obscure government databases to learn the truth as this monograph attempts to do.

Like most other federal government programs, refugee resettlement has grown and metastasized over the years into a giant malignancy. It is increasingly expensive at the federal, state, and local level, and imposes significant other burdens on local communities, like corruption, crime, cultural clashes, disease, and terrorism.

Who Is Eligible for Resettlement?

According to the U.S. Citizenship and Immigration Service (USCIS), refugees are:

> [P]eople who have been persecuted or fear they will be persecuted on account of race, religion, nationality, and/or membership in a particular social group or political opinion.[194]

Those who meet the definition include refugees (those seeking protection in the United States who are not already in the country), asylum seekers or asylees (those who apply for asylum after coming to the U.S.), Cuban/Haitian Entrants, Special Immigrant Visas (SIV) and Trafficking Victims. The Unaccompanied Alien Children (UAC) program is also administered by the Office of Refugee Resettlement, although UACs do not meet the definition of "refugee."

The actual totals are reflected in Table 11. So, for example, in FY 2016, 84,995 refugees were resettled, but the total number of immigrants resettled through the refugee resettlement system was over 257,000, about a quarter of all immigrants given legal permanent resident status in 2016.

Table 11

Fiscal Year	Refugee Ceiling	Refugees	SIV[1]	Cuban/ Haitian[2]	Asylees[3]	Trafficking Victims	UAC[4]	Total
1980	231,000	207,116	0	0	1,104	0	0	208,220
1981	217,000	159,252	0	0	1,175	0	0	160,427
1982	140,000	98,096	0	0	3,909	0	0	102,005
1983	90,000	61,218	0	0	7,215	0	0	68,433
1984	72,000	70,393	0	0	8,278	0	0	78,671
1985	70,000	67,704	0	0	4,585	0	0	72,289
1986	67,000	62,146	0	0	3,359	0	0	65,505
1987	70,000	64,528	0	0	4,062	0	0	68,590
1988	87,500	76,483	0	0	5,531	0	0	82,014
1989	116,500	107,070	0	0	6,942	0	0	114,012
1990	125,000	122,066	0	0	8,472	0	0	130,538
1991	131,000	113,389	0	1,091	5,035	0	0	119,515
1992	131,000	132,531	0	12,924	6,307	0	0	151,762
1993	142,000	119,448	0	4,152	9,543	0	0	133,143
1994	121,000	112,981	0	14,364	13,828	0	0	141,173
1995	112,000	99,974	0	32,238	20,703	0	0	152,915
1996	90,000	76,403	0	17,331	23,532	0	0	117,266
1997	78,000	70,488	0	5,326	22,939	0	0	98,753
1998	83,000	77,080	0	13,551	20,507	0	0	111,138
1999	91,000	85,525	0	20,848	26,571	0	0	132,944

Refugee Resettlement Program Numbers

Fiscal Year	Refugee Ceiling	Refugees	SIV[1]	Cuban/ Haitian[2]	Asylees[3]	Trafficking Victims	UAC[4]	Total
2000	90,000	73,147	0	19,441	32,514	0	0	125,102
2001	80,000	69,304	0	15,950	39,148	0	0	124,402
2002	70,000	27,110	0	16,734	36,937	0	0	80,781
2003	70,000	28,422	0	11,837	28,743	151	4,792	73,945
2004	70,000	52,868	0	27,981	27,376	163	6,200	114,588
2005	70,000	53,813	0	17,571	25,304	231	7,800	104,719
2006	70,000	41,279	0	24,217	26,352	231	7,746	99,825
2007	70,000	48,281	0	18,492	25,318	303	8,212	100,606
2008	80,000	60,192	666	20,235	23,022	310	7,211	111,636
2009	80,000	74,654	2,332	20,022	22,303	280	6,639	126,230
2010	80,000	73,311	2,108	21,496	19,771	549	8,302	125,537
2011	80,000	56,424	719	22,982	23,569	661	7,120	111,475
2012	76,000	58,238	3,312	21,000	27,948	469	13,625	124,592
2013	70,000	69,925	1,902	28,560	24,996	506	24,668	150,557
2014	70,000	69,987	10,240	31,871	23,369	749	57,496	193,712
2015	70,000	69,933	7,226	71,618	26,011	872	33,726	209,386
2016	85,000	84,994	12,269	87,111	20,340	797	59,170	264,681
*2017	50,000	53,716	19,321	**88,036**	26,568	**500**	40,810	**228,951**
*2018	45,000	22,491	10,256	19,458	34,249	500	49,100	136,054
Total	3,641,000	3,071,980	70,351	**706,437**	**717,435**	**7,272**	342,617	**4,916,092**

Sources: Proposed Refugee Admissions, FY 2019, p. 9;

(www.wrapsnet.org) Admissions & Arrivals - 2018 refugees & SIVs

2016 Office of Refugee Resettlement Annual Report to Congress

* FY 2017/2018 estimates in **bold** - author estimates

[1] Includes SIVs and family members; FY 2017/2018 SIVs only

[2] 2010 Excludes 697 Haitian children; 2017-18 estimates based on VOLAG CHEP spending

[3] 2018 estimates based on approvals from EOIR and USCIS Asylum Office workload reports as of 9/30

1980-1989 asylum figures exclude approvals by EOIR

[4] UAC FY 2012-2018 UAC referrals from DHS

A few particulars are worth mentioning. First, refugee numbers have declined dramatically. President Trump limited refugee resettlement to 53,716 in FY 2017 and only 22,498 were resettled in 2018—the lowest annual number since the program began.

Yet some other components of the overall program remain high. Asylum cases have increased, and while UAC numbers are down somewhat this year, they still remain historically high, and if trends continue, FY 2019 will be a record high year for UACs. In the first two years of the Trump presidency, total program numbers were reduced to an estimated 121,817, a 53 percent reduction from 2016.

It's a big improvement from the last few Obama years, but only a little better than historical averages, and still represents an annual influx of immigrants equivalent to a large U.S. city. Furthermore, with a future administration, these numbers could be reversed in a moment, because the underlying legislation has not changed. The only permanent solution to this massive invasion is to abolish the refugee resettlement program altogether and restore it to the private, charitable activity it once was.

Following is a brief rundown on the different elements encompassed by the overall refugee resettlement program.

Cuban Haitian Entrant Program (CHEP)

CHEP was created by the Refugee Education Assistance Act of 1980 in response to the Mariel Boat Lift, in which 125,000 Cubans and over 40,000 Haitians attempted to immigrate en masse by boat to the U.S.[195] At that time, Fidel Castro emptied his prisons, allowing hardened criminals to join the exodus. Also included in the mix were numerous Cuban intelligence officers. President Carter let them all in. Few if any were deported.[196]

CHEP is a form of humanitarian parole, which allows entry of otherwise inadmissible aliens for humanitarian reasons. CHEP offers benefits to Cubans and Haitians on par with other refugee groups. The program is managed by Church World Service and the U.S. Conference of Catholic Bishops with funding provided by the USCIS.[197] CHEP beneficiaries receive the same benefits available from HHS that normal refugees do.

HHS spending for CHEP is buried in those numbers, but for example, in 2016, HHS provided $18.5 million for CHEP as reported in Table 12 below.[198] And note how broadly these monies are distributed to organizations other than CWS and USCCB.

Table 12

Table II-4: FY 2016 Cuban/Haitian Program Grantees

GRANTEE	STATE	AMOUNT
Arizona Department of Economic Security	Arizona	$192,396
California Department of Social Services	California	$122,312
Florida Department of Children and Families	Florida	$15,121,792
Catholic Charities of Louisville	Kentucky	$475,168
Catholic Charities of Southern Nevada	Nevada	$525,500
New Jersey Department of Human Services	New Jersey	$192,664
New York Office of Temporary and Disability Assistance	New York	$166,416
North Carolina Department of Health and Human Services	North Carolina	$104,452
State of Oregon	Oregon	$95,252
Commonwealth of Pennsylvania	Pennsylvania	$123,392
Texas Health and Human Services Commission	Texas	$1,348,656
TOTAL		$18,468,000

Source: FY 2016 Office of Refugee Resettlement Report to Congress

Prior to normalization of relations with Cuba, the following groups were eligible for CHEP:

- Cubans who arrive directly from Cuba through the visa lottery system (Special Cuban Migration program) or the Cuban Family Reunification Parole Program;
- Cuban entrants who arrive by raft (balseros) and are processed through U.S. Customs and Border Protection (CBP);
- Cuban entrants who cross the U.S./Mexican border (Southwest Border Crossers);
- Cuban entrants who arrive at the Miami International Airport and are released by immigration authorities;
- Cuban and Haitian minors released from immigration custody; and
- Cuban Medical Personnel and their families.

In the 1990s, the Clinton administration tried to limit Cubans attempting to reach America by boat with the so-called "wet foot/dry foot" policy. Only those Cubans who successfully reached American shores (dry-foot) would be granted parole. If intercepted by U.S. authorities at sea (wet-foot), they would be returned to Cuba. At that time, the U.S. government also created a special visa lottery for Cubans that would guarantee a floor of 20,000 Cuban migrants per year. This was a concession to Cuba in response to a threat by Fidel Castro to provoke another Mariel boat lift. Castro *wanted them to come here*. What does that tell you? Lotteries were held in 1994, 1996, and 1998, with a total of 541,000 applicants. As of 2015, they were still being processed.[199]

In December 2014, President Obama normalized relations with Communist Cuba. Just a few days prior to leaving office in 2017, Obama cancelled wet-foot-dry-foot as part of the normalization process.[200] He also ended the special parole for Cuban medical personnel, and now Cuban illegals crossing the Southwest Border are treated the same as all other illegals.

In anticipation of these changes, the CHEP program exploded in 2015 and 2016, as shown in the refugee resettlement program numbers table. While actual CHEP numbers for FY 2017 and 2018 are not available at publication time, spending levels are. FY 2017 USCIS spending was a record high, suggesting a record high number of CHEP entrants. Similarly, the low spending for 2018 suggests a big reduction in entrants. The estimates for 2017-18 were projected based on these dollar spending levels as shown in Table 13.

Table 13

USCIS Grants for CHEP			
	CWS	USCCB	Total
2011	$3,950,000	$3,950,000	$7,900,000
2012	$3,033,867	$2,706,146	$5,740,013
2013	$3,950,000	$4,937,500	$8,887,500
2014	$3,950,000	$3,932,961	$7,882,961
2015	$5,328,430	$5,447,285	$10,775,715
2016	$9,092,239	$9,039,881	$18,467,999
2017	$9,612,676	$9,730,932	$19,343,608
2018	$2,551,215	$2,334,863	$4,886,078

Source: USASpending.gov

Asylum

Asylum is broken down into two categories: affirmative and defensive. Affirmative asylees are those who formally apply for asylum status at our nation's borders. Defensive asylees are people in deportation proceedings who request asylum status to avoid deportation. Affirmative asylum cases are decided by USCIS; the U.S. Department of Justice's Executive Office for Immigration Review (EOIR) decides defensive asylum cases.

Chart 3

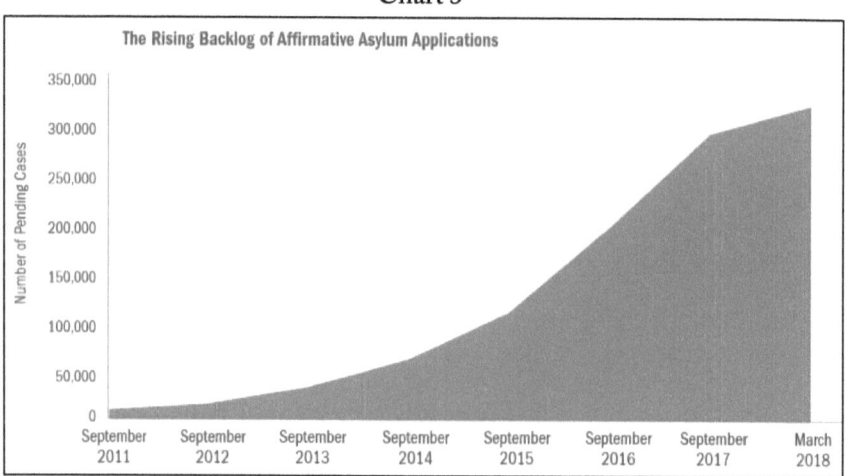

Source: 2018 Annual Report: Citizenship and Immigration Services Ombudsman, p. 42.

Asylum applications have exploded in recent years, as shown in the above chart of affirmative case backlogs. At the end of FY 2018, the U.S. Citizenship and Immigration Services' affirmative asylum backlog was about 320,000 cases representing 492,000 individuals.[201] The EOIR backlog, which includes defensive asylum and other types of deportation cases, was 786,303 for FY 2018.[202] So today we are looking at a backlog of over 1 million. The average wait time in immigration court is over 1,000 days. In New Jersey and California, the wait time averages 1,300 days.[203] Most will just disappear into the country.

Like refugee resettlement, the asylum program is also rife with fraud.[204] The Trump administration has tightened it up, which, as shown in the Affirmative Backlog chart, has slowed the growth in the backlog, but the country still must deal with those in the pipeline.

Table 14, derived from the USCIS 2016 Yearbook of Immigration Statistics describes the top countries whose nationals received asylum in 2016.* Interestingly, the "Russia" category in the table includes a separate line item labeled "Former Soviet Union." It is not explained why there are two separate categories, but this likely results from the post-USSR establishment of 15 individual, independent states. Communist China has topped the list for every year since 2007, with a total of 69,423 asylum grantees since then. Recall from the earlier discussion that many of the Chinese nationals in the U.S. are considered assets by Chinese intelligence.

Table 14

Asylum Grantees FY 2016		
Country	Asylees	% Total
China (PR)	4485	21.9%
El Salvador	2157	10.5%
Guatemala	1949	9.5%
Honduras	1505	7.4%
Mexico	919	4.5%
Egypt	839	4.1%
Syria	735	3.6%
Iraq	637	3.1%
Russia	416	2.0%
Venezuela	355	2.4%
All Others	6458	30.3%
Source: Yearbook of Immigration		
Statistics 2016 - Tables 17 & 19		

---

* Tables 17 and 19.

China also has a very active anchor baby program, bringing thousands of pregnant women to the U.S. specifically to give birth every year. It has become an industry, charging $40,000 to $80,000 per person for wealthy pregnant Chinese women. [205] Considering that most wealthy Chinese nationals are closely connected with the government in some capacity, this is another potential source for exploitation by Chinese intelligence.

Furthermore, anchor babies provide a major point of access for illegal aliens. There are 300,000 to 400,000 children born in the U.S. to illegal aliens every year. The illegal parent is much less likely to be deported than others, and this perception fuels the willingness of illegal alien mothers to cross borders to give birth in the U.S. [206] Once fully established, these families contribute to the chain migration that now comprises the vast majority of all U.S. immigration.

Unsurprisingly, the next highest ranking comes from the three Central American nations now flooding our border in an unending stream of caravans. Finally, there are some successful asylum cases from countries you would never expect, including at least 43 since 2007 from Canada, 270 from the island of Fiji, 171 from Greece, 151 from Israel, 405 from Jamaica, and at least 16 from the tiny South Pacific island of Niue, with a total population of 1,624. What kind of persecution could these people possibly have faced from these countries that would cause them to seek safe haven in the U.S.? Persecution *in Canada*? And if those nations didn't tolerate them, exactly whom are we allowing in?

Special Immigrant Visas (SIV)

The SIV program awards refugee status to Iraqis and Afghans who have helped the U.S. military as interpreters and translators during military operations in those countries. Many of these individuals face the threat of death if they remain in their own countries. In recent years, their numbers also have soared. This is one of the more legitimate refugee resettlement programs. There is a large backlog of requests from this group as well, and some have died at the hands of our enemies while waiting for relief. Yet legislators do nothing to stem the flood of illegals crossing the border every day.

Trafficking Victims

This program helps victims of a severe form of trafficking, *i.e.*, those who are lured into sex trafficking and become essentially slaves of the sex trade. Not mentioned in the table, but also handled by the refugee program, are victims of torture. ORR provides special grants to organizations assisting such people.

LGBT Refugees

While not counted as a separate line item, there is even a "Rainbow Welcome Initiative" funded by the Heartland Alliance International, LLC, a government contractor, to meet the special needs of lesbian, gay, bisexual, and transgendered (LGBT) refugees and asylees. Government funds 92 percent of this non-profit's $18 million annual budget, according to Heartland's 2017 tax return. CEO Evelyn Diaz makes $365,000 per year in pay and benefits. The former CEO, Sid Mohn, is still on the payroll taking home $137,000. Combined, the top four officers plus the former CEO make over $1.1 million per year—almost all paid for by the U.S. taxpayer.[207] Heartland is an affiliate of the US Committee for Refugees and Immigrants, one of the nine VOLAGs.

UACs

The Unaccompanied Alien Children program has grown into the largest single component of the overall domestic refugee resettlement program. While Mexican illegals can be immediately sent home, immigration law requires the U.S. government to hold any underage individual from a non-contiguous country. This is why so many are from Central America. UAC contractors are paid to house those minors who are caught.

Beginning in 2012, UAC numbers began to explode after former president Obama instituted the DACA program that year. With the massive numbers of border crossers today and the highly organized nature of the caravans, there seems little doubt that DACA was intended to spur mass migration from Central and South America.

Criminal gangs saw this as an opportunity to exploit immigration law. Minors are rarely prosecuted for carrying drugs across the border, so have been recruited by the cartels to act as mules.[208] The mass of illegals, both minors and families, also serves to tie down Border Patrol, so the mules can get through (especially in places with no border wall).

Unaccompanied minors are housed in facilities run by contractors much like the VOLAGs. They stay an average of 57 days before being transferred into the care of a foster family or relative. While in the facilities they are provided:[209]

- Classroom education
- Mental and medical health services
- Case management
- Socialization and recreation
- Family reunification services that facilitate safe and timely release to family members or other sponsors that can care for them

Seventy-six percent of UACs are between 15 and 17 years old. Very few are returned and most join the ranks of other illegal aliens in the U.S. to await deportation hearings.

Deportations

The Left disingenuously claims that President Obama deported record numbers of illegals, anointing him with the title "Deporter in Chief." But unsurprisingly, this was disingenuous.[210] The Los Angeles Times called it "misleading." That's an understatement.

Illegal aliens are deported either through removals, which is a formal process requiring the decision of an immigration judge, or returns, where a border agent can simply send someone apprehended within 100 miles of the border back if the illegal does not have documents or if the documents are fraudulent. Since 1996, there is also something called "expedited removals," which are essentially the same as returns but with a simple process for documentation.

Under prior administrations, these people were usually characterized as "voluntary returns," but Obama reclassified them as expedited removals. Table 15 tells the whole story. These are the latest data available. As with practically everything else about his administration, this minor change was deliberately deceptive, allowing Obama to claim to be serious on enforcement, when in fact he

Table 15

ALIENS REMOVED OR RETURNED (Fiscal Years 2000-2016)			
	Removals	Returns	Total
2000	188,467	1,675,876	1,864,343
2001	189,026	1,349,371	1,538,397
2002	165,168	1,012,116	1,177,284
2003	211,098	945,294	1,156,392
2004	240,665	1,166,576	1,407,241
2005	246,431	1,096,920	1,343,351
2006	280,974	1,043,381	1,324,355
2007	319,382	891,390	1,210,772
2008	359,795	811,263	1,171,058
2009	391,283	582,584	973,867
2010	381,593	474,166	855,759
2011	385,778	322,073	707,851
2012	415,900	230,333	646,233
2013	433,034	178,663	611,697
2014	405,589	163,223	568,812
2015	326,962	129,429	456,391
2016	340,056	106,167	446,223

Source: Table 39 Yearbook of Immigration Statistics FY 2016

was allowing hundreds of thousands of deportable illegals to remain under DACA and DAPA. Overall, Obama sent home half the number of illegals that President G.W. Bush did, and in fact, you have to go back to the 1970s to find overall deportation numbers as low as the Obama years.

Other Programs

As part of the Immigration Act of 1990, the same law that gave us the Diversity Visa Lottery, Congress created "Temporary Protected Status" (TPS) to grant temporary legal status to people in the U.S. when their home countries were deemed unsafe to return to. The program was initially spurred largely by civil wars and natural disasters in Central America, when 1.1 million Salvadorans—one-fifth of that nation's population—migrated, most illegally, to the U.S.[211]

TPS enrollees are given status in 6- to 18-month increments. While it is supposed to be "temporary," beneficiaries usually simply re-enroll when their status expires. Many have been here since the 1990s. That status now applies to the following 11 countries. The dates in parentheses indicate when nationals of these countries were declared in need of "temporary" protection: El Salvador (2001), Haiti (2010), Honduras (1999), Nepal (2015), Nicaragua (1999), Somalia (1991), Sudan (1997), South Sudan (2011), Syria (2012), and Yemen (2015). The law was supposed to prevent TPS enrollees from getting green cards and sponsoring relatives for admission, but Obama undermined this with Executive Orders.[212] As of October 12, 2017, the latest data available, there were 436,866 TPS enrollees.[213]

The Diversity Visa is a lottery that allows about 50,000 individuals from participating nations to become legal permanent residents each year. Most of the participating nations recently are less developed, guaranteeing a flow of needy, third-world populations to add to America's "diversity." And while there is no specific resettlement program providing special benefits for lottery winners, they are eligible for all forms of welfare.

Numerous efforts have been launched to end the program. The November 2017 truck-ramming terrorist attack in New York City by Uzbek Muslim Sayfullo Saipov (who entered the U.S. in 2010 on a 'diversity visa'), was only the most recent by a lottery winner. In 2002 another "winner," Hesham Mohamed Ali Hadayet, killed two people at Los Angeles International Airport. He was actually an illegal alien who had been denied asylum. But he obtained legal status anyway, because his wife had won the lottery. And lottery winners, like all other legal permanent residents, can invite their relatives (chain migration).[214]

In December 2013, the Obama administration announced an in-country refugee program for Central American Minors (CAMs), allowing those under 21 years of age from El Salvador, Guatemala, and Honduras direct travel to the U.S. While those countries suffer high crime and poor economic conditions, afflicted populations do not rise to the definition of "refugee." By offering this status, the Obama administration deliberately—and illegally—expanded the definition. It has been called a "rogue family reunification program,"[215] one thankfully ended by President Trump.

Welfare Costs

Refugee populations impose huge fiscal burdens on federal, state, and local governments aside from direct program costs. Costs include crime, English language classes, overburdened public housing, terrorism, translation services, and welfare programs.

When the 1980 Refugee Act was first passed, the federal government promised to cover 36 months of the states' share of food stamps, Medicaid, Temporary Assistance for Needy Families (TANF—the federal government's primary cash assistance program), Refugee Cash Assistance (RCA), and Refugee Medical Assistance (RMA), provided to resettled refugees—a huge subsidy.

Today it covers only 8 months of RCA and RMA and no other state costs. Refugees rely heavily on state local assistance. These costs have exploded.

Refugees use welfare at astronomical rates compared with U.S. citizens. This might be understandable for a few years, given the need to adjust to life in America, but there are numerous federal programs supposedly designed to make them rapidly "economically self-sufficient."

Refugee advocates make bold claims about how quickly refugees get on their own feet, for example, boldly claiming economic self-sufficiency within months of arrival. These claims are belied by the statistics. Refugees remain reliant on many forms of welfare at higher rates than Americans, and even other immigrants, for life. The following two charts tell the story. Note that as far back as 1980, refugee welfare use still exceeds that of U.S.-born citizens.

Chart 4

Program	1 2015	2 2014	3 2013	4 2012	5 2011	All Years	U.S. Rates[2,3]
2015 Refugee Welfare Use[1] **Based on Number of Years in U.S.**							
Temporary Assistance for Needy Families (TANF)	40.3%	19.6%	12.7%	7.5%	6.4%	18.0%	1.2%
Supplemental Security Income	17.7%	19.2%	25.7%	29.3%	22.8%	22.6%	3.0%
Refugee Cash Assistance (RCA)	24.9%	1.9%	1.0%	0.0%	1.5%	6.1%	NA
General Assistance	23.0%	14.8%	12.6%	8.8%	6.4%	13.5%	<1%
Medicaid/Refugee Med. (RMA)	67.7%	56.7%	48.9%	36.4%	33.5%	49.4%	15.3%
Food Stamps	92.5%	77.5%	74.2%	64.7%	60.0%	74.6%	14.2%
Public Housing	8.8%	12.0%	21.4%	16.6%	19.5%	15.5%	4.2%

[1]Source: 2015 Office of Refugee Resettlement Report to Congress
[2]Sources: HHS, SSA, U.S. Census, USDA
[3]U.S. Rates: TANF, 2014; SSI & Food Stamps, 2015; Medicaid & Public Housing, 2012

Chart 5

Refugee Long Term Welfare Use						
	2011 - 2015	2006 - 2011	2000 - 2005	1990 - 1999	1980 - 1989	U.S. Born
Food Stamps	74.6%	42.0%	29.0%	24.0%	16.0%	11.0%
Cash Assistance[1]	44.7%	7.0%	2.7%	2.8%	2.2%	1.6%
Medical Assistance[2]	49.4%	24.0%	16.0%	14.0%	13.0%	11.0%

[1] Cash asistance = TANF, RCA, state & local general assisance

[2] Medical Assistance = Medicaid, RMA, other state and local medical

Sources: Integration Outcomes of Refugees, Successes and Challenges

Migration Policy Institute. June 2015;

FY 2015 Office of Refugee Resettlement Report to Congress

So how do we reconcile these conflicting statements? As this author and many others argue, the entire program deliberately misleads and obscures facts. Advocates can claim "economic self-sufficiency" because the Office of Refugee Resettlement created a special definition of "economic self-sufficiency" applicable only to refugees. It states:

> Economic self-sufficiency means earning a total family income at a level that enables a family unit to support itself without receipt of a cash assistance grant.[216]

This definition is important for what it *does not* say. Refugees who are employed and thus unable to obtain welfare cash assistance can still obtain an endless list of other benefits, like Medicaid, food stamps, housing subsidies, WIC, energy assistance and countless other public benefits and still be considered "self-sufficient." Also, the regulation specifies that "cash assistance" is limited to TANF, the main cash welfare program, and RCA. It does not include General Assistance, available from many local governments, or Supplemental Security Income (SSI). SSI is supposed to be for the elderly and disabled, but refugees use SSI at very high rates, as indicated in Chart 5.

Not knowing this, you might be impressed when a refugee advocate brags that, for example, "84 percent of refugees are self-sufficient after six months." Kirk Peterson, a correspondent for the Episcopal Church, which runs one of the nine VOLAGs, cited this statistic in an August 2018 article.[217] But earning under $10 per hour—as the average refugee does—while taking the many public benefits he/she still qualifies for, is not being economically self-sufficient.[218]

Numerous estimates of refugee welfare costs have been produced since the first edition of The Red-Green Axis. But in 2018, the government produced its very own estimates.[219] And because HHS administers most of the welfare programs in question, and has access to data unavailable outside the agency, this may be the most accurate to date. Table 16 below summarizes its findings.

Table 16

Estimated HHS-Related Expenditures by Program, 2005-2014 (in millions of 2014 dollars)						
	Refugees and asylees			Refugees and asylees plus spouses and children		
	Total	Federal	State	Total	Federal	State
Medicaid/CHIP	$47,554	$26,146	$21,408	$65,338	$35,924	$29,414
Medicare	$39,251	$39,251	$0	$45,811	$45,811	$0
ORR Transitional Assistance and Medical Services	$3,245	$3,245	$0	$3,245	$3,245	$0
Disproportionate Share Hospital (DSH) Payments	$2,919	$2,919	$0	$5,348	$5,348	$0
ORR Social Services	$1,609	$1,609	$0	$1,609	$1,609	$0
TANF	$993	$541	$452	$2,045	$1,114	$931
ORR Targeted Assistance	$508	$508	$0	$508	$508	$0
Low Income Home Energy Assistance Program (LIHEAP)	$220	$220	$0	$299	$299	$0
Health Centers	$186	$186	$0	$289	$289	$0
Child Care Subsidies	$113	$62	$51	$1,154	$634	$519
ORR Preventive Health	$52	$52	$0	$52	$52	$0
Total	$96,650	$74,739	$21,911	$125,696	$94,832	$30,864

To summarize, over the 10-year period from 2005-2014, the welfare and related costs for refugees, asylees, and their families were $12.5 billion annually. This measurement includes all categories under the "refugee resettlement" roof except UACs.

Many costs, however, were excluded from this analysis:

- Social Security
- Social Security Disability Insurance (SSDI)
- Supplemental Security Income (SSI)
- National School Lunch Program
- Supplemental Nutrition Assistance Program (SNAP)
- Woman, Infants, and Children (WIC) Special Supplemental Nutrition Assistance
- General K-12 public education spending
- Public funding for higher education
- Criminal justice and corrections cost
- Housing assistance
- Child Care Tax Credit
- U.S. Earned Income Tax Credit
- State Earned Income Tax Credits
- State and local general assistance programs
- Other state and local government costs

The Federation for American Immigration Reform (FAIR) recently published an estimate of refugee costs covering the first five years of their resettlement. It includes probably the most detailed and complete estimate of refugee welfare costs yet produced.[220] The tally includes some of the costs excluded in the HHS study:

- Public Housing
- Supplemental Security Income (SSI)
- Earned Income Tax Credit and Additional Child Tax Credit
- English as a Second Language programs

These programs add another $1.2 billion to the HHS annual estimate, when all the categories under the "refugee" roof except UACs are included. But the FAIR study also lists many costs not calculated:

- Social Security Disability Insurance
- WIC
- Criminal justice and corrections cost
- Job Opportunities for Low Income Individuals (JOLI)
- Postsecondary Education Loans and Grants
- State and local housing assistance
- Special education programs
- Social services programs
- State Earned Income Tax Credits
- Other state and local government costs

So, between these two studies, we can calculate an annual cost covering those refugees resettled in the U.S. in the past five years at $13.7 billion. This cost excludes UACs and covers 792,482 refugees. Consider that, since the program began in 1980, we have resettled 4.6 million people, excluding UACs.

It is beyond the scope of this paper to estimate the annual cost for all the people resettled since 1980. Use of these services trails off slowly for refugee groups who have been here for longer periods of time than these studies cover and some of the people have since died. The total annual cost, however, will be substantially more than $13.7 billion.

Add to that the costs that have not been included, then add the chain migration of similarly needy relatives, then add all the other immigration programs that cater to third world, low-skilled individuals like UACs, the Diversity Visa Lottery program and TPS, and finally, add on top of all that FAIR's $115.9 billion estimated annual cost of illegal immigration, and you begin to see the magnitude of the problem. The total cost represents anywhere from 15 to 20 percent or more of our $1 trillion annual budget deficit.

Voluntary Agencies (VOLAGs)

VOLAGs are private, tax-exempt organizations that resettle refugees for the U.S. government. The VOLAGs are:

- Church World Service (CWS);
- Domestic and Foreign Missionary Society of the Protestant Episcopal Church (DFMS), also called Episcopal Migration Ministries (EMM);
- Ethiopian Community Development Council (ECDC);
- HIAS, Inc, (formerly Hebrew Immigrant Aid Society);
- International Rescue Committee (IRC);
- Lutheran Immigration and Refugee Service (LIRS);
- U.S. Conference of Catholic Bishops (USCCB);
- U.S. Committee for Refugees and Immigrants (USCRI);
- World Relief Corporation of the National Association of Evangelicals (WRC).

VOLAGs utilize a network of subsidiaries called "affiliates" who perform most of the actual resettlement work. This includes providing the following services to refugees for the first 30-90 days of their resettlement in the U.S.:[221]

- Decent, safe, sanitary, affordable housing in good repair
- Essential furnishings
- Food, food allowance

- Seasonal clothing
- Pocket money
- Assistance in applying for public benefits, social security cards, ESL, employment services, non-employment services, Medicaid, Selective Service
- Assistance with health screenings and medical care
- Assistance with registering children in school
- Transportation to job interviews and job training
- Home visits

The VOLAGs work the administrative end, distributing State Department resettlement dollars and deciding where to relocate refugees. Refugees get top priority for housing. As a result, many Americans go homeless or are otherwise denied public housing for extended periods. In New Hampshire for example, where refugee resettlement has stressed many communities to the breaking point, the wait time for public housing is eight years.[222]

UAC Contractors

Two more large contractors, Baptist Child & Family Services (BCFS) and Southwest Key Programs, Inc. (SW Key), focus primarily on UACs and families. There are hundreds of other UAC contractors, but most are much smaller, and resettling illegal alien minors is only a portion of their endeavors. The VOLAGs LIRS, USCCB and USCRI also resettle UACs.

Federal Refugee Resettlement Grants

The nine VOLAGs, their many affiliates, and UAC contractors all receive funding from the federal government to resettle the various refugee categories. Most funding comes in the form of grants. Prime awards are grants directly from the federal government to the state or the contractor. Sub-awards are those given to contractors by other contractors or state governments that received the prime grant. Table 17 enumerates prime grants to VOLAGs for refugee resettlement and related programs. This excludes UAC funding for LIRS, USCCB and USCRI, which are shown in Table 18.

Table 17

					VOLAGS				
		VOLAG Grants ($ Millions)							
	CWS	DFMS	ECDC	HIAS	IRC	LIRS	USCCB	USCRI	WRC	Total
2008	$23.1	$4.4	$5.2	$10.8	$55.3	$17.5	$11.0	$6.3	$11.7	$145.4
2009	$23.0	$10.0	$6.3	$13.4	$60.7	$27.8	$44.5	$21.5	$14.5	$221.7
2010	$34.1	$14.0	$10.3	$16.3	$65.8	$28.5	$57.4	$30.6	$9.8	$266.9
2011	$33.5	$12.1	$11.4	$14.3	$70.0	$24.4	$59.8	$29.7	$19.9	$275.0
2012	$36.1	$13.6	$11.0	$15.5	$73.2	$27.8	$56.6	$31.1	$19.8	$284.6
2013	$39.9	$14.9	$13.1	$18.6	$78.8	$31.5	$64.2	$34.0	$21.1	$316.0
2014	$44.1	$16.7	$14.8	$17.7	$89.7	$35.9	$70.1	$38.3	$25.4	$352.8
2015	$46.7	$17.4	$15.1	$24.2	$90.3	$35.3	$71.7	$42.8	$24.9	$368.2
2016	$64.8	$20.5	$18.9	$24.1	$103.7	$43.7	$94.3	$50.6	$33.8	$454.4
2017	$54.5	$16.0	$15.2	$22.6	$105.1	$33.9	$77.6	$75.0	$21.2	$421.1
2018	$45.9	$10.5	$12.2	$22.0	$97.2	$33.5	$55.0	$49.5	$18.6	$344.3
Total	$445.8	$150.0	$133.3	$199.5	$889.9	$339.9	$662.0	$409.5	$220.6	$3,450.6

Source: USASpending.gov

Some of the VOLAGs, for example the ECDC, focus almost entirely on refugee resettlement. Others, like USCCB, IRC, CWS and WRC, have a broader mission.

Of the latter, the Catholic Bishops is the largest. As the table shows, USCCB has received a total of $662.0 million for resettlement purposes, excluding UACs, since 2008. With the numerous lawsuits swirling around the Church's sex scandals, it is not surprising that the USCCB has become one of the Left's biggest open borders enthusiasts.

The USCCB participates in myriad other federal grant programs as well, however, including Global AIDS, Food For Peace Development Assistance, USAID Foreign Assistance, and even the John Ogonowski and Doug Bereuter Farmer-to-Farmer Program, which provides volunteer technical assistance to farmers in developing countries.[223] While it took in only $55 million in FY 2018 for refugee resettlement, that year it received a total of $561 million for all its activities. Since 2008, USCCB has received a total of $4.3 billion for all purposes from the federal government.[224]

IRC also engages in other activities for the U.S. government, but does not take in nearly as much as USCCB. The FY 2018 total from all U.S. government sources was $202.2 million, with less than half devoted to domestic and overseas refugee programs.[225] IRC has received $913 million for refugee resettlement since 2008, and a total of $1.7 billion from the feds over the same period.

CWS has received a total of $456.7 million for all services from FY 2008-2018 of which $436.1 million was for domestic and overseas refugee programs. [226] World Relief has received $220.6 million for refugee resettlement and $282.1 million for all purposes since 2008.[227] For all VOLAGs, the federal government has awarded $3.5 billion in prime grants since 2008.

Because they are non-governmental organizations (NGOs), VOLAGs lobby for advantageous changes to law and build allies in Congress and the bureaucracy, all fertilized by an open spigot of taxpayer dollars. They could not pursue this agenda so aggressively and so overtly were they government agencies.

While 6 of the 9 VOLAGs are affiliated with religious groups, it is a false notion that they are charitable organizations doing the Lord's work. Prior to the 1980 Refugee Act, some of these VOLAGs may have provided funding for resettlement operations through private charitable donations and church tithes.

Today they are federal contractors, relying on the government for support. As such they are not allowed to proselytize at all. They do the government's bidding, whether it honors religious principles or not. In fact, as we shall see, these "religious" contractors quite plainly violate scriptural teaching to receive federal dollars while promoting mass immigration.

Table 18

			Catholic					Other	
	BCFS	SW Key	Charities	LIRS	LSS	USCCB	USCRI	UAC	All UAC
2008	$0.0	$30.7	$8.4	$3.5	$9.6	$7.7	$0.0	$31.2	$91.1
2009	$6.6	$27.8	$8.7	$3.7	$4.4	$5.8	$0.0	$37.8	$94.7
2010	$10.6	$32.5	$8.7	$6.3	$5.5	$5.8	$0.0	$52.8	$122.2
2011	$17.0	$35.6	$7.7	$6.1	$5.8	$8.7	$0.7	$54.3	$136.1
2012	$64.9	$50.2	$7.1	$7.2	$4.9	$6.2	$0.6	$74.0	$215.1
2013	$58.4	$88.2	$8.3	$17.7	$7.7	$11.6	$4.8	$107.8	$304.5
2014	$197.0	$160.1	$10.7	$20.4	$18.1	$11.7	$2.0	$273.5	$693.5
2015	$71.1	$163.8	$10.3	$19.2	$21.4	$9.8	$5.9	$285.6	$587.2
2016	$200.7	$211.4	$10.4	$16.3	$16.1	$9.9	$5.4	$257.8	$727.9
2017	$214.4	$285.5	$12.4	$23.9	$25.5	$10.7	$5.6	$368.9	$946.9
2018	$440.1	$626.1	$14.1	$22.3	$30.8	$12.6	$5.8	$395.4	$1,547.2
Total	$1,280.8	$1,711.8	$106.8	$146.6	$149.8	$100.6	$30.8	$1,939.1	$5,466.2

UAC Contractor Grants ($ Millions)

Source: Department of Health and Human Services

Table 18 shows HHS grants to the main UAC contractors. The two largest by far are BCFS and SW Key. While all UAC contractors have seen rapid growth in receipts, their budgets have exploded with the growth in housing needs for the illegal alien minors flooding the border.

Prior to 2012, about 8,000 illegal alien minors were being housed. After DACA that jumped to about 44,000 a year.

The table shows how much the VOLAGs, LIRS, USCCB and USCRI take in via the UAC program. The "other" category contains grants to many smaller contractors, too numerous to include here.

Two refugee VOLAG affiliates, Lutheran Social Services (LSS) and Catholic Charities, receive millions in both prime and sub-grants for refugee resettlement. In many ways they could be considered VOLAGs in their own right. They also act as prime contractors for the UAC program. Their UAC grants are shown here. As the table shows, UACs have added substantially to their bottom line, with UAC grants alone totaling $256.6 million for the two organizations since 2008.

Additionally, much like their senior partner, the U.S. Conference of Catholic Bishops, the many Catholic Charities affiliates across the U.S. receive grants from many different federal programs, such as Head Start, Section 8 Housing, homeless veterans programs, and others, in addition to refugee and UAC resettlement. In FY 2018 alone, Catholic Charities programs in the U.S. collected a total of $118 million in prime grants and another $1.3 million in Veterans Administration contracts.[228]

And even that isn't the end of it. There is Catholic Community Services, Catholic Social Services, Inc., the Catholic Legal Immigration Network and others, all of which receive resettlement and/or UAC grants. The Catholic Church does big business with the federal government and throws its weight around to protect its refugee resettlement franchise.

Note that starting in 2014, UAC program grants exceeded those for refugee resettlement. This remains true to the present time. While the Trump administration has successfully reduced the flow of refugees and some other groups, with a corresponding reduction in resettlement grants, illegal aliens continue to flood the border. Border crossings did fall to historic lows for the first few months after President Trump took office. But, as discussed earlier, illegal crossings quickly shot back up to near historic highs by the end of FY 2017 and remain high to the present time.[229]

As shown in Table 19, VOLAGs and UAC contractors receive on average almost 80 percent of their revenues from government. Many receive virtually all support from government. As actual churches DFMS and USCCB are not required to publicize this information.

Doing Well by Doing Good

This is big business. Top management typically receives salary and benefit packages well into six figures. Table 20 lists the CEO compensation for the VOLAGS and main UAC contractors, as available. This information is provided on the most recent IRS Form 990 non-profit annual tax return most of them must file.

Table 19

Percentage of Revenues Received from Government ($ Millions)			
	Govt Grants	Total Revenues	% Grants
VOLAG			
CWS	$68.4	$95.8	71.5%
DFMS	NA	NA	NA
ECDC	$18.3	$19.1	95.8%
HIAS	$24.5	$45.3	54.1%
IRC	$493.6	$736.8	67.0%
LIRS	$64.7	$69.2	93.5%
USCCB	NA	NA	NA
USCRI	$53.6	$59.2	90.5%
WRC	$51.1	$79.2	64.5%
UAC Contractor			
BCFS	$287.9	$300.3	95.9%
SW Key	$240.2	$242.6	99.0%
Total	$1,302.2	$1,647.4	79.0%
Source: Most recent IRS 990 tax filings			

Table 20

CEO Compensation		
VOLAG	CEO	Latest 990
CWS	Rev. John L. McCullough	$345,366
DFMS	Not publicized	NA
ECDC	Tsehaye Teferra	$357,605
HIAS	Mark Hetfield	$343,630
IRC	David Miliband	$671,749
LIRS	Linda Hartke	$327,876
USCCB	Not publicized	NA
USCRI	Lavinia Limon	$300,194
WRC	Stephan Bauman	$132,740
UAC Contractor		
BCFS	Kevin Dinnin	$502,614
SW Key	Juan Sanchez	$786,822

These filings usually lag by a year or more so most of the information in the table is at least one year old. USCRI's Lavinia Limon and Linda Hartke of LIRS have since been replaced. It is also important to note that, while substantial, these salaries would not normally be out of line for a corporate CEO. But these are tax-exempt entities that merely administer federal grants—something most of them can do in their sleep. They are little more than glorified clerks.

The denominations represented, whether churches or church affiliates, all promote leftwing policies. Many reflect the "Social Gospel" *i.e.*, the effort to marry socialist ideas with Christian doctrine. Many are directly or indirectly connected to communists (Marxists?) and communist agendas. While some individual Catholic churches and dioceses remain traditional, much of the hierarchy, including the current Pope, reflect the teaching of so-called "liberation theology," a KGB creation, according to former Romanian intelligence chief, Ion Pacepa.[230]

Consonant with leftist strategies in all spheres, these organizations purposefully manipulate language and subtly misinterpret Gospel to rationalize their advocacy. So now, within their mission statements you frequently read the newest refugee/immigrant mantra, *"welcoming the stranger."* Then, with decidedly un-Christian vitriol, they savage anyone who questions their motives as "racists," "xenophobes," etc. (More about this later.)

VOLAG Profiles

Church World Service (www.churchworldservice.org) — CWS is a subsidiary of the National Council of Churches (NCC), which was formed from the communist front Federal Council of Churches in 1950. The Federal Council was one of the early promoters of social gospel. That tradition was carried forward by the NCC where communist and socialist ideology found a natural home. NCC is today the U.S. subsidiary of the World Council of Churches, co-opted by the Soviet KGB in the 1970s.[231] The NCC also promotes Marxist liberation theology.

According to its website, (http://nationalcouncilofchurches.us), the NCC represents 37 denominations with 45 million people in over 100,000 U.S. congregations and has subsidiaries in all 50 states and the District of Columbia. The subsidiary Virginia Council of Churches' effort to place refugees in Hagerstown, MD, motivated Maryland resident Ann Corcoran to launch her now famous Refugee Resettlement Watch blog. This story is recounted in her book, Refugee Resettlement and the Hijra to America.[232]

NCC has been used as a vehicle to subvert American churches on behalf of the communist cause for decades. Parishioners would be shocked to know that their tithe dollars have supported communist guerrilla armies in Zimbabwe, Namibia, Mozambique, Angola, Nicaragua, El Salvador and elsewhere. (Or maybe not?) CWS provided financial aid to the communist governments of Poland and Yugoslavia before the wall (Iron Curtain?) fell.[233]

The NCC strongly supports communist Cuba and normalization of relations. At the behest of the state-controlled Cuban Council of Churches, NCC assisted Cuba in demanding the return of Elian Gonzales, the Cuban refugee youth who escaped Cuba with his mother on a raft in 1999. His mother drowned, but Elian was rescued and taken in by the Miami Cuban community.[234] Who can ever forget this photo of a night raid where Elian was ripped out of the arms of his protectors and forced to return to Cuba.

Unsurprisingly, CWS is one of two VOLAGs primarily responsible for the Cuban/Haitian Entrant Program. Some of these Cuban "refugees" are almost certainly intelligence agents, saboteurs and/or agitators, who join the refugee flow to establish bases in the U.S.

Table 21 lists the member churches of the NCC. If you belong to one of these churches, understand that it is being used to subvert and ultimately destroy Christianity, and your tithe dollars are being used to promote international communism. If you are a member of one of these churches, discontinue tithing and consider another church.

Most, if not all, of these churches are also involved in the Interfaith Dialogue movement. This is a Red-Green Axis influence operation designed to undermine traditional faiths and interject Islamic supremacist concepts. It claims to work toward "Building Bridges," and some programs are specifically so-named.[235] But as Center for Security Policy President Frank Gaffney noted:

> While the interfaith dialogue movement presents itself as a laudable effort to 'bridge' the distance between faiths, those more familiar with the doctrine of the Muslim Brotherhood know that the actual agenda of too many such efforts is, in fact, modeled after the well-known dictum of Sayyid Qutb, who candidly reminded Muslims that such a 'bridge' is 'only so that the people of Jahiliyyah [society of unbelievers] may come over to Islam.[236]

Table 21

1. African Methodist Episcopal Church	15. Greek Orthodox Archdiocese of America	27. Polish National Catholic Church
2. The African Methodist Episcopal Zion Church	16. Hungarian Reformed Church in America	28. Presbyterian Church (U.S.A.)
3. Alliance of Baptists	17. International Council of Community Churches	29. Progressive National Baptist Convention, Inc.
4. American Baptist Churches in the USA	18. Korean Presbyterian Church Abroad	30. Reformed Church in America
5. Armenian Church of America, Eastern and Western Dioceses	19. Malankara Orthodox Syrian Church, American Diocese	31. Religious Society of Friends, Friends United Meeting
6. Assyrian Church of the East		32. Religious Society of Friends, Philadelphia Yearly Meeting
7. Christian Church (Disciples of Christ) in the United States and Canada	20. Mar Thoma Church	33. Serbian Orthodox Church in North and South America
8. Christian Methodist Episcopal Church	21. Moravian Church in America, Northern and Southern Provinces	34. The Swedenborgian Church of North America
9. Church of the Brethren	22. National Baptist Convention of America, Inc.	35. Syrian Orthodox Church of Antioch, Archdiocese of the Eastern United States
10. Community of Christ	23. National Baptist Convention, USA, Inc.	
11. Coptic Orthodox Archdiocese of North America	24. National Missionary Baptist Convention of America	36. Ukrainian Orthodox Church of the USA
12. Ecumenical Catholic Communion	25. Orthodox Church in America	37. United Church of Christ
13. The Episcopal Church (USA)	26. Patriarchal Parishes of the Russian Orthodox Church in the USA	38. The United Methodist Church
14. Evangelical Lutheran Church in America		

CWS boasts its radicalism front and center on its website. Under its "Supporting Immigrants and Refugees" menu option, three services are offered: legal help, travel loans, and the sanctuary movement. Clicking through to the third option takes you to a different website, Sanctuary Movement (www.sanctuarynotdeportation.org). Its agenda is bold and clear:

> As faith allies, we are called to be in solidarity through rapid response mobilization to stop these raids, stop these deportations and support impacted communities. In the face of President Trump's extremist anti-immigrant agenda, we must respond with a prophetic and bold voice.

Your tax dollars are supporting this. And the photo below of a CWS protester should cure you of any hope that this is a legitimate Christian organization.

NCC President and General Secretary Jim Winkler is a typical radical leftist. He called for impeachment of President Bush in 2006. He co-chaired the board of Healthcare Now! with steelworkers' president Leo Gerard, who advocated violence against tea partiers, and the socialist Quentin Young. Young was Obama's 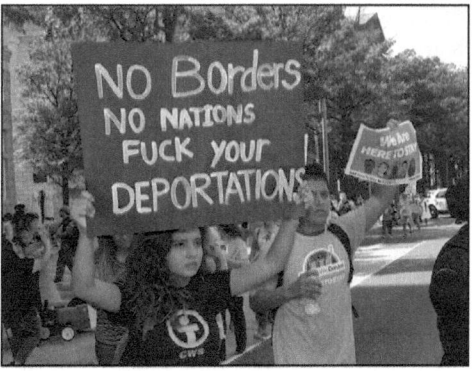 personal physician for 20 years and Obama's mentor on single-payer healthcare whose ideas formed the inspiration for Obamacare.[237]

It is no surprise to find CWS at the heart of the open borders crowd. It profits from the refugee program while the influx of refugees serves the Left's subversive agenda. In addition to revenue streams from government, CWS has received funding from Soros, Ford, Tides, the Vanguard Fund and many others.

U.S. Conference of Catholic Bishops (www.usccb.org) — USCCB is formally listed as one of the nine VOLAGs, while many of the 164 local chapters of Catholic Charities [238] are listed as affiliates. These Catholic Charities offices, however, obtain direct grants for the UAC program, independent of the VOLAGs. Catholic Charities offices are also affiliates of more than one VOLAG, making a comprehensive evaluation of program participation more difficult. This is just one of many illustrations of how this program is convoluted and difficult to describe accurately in full.

These nominally Catholic organizations are the largest resettlement contractors, with hundreds of offices spread throughout the country. They are prominent members of the open borders/amnesty movement. The Catholic Campaign for Human Development (CCHD) is the grant making vehicle of the USCCB. It was founded in Chicago in 1969 with the help of radical Left organizer Saul Alinsky specifically to fund Alinsky's Industrial Areas Foundation (IAF).[239] CCHD has been a radical leftist funding vehicle ever since, giving millions to ACORN, the radical training school, Midwest Academy, and others. IAF continues to receive the largest percentage of CCHD grants of any CCHD grantee.[240]

USCCB founded the Catholic Legal Immigration Network, Inc. (CLINIC), a $7 million subsidiary which assists illegal aliens based on "the Gospel value of welcoming the stranger." CLINIC receives funding from the government to provide legal services to immigrants and advocate on behalf of immigrants. It aggressively promotes international socialism as envisioned by the UN migrant compact, believing that "all goods of the earth belong to all people. When persons cannot find employment in their country of origin to support themselves and their families, they have a right to find work elsewhere in order to survive. Sovereign nations should provide ways to accommodate this right."[241]

Catholic Charities promotes liberation theology. It spread rapidly in Central and South America during the 1980s and was supported vigorously by certain Catholic denominations there, most notably the Jesuits and Maryknoll order. This explains much of the Central American Church's involvement with communist revolutionaries. During the Reagan administration, Catholic groups helped hundreds of thousands of Salvadorans to enter the U.S. illegally from the southern border. The Catholics' explicit purpose was to oppose President Reagan's foreign policy in Central America.[242] Unsurprisingly, USCCB is the other VOLAG managing the Cuban/Haitian Entrant program.

A good source for information about the Left's infiltration of our churches can be found at Exposing Marxism in the Church (www.religiousleftexposed.com) created by veteran investigative journalist, Cliff Kincaid.

HIAS, Inc. (formerly Hebrew Immigrant Aid Society, www.hias.org) — HIAS describes itself as a "major implementing partner of the United Nations Refugee Agency and the U.S. Department of State." HIAS claims to be the oldest refugee resettlement agency in the world. It provides pro bono legal services for Asylum applications and Removal hearings. Services include "Filings with USCIS, Representation at Asylum Interviews (Credible Fear Interviews, Reasonable Fear Interviews), Representation before the Immigration Court, Representation before the Board of Immigration Appeals (BIA), and Federal court appeals." HIAS lists its values as "Welcoming, Dignity and Respect, Empowerment, Excellence and Innovation, Collaboration and Teamwork, and Accountability."[243]

HIAS President Mark Hetfield is an extreme leftist who is constantly at the center of controversy. In August 2018 he made a trip to the border to protest on behalf of the migrant caravans, and regularly participates in protests against Trump immigration policies. [244] He advocated placing virulently antisemitic Islamic apologist Linda Sarsour on an antisemitism panel in 2017, and signed a letter of support for Sarsour.[245] He is associated with J-Street, a phony "Jewish" organization that promotes the Palestinian cause in opposition to Israel. J Street's board chairman is Morton Halperin, another hardcore leftist with a lifetime of anti-American activity under his belt. He was at one time described in State Department files as a Soviet or Communist agent.[246]

In 2016, HIAS received $24.5 million from government grants—54 percent of revenues totaling $45.3 million. Because VOLAGs are considered "non-profits" for tax purposes, there is no profit line in their income statements; however, HIAS has managed to amass net assets of at least $45.9 million, so it is very clear that HIAS normally takes much more in than it needs to carry out its mission.[247]

HIAS Launches "Hate" Offensive

Edition I of this book described the HIAS pamphlet, *Resettlement at Risk: Meeting Emerging Challenges to Refugee Resettlement in Local Communities.*[248] This 30-page screed was underwritten for $35,000 by the J.M. Kaplan fund (of Welch's Grape Juice fame), a prominent open-borders funder. It cited Ann Corcoran's Refugee Resettlement Watch blog as an example of the pushback resettlement organizations were beginning to face from citizens. The report recommended going on the warpath against such opponents and targeting them with the professional smear shop, the Southern Poverty Law Center (SPLC).

Over the past three years, this has metastasized into an aggressive effort by the Red-Green Axis, including members of Antifa, the SPLC, CAIR, Black Lives Matter, and other leftwing and Muslim Brotherhood groups to silence their critics. For years, the SPLC was regularly cited in mainstream print and other media as a credible source for smearing anyone willing to speak out against any aspect of the Left/Islamic agenda. It has been used by Amazon.com to rate publications and even the supposedly non-partisan Guidestar.org, an aggregator on information about tax-exempt foundations. Such labeling could be disastrous for any non-profit reliant on private donations. Guidestar, however, discontinued this practice after an uproar of objections.[249]

In 2016, this author traveled to Rutland, Vermont, twice to speak about the federal refugee resettlement program. Then-Rutland Mayor Christopher Louras had just announced the opening of a refugee resettlement program that behind the scenes he had secretly conspired to create over the prior year.[250] Residents were understandably outraged. The local newspaper, the *Rutland Herald*, discredited the presentation as follows:

> The Center for Security Policy, with which Simpson is affiliated, has been called a conspiracy-oriented mouthpiece for the growing anti-Muslim movement in the United States by the Southern Poverty Law Center.[251]

Another article characterized this author and Ann Corcoran as members of "Hate" groups whose writings appear in "hate publications like American Thinker," as characterized by the SPLC.[252] In each case, this author penned a rebuttal challenging their accusations. They refused to publish any of them.

International Rescue Committee (www.rescue.org) — IRC is run by British Labor Party politician, David Miliband. His brother, "Red Ed" Miliband, Labor's pick for prime minister, lost in UK's 2015 recent election. Miliband's father was a hardcore Marxist. Those roots haven't prevented Miliband from enjoying the benefits of capitalism. At over $670,000, Miliband's annual compensation is the highest of all the VOLAG leaders.

IRC was investigated by the U.S. Agency for International Development's Office of Inspector General for bid-rigging on USAID contracts in Turkey. OIG reported to Congress in 2016 that five Turkish companies and seven officers were banned from further government business. Two individuals working for IRC were fired after taking bribes.[253] USAID's June 2016 report identified another case of fraud with Afghanistan staff who inflated prices and steered contracts to family members. Six IRC staff were dismissed.[254]

David Miliband, left, giving George Soros an IRC award (IRC photo).

In 2016 IRC opened an office in Missoula, Montana, the only refugee resettlement center in the Mountain State. Despite complaints from all the VOLAGs regarding the reduced refugee targets for 2017 and 2018, this office remains open. IRC and Miliband have friends in George Soros, the Clintons, and other well-connected leftists.

World Relief Corp. (www.worldrelief.org) — Initially founded in 1947 as *War Relief of the National Association of Evangelicals* to address humanitarian needs of post-war Europe, it was renamed World Relief in 1950. WRC describes itself as the largest evangelical refugee resettlement agency in America. It serves in "education, health, child development, agriculture, food security, anti-trafficking, immigrant services, micro-enterprise, disaster response and refugee resettlement."

To advance the "Welcoming" propaganda effort, WRC has published a free PDF, *Welcoming the Stranger*. [255] It is affiliated with the leftwing Evangelical Immigration Table and Refugee Council USA (a lobbying group for the VOLAGS).

WRC received government grants totaling $18.6 million FY 2018, down 12 percent from 2017 and 45 percent from 2016. Private foundation supporters include the Vanguard Charitable Foundation, Mustard Seed Foundation, Soros Fund Charitable Foundation, Pfizer Foundation, Global Impact, and many others.

Lutheran Immigration and Refugee Service (www.lirs.org) — LIRS has been involved in refugee resettlement for decades. Its 2016 tax return lists Lutheran Social Services and many unrelated affiliates nationwide receiving refugee resettlement grants from LIRS. Numerous Catholic Charities dioceses are also listed as recipients. In addition to refugee resettlement, LIRS has been actively involved in processing UACs.

Former LIRS CEO Linda Hartke was at the helm from 2010 to 2018 and seemed to be a fixture at LIRS. She was forced out, however, following revelations of extensive financial mismanagement and harassment exposed by Breitbart News. According to Breitbart, investigations looked into "wasteful spending, concealment of taxable income, timesheet fraud, budget grant fraud and large severance and settlement payouts to avoid public and board reporting."[256]

But, as usual, and despite evidence of rampant wrongdoing, Hartke landed on her feet and received glowing statements from LIRS board members with her sendoff. The Left always protects its own. And there is no doubt about her ideology. It needs to be constantly reemphasized that VOLAG leaders are not merely government contractors, but partisans with a leftwing, open-borders agenda. She is now on the Board of Trustees of the Center for Migration Studies. Her bio describes previous work for Church World Service, chief of staff to leftist Massachusetts Democratic Rep. Chet Atkins, and as executive director of the Ecumenical Advocacy Alliance, "a global network of churches and agencies engaged in advocacy."[257]

Ecumenism, by the way, seeks to blend various religions. Starting in the early 20th Century, it represents one of the earliest efforts to subvert the Christian churches. Today's evolution of the ecumenical movement is the Interfaith Dialogue discussed earlier—a much more muscular effort that seeks to undermine Christian teachings by supplanting them with those of Islam, all advocated under the Coexist banner.

LIRS's replacement for Hartke is Krishanti O'Mara Vignarajah, who came to the U.S. as a baby when her parents fled their native Sri Lanka to avoid the civil war. So, LIRS will continue the trend of using former refugees to lead resettlement agencies. Vignarajah is also the former policy director for Michelle Obama and ran for governor of Maryland in 2018 as a Democrat. She is the first non-Lutheran to run LIRS in its 80-year history.[258] So, whereas Hartke was a covert leftist and "Christian" in name only, LIRS is not even pretending to be Christian any more and no longer bothers to hide its leftist tilt.

LIRS receives funding from the Open Society Institute, the Ford Foundation, Global Impact, Fidelity Investment Fund, Bank of America Fund, Annie E. Casey Foundation, and many others, but almost all support is provided by government grants. LIRS received 93.5 percent of its income from government grants in FY 2016.[259] Its FY 2018 government funding was $55.9 million, down slightly from the $60 million it received in 2016. LIRS received almost 40 percent of its 2018 government grants from the UAC program. The percentage of its business from UACs has grown considerably since 2008, when only 17 percent was derived this way.

U.S. Committee for Refugees and Immigrants (USCRI) (www.refugees.org) — USCRI first formed as the International Institute in 1911, a brainchild of the YWCA, and became a VOLAG in 1977. Today, USCRI has 12 branch offices in the U.S. and one in El Salvador. It receives over 90 percent of revenue from government contracts. USCRI took credit for inspiring the Obama administration's Central American Minors program.[260] Fortunately, that program was ended by President Trump. But USCRI has been at the forefront of the refugee resettlement program for decades and its leaders helped shape ORR policies toward refugees and illegal minors—a conflict of interest if there ever was one.

Revolving Door

VOLAG directors and agency heads frequently change places, creating an incestuous revolving door among a group of leftists all pushing the open borders agenda while earning very high incomes at taxpayer expense. For example, current USCRI director Eskinder Negash was director of ORR from 2009-2015. In hiring Negash to run USCRI, board chairman Gene DeFelice stated, "I am pleased to announce that after an extensive national search that included a number of interested candidates, the Board of Directors has unanimously appointed Mr. Eskinder Negash as Chief Executive Officer."[261]

Eskinder Negash

Negash worked for the USCRI from 2002 to 2009 as Chief Operating Officer.[262] He also worked as VP and chief administrative officer at the International Institute, which is an affiliate of USCRI, for 15 years. His work with USCRI spans 22 years. In 2016, he was listed as a senior vice president at USCRI, earning $146,000.[263] It is difficult to believe that USCRI did "an extensive national search," if they did any search at all. More likely Negash just moved a few offices down the hall.

Former president and CEO Lavinia Limon also typifies the revolving door among VOLAG leaders. Limon served as the Director of the Office of Refugee Resettlement during the Clinton administration from 1993 to 2000, "designing and implementing programs to assist newly arriving refugees in achieving economic and social self-sufficiency." She then moved to the National Immigration Forum where she directed NIF's Center for the New American Community for a short while before joining USCRI in 2001.

Independent Audit Needed

Limon left USCRI in October of 2017, a fact that was not publicized until three months later, and then only in a letter by Gene DeFelice, chairman of the USCRI board of directors, who said she was retiring.[264] But in another twist, it turns out Limon has not retired at all, but moved on to a mysterious USCRI affiliate titled Immigration and Refugee Services of America (IRSA).

IRSA has received refugee resettlement grants totaling $104.6 million since 2008, including $19.6 million in 2018, (see Table 22, below). IRSA is listed as a USCRI affiliate in the 2016 VOLAG affiliate directory as working in two locations, Brooklyn, NY and Miami, FL, but it is not a stand-alone affiliate.[265]

In Brooklyn, IRSA is listed alongside Camba Inc., a large tax exempt which receives about 90 percent of its $100 million plus annual revenue from New York City and state government.[266] Camba lists USCRI as one of its supporters but doesn't mention anything about IRSA. Similarly, in Florida, IRSA is listed alongside Youth Co-Op, Inc., another tax exempt which receives 99 percent of its revenues from state and local government, but Youth Co-Op does not mention IRSA either, only USCRI. Both Camba and Youth Co-Op provide various programs to assist illegal aliens, all with taxpayer dollars. Yet another way we fund the open borders agenda without knowing it.

Even more strange, the latest USCRI tax return (2016), lists all of the affiliates that receive funding from USCRI. Both Camba and Youth Co-Op are listed, but IRSA is nowhere to be found.

The State Department's archives list IRSA as a VOLAG, ironically, as of April Fools Day, 2001.[267] It is not, however, one of the nine current VOLAGs. IRSA is not listed among 501(c)(3) charitable organizations at Guidestar.org, which keeps files on tax-exempts, and IRSA does not publish an annual report.

Two reviews of IRSA found in a Google search provide a Washington, D.C., address and phone number, nothing in New York or Florida, but repeated calls at all hours get a busy signal. Two separate IRSA websites are referenced in these reviews, www.refugeesusa.org, and www.irsa-uscr.org. Both are defunct placeholder blogs with no reference to IRSA and no current information of any sort.

Bloomberg's review describes IRSA as "a charitable organization that focuses on defense of human rights, builds communities, fosters education, promotes self-sufficiency, and forges partnerships through an array of programs."[268] The other review was written in 2008 by Melanie Nezer, currently Senior Vice President for Public Affairs at HIAS.[269] Nezer was apparently employed by IRSA in 2008 and described it as "the oldest and largest non-sectarian network of organizations serving immigrants, refugees, and other foreign-born people worldwide."[270]

But it gets weirder still. Lavinia Limon is listed by *Bloomberg* as IRSA's current director, *along with Negash*, who supposedly took Limon's place at USCRI.[271] Officer compensation is not listed, but having received over $100 million since 2008, IRSA is paying someone good money. For what? Is IRSA some kind of slush fund flying under the radar because no one pays attention to this politically coddled, convoluted, Byzantine network of programs?

Is Negash actually employed by both USCRI and IRSA? Can he faithfully perform the duties of COO at IRSA while being CEO at USCRI? How long has he been at IRSA? It doesn't say. What exactly is going on here? There have been frequent requests to audit the refugee resettlement program, especially the contractors. IRSA is an organization that screams to be audited at the very least, if not investigated for possible criminal activity.

Limón made about $300,000 per year as CEO, according to USCRI's 2016 tax filing.[272] Her brother, Peter Limón, had worked for USCRI as director of field offices in earlier years, but by 2016, he was out. Maybe USCRI has had enough of the Limons but can't quite let them go completely. One anonymous blog commenter who identified himself as a former USCRI employee says, "It's a family operation all right. I'm a former employee. As we used to say, 'When life gives you Limones ... keep your head down and don't ask questions ... or else ...'"*

USCRI receives private funding from the Ford Foundation, California Community Foundation, Robert Wood Johnson, Nissan, the Oak Foundation, Western Union, and others. USCRI received $55.3 million in FY 2018, virtually unchanged from 2016, but a big drop from 2017, when it received $80.6 million, its largest grant level ever. While USCRI does resettle some UACs, this big boost in 2017 was not from the UAC program. When every other VOLAG took reductions in FY 2017, it is strange to say the least that 2017 should be USCRI's banner year. Of all the VOLAGs, USCRI should be number one on the auditor's list.

---

* See: 1st comment by Anonymous at Peter Huston, "Is USCRI Albany a successful organization?" *PeterHuston*, May 6, 2011, accessed May 1, 2015, http://peterhuston.blogspot.com/2011/05/is-uscri-albany-successful-organization.html.

Domestic & Foreign Missionary Society (DFMS) — Officially known as the Domestic & Foreign Missionary Society of the Protestant Episcopal Church USA, it is also called Episcopal Migration Ministries (EMM). EMM has its own website (www.episcopalmigrationministries.org). All government databases, however, refer to DFMS. But EMM is the title DFMS has given to its work. Repeating the "welcoming" mantra, EMM lists its first order of business as Welcoming Services: "Episcopal Migration Ministries' affiliate partners provide refugees with the information and services they require to thrive in their new communities within just months after arriving."

DFMS/EMM is one of the smaller VOLAGs and saw a precipitous drop of almost 50 percent since 2016 in government grant revenues for refugee resettlement. A greater decline than all other VOLAGs. As with all other VOLAGs, however, 2016 was a high watermark over the past ten years at least. FY 2017 revenues were in keeping with prior years, and its EMM website brags resettling 3,187 refugees that year on revenues of $16 million, or just over $5,000 per refugee. According to the VOLAG, it has reduced its number of affiliates from 30 to 14.[273]

Until 2018, EMM was run by Rev. Canon E. Mark Stevenson, pictured below holding up a sign that says, "I #supportrefugees because:" and then lists various bible passages, all of which are deliberately misinterpreted by advocates to justify resettlement. (For an example of this, see the section on Welcoming America.) This is no surprise for the Episcopal Church, which has probably drifted further left than any of the other Protestant denominations.

Rev. Canon E. Mark Stevenson

The Episcopal Church makes no bones about its agenda and acknowledges that President Trump's efforts to curtail refugee resettlement have struck a nerve. VOLAGs object when accused of being paid by the head to resettle refugees, but here he is acknowledging it and complaining to boot:

> When President Trump introduced a travel ban and moratorium on refugee resettlement during his first week in office, it threatened the very existence of EMM, which receives most of its funding from the federal government based on the number of refugees it resettles.[274]

Stevenson bragged about how efficient the refugee resettlement program was, saying: "One of the things that we do well is refugee resettlement .... We do it inexpensively, we do it effectively, we do it efficiently."[275]

Rev. Stevenson was promoted to a top leadership position in the Episcopal Church and appointed his deputy, Demetrio Alvero, to direct EMM. The EMM website provides no information about Alvero, nor does a Google search or LinkedIn.

Ethiopian Community Development Council (ECDC) (www.ecdcus.org) — Founded in 1983 to serve the growing U.S. Ethiopian community, it began its resettlement program in 1991. Competing with EMM as the smallest of the VOLAGs, ECDC received $12.2 million from government contracts in 2018. ECDC receives about 95 percent of total revenues from government. In addition, ECDC has received donations from the Open Society Institute, Komen Foundation, the United Way, Tides Foundation, even Citi Foundation (CitiBank), and others. ECDC provides the regular menu of services to refugees and is involved in other contractual services as well. For example, the ECDC Enterprise Development Group provides SBA Microloans for new minority businesses.

ECDC founder and director Dr. Tsehaye Teferra is an Ethiopian immigrant who came to the U.S. as a UNESCO Fellow in 1972. He received his PhD at Georgetown University in sociolinguistics. Like all other VOLAG directors, he is a leftist, deeply entrenched in the movement. He is a founding member of the Arlington County, Virginia, Multicultural Commission, and works on the county Equal Employment Opportunity Commission, the Task Force for Arlington's Future, and the County's Diversity Dialogue Task Force. He also served as a board member of the far-left InterAction, "A United Voice for Global Change," a position USCRI's Negash now holds.[276] The Obama White House named him one of its Champions of Change.[277]

Unaccompanied Alien Children Contractors

Baptist Child and Family Services (BCFS) (www.bfcs.net) — Texas-based BCFS partners with HHS, DHS, USAID, the Justice and Labor Departments and numerous Texas and other state agencies, but its primary focus is the UAC program. BCFS receives almost all of its income through government grants—about 96 according to its most recent tax return. (See Table 18.)

BCFS vies with Southwest Key Programs as the largest illegal alien minor (UAC) contractor. In 2018 it received $440 million to house and resettle illegal alien minors (UAC). The biggest expense for UAC contractors is temporary housing for the illegal minors. In *Red Green Axis edition I*, we discussed how BCFS had planned to spend $50 million for a luxury hotel for the minors but was stopped through public pressure.

Southwest Key Programs, Inc. (www.swkey.org) — Southwest Key describes itself as an "Unaccompanied minors program" that serves "youth who enter the United States without parents or adult guardians and have been detained by immigration officials...." It operates 87 different programs, which is many more than the 64 programs it ran when the predecessor of this book came out. It calls itself one of the largest providers of shelter services for UACs in the country.[278]

Southwest is led by Dr. Juan Sanchez, a well-connected Hispanic activist who founded the organization in 1987. He received $787,000 in pay and benefits in 2016. Dr. Sanchez's biography claims that he serves on the board of the National Council of La Raza (UnidosUS). Dr. Sanchez also claims to have received a "Rising to the Challenge Social Justice Award" from LULAC.

Government provides 99 percent of Southwest Key's revenue, an eye-popping $626 million in 2018. Between 2008 and 2018, the group received $1.7 billion to house and place illegal alien minors. Over the past few years, Southwest Key has taken in more than BCFS in governmental receipts for resettling illegals.

Southwest Key also operates five for-profit "social enterprises," a Mexican restaurant, "Green" energy and construction, maintenance and workforce development, all of which are supposed to feed profits back to SW Key. Their tax returns, however, show only meager income from sources other than government grants. And SW Key gets a lot of money that way. In FY 2016, income exceeded expenses by over $16.5 million, and net assets were over $60 million.[279] This is the Left's favorite business model: an organization wholly reliant on taxpayer dollars, that receives and spends millions, and can become engaged in profit-making enterprises with little or no downside risk, because the taxpayer is covering everything.

Special Grants

There are numerous grants offered by ORR to support and assist refugees in every aspect of their lives. [280] There are grants for building community gardens, home-based childcare businesses, and many others. They are administered by VOLAGs, affiliates and other organizations. For some small NGOs, administering these grants is their sole source of employment. They are often run by former refugees. For refugee advocates, these programs provide the means for a self-fulfilling prophecy of refugee financial success and assure that refugees have a big leg up in competition for employment and business. All funded at taxpayer expense. An incomplete list of such grants and recent funding follows:

> Ethnic Community Self Help — Community building among refugee communities and cultural adjustment and integration. FY 2019: $3.7 million for 20 grants averaging $187k each.

> Individual Development Accounts — Provides dollar-for-dollar matching grants of up to $2,000 per refugee or $4,000 per refugee family for each dollar deposited in a savings account. FY 2019: $4.3 million for 18 grants of about $240k each.

> Microenterprise Development — Finances refugees to develop, expand or maintain their own businesses and become financially independent. FY 2019: $4.2 million for 21 grants of about $200k each

> Preferred Communities — Preferred communities are supposed to provide more opportunities for early employment and sustained economic independence. In addition, they support special needs populations. As of 2015, there were 96 preferred communities in 31 states. Administered by VOLAGs and affiliates. FY 2019: $10.7 million for 9 grants of about $1.1 million each.

> Refugee Agricultural Partnership Program — Provides grants for small refugee agriculture businesses, *i.e.*, farm stands and family farms. Michelle Obama called it "a model for the nation, for the world." FY 2019: $1.5 million for 13 grants in 10 states.

> Refugee Health Promotion — In addition to Medicaid, Medicare and Refugee Medical Assistance, refugees are eligible to benefit from these grants provided to state health agencies and some refugee contractors. Provides health screening, preventative care and other medical services. FY 2019: $4.6 million for 41 grants of about 112k each.

> Refugee Social Services — Provides daycare for children, interpreters, citizenship and naturalization, job searches and more. Funding NA.

> School Impact — Provides funding for activities such as ELL, tutoring, parental involvement programs, interpreters and other services. FY 2019: $14.6 million in to 38 states ranging from $75k to $1 million.

Given the massive amounts being spent at the state and local level on approximately 4.8 million students nationwide, this program is a drop in the bucket, and communities nationwide complain about ELL costs.

Services to Older Refugees — State grants provide services to help elderly refugees live independently, assure access to all social services, as well as naturalization services. FY 2019: $5.0 million to 39 states—grants range from $75k to $325k.

VOLAG Affiliates

According to a February 14, 2018 report by Reuters, at the end of 2017, there were 324 affiliate offices across the country. Reuters' announced, fittingly on Valentine's Day, that at least 20 offices were slated for closure and another 40 would reduce operations to adjust for President Trump's lower refugee caps. A graphic compiled in this report listed 55 offices that would either close or receive no new refugees, and another 22 joint sites where one or more affiliates would close, a reduction from 324 to 256. It also claimed that eleven planned offices will not open.[281] This is welcome news, but note that in the Reuters report, all the closures are prospective. The VOLAGs have bitterly complained that the refugee slowdown has forced affiliate offices to close, and while some clearly have, there are new offices that did not exist when the first edition of this book was published in 2015. As you will read below, many also continue to operate, despite having nothing to do, in anticipation of an uptick when the political winds change.

Furthermore, in another demonstration of the refugee program's secretive nature, the State Department's VOLAG affiliate directory, usually found on its Refugee Processing Center website (www.wrapsnet.org), has been removed. An old directory, dated December 13, 2016, is buried in the State Department's Travel website and was only found through a Google search.[282] So it is impossible to confirm how many offices have actually closed since, and they probably want to keep it that way.

Most VOLAG affiliates likely have found different ways to keep their doors open. One such case is described here. VOLAG affiliate Catholic Charities of Onondaga County (CCOC) is one of many Catholic Charities branch offices of the Roman Catholic Diocese of Syracuse, New York. As such, CCOC does not file its own IRS return. It does, however, publish its own annual reports. In 2016, the latest report available, CCOC took in $17.4 million, $12.7 million of which was received from government.[283] The report does not specify which level of government, but sources at the CCOC confirmed that it receives funding from federal, state, and local government.[284]

According to Foundation Search, CCOC also receives millions from thousands of private donors, including organizations such as Allstate, Amazon, AT&T, Bank of America, Bristol Myers, Citizens Bank, Exelon, GE,

Honeywell, IBM, M&T Bank, United Technologies, United Way, and many more.

An August 2018 story in the Syracuse, New York, *Post Standard* described how CCOC expects to lose $600,000 from its refugee resettlement program as a result of historically low refugee numbers and a corresponding reduction in federal funding since President Trump took office. The article states that resettlement staff of Catholic Charities of Onondaga County has been reduced from 6 full-time and one-part time to one each full- and part-time.[285]

The New York State government has stepped in to shore up funding. The article quotes CCOC CEO Mike Melara, who believes that refugee resettlement will resume apace when a new, presumably pro-refugee, administration replaces the current one. "[L]ocally, we don't want to get depleted to the point where we can't resettle refugees," he said.[286] So despite having little to do, the goal is to keep staffing levels up in anticipation of future increases—*at taxpayer expense.*

CCOC's parent, the Diocese of Syracuse, lists income of $61.4 million in its 2016 tax filing, with government grants totaling $26.9 million and net assets exceeding $21 million. Revenues for 2016 alone exceeded expenses by $3.5 million.[287] Clearly, the organization is flush with cash, gets huge amounts from the government, and has no problem raising money from a broad base of private donors.

Why should taxpayers be providing additional support to keep CCOC's offices open where little work is being accomplished on the hope that when political winds change, those employees will have something to do?

This little story provides a window into how refugee contractors and their political allies rip off the public in just one locale, and how difficult it is to uncover the financing. It also shows how the political system supports the resettlement program well beyond the boundaries set by federal law, and suggests how resettlement contractors are incentivized to support political candidates and parties that will keep these programs alive, *not* because it is in the public interest, but because it keeps the dollars rolling in. Replicate this situation all over the country to get a sense of the true dimensions of this problem.

It is difficult to evaluate local government spending for refugee resettlement because it varies widely among jurisdictions and is buried among tens of thousands of local budget documents. But CCOC's experience is not unique. For example, HIAS affiliate HIAS PA received $1,647,019 from government entities in 2016, according to its latest tax filing.[288] It does not specify the governmental source; however, HIAS PA's annual report covering that period describes local government donations that included the Philadelphia Department of Human Services, the Philadelphia School District, even the Mexican Consulate of Philadelphia, and numerous other local organizations with pass-through funding from the Office of Refugee Resettlement and other federal government programs.[289]

Additionally, like CCOC, HIAS PA receives donations from numerous private sponsors, including the United Way. Many VOLAG affiliates will likely stay afloat in these lean years with this kind of support. The only way to remove the adverse incentives created by the refugee resettlement program is to abolish the use of private contractors altogether.

A BILLION-DOLLAR TAXPAYER-FUNDED ADVOCACY INDUSTRY

The Office of Refugee Resettlement (ORR) offers a multitude of grants for refugees and Unaccompanied Alien Children (UAC) to many other NGOs in addition to the VOLAGs and their affiliates. It has created a billion-dollar taxpayer-funded advocacy industry that has experienced explosive growth. Chart 6 shows total ORR grants for refugees and UACs since 2008.

Chart 6

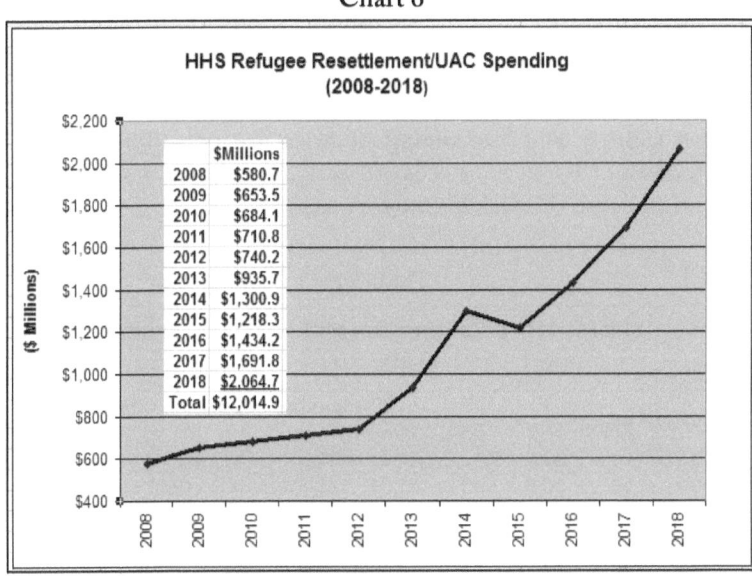

There is a total of eight programs specifically for refugee groups and the Unaccompanied Alien Children program. These are as follows:

- State Administered programs, ($4.1 billion since 2008)
- Voluntary Agency ($703.3 million since 2008)
- Discretionary Grants ($726.9 million since 2008)
- Targeted Assistance ($415.6 million since 2008)
- Wilson-Fish ($313.5 million since 2008)
- Services to Victims of a Severe Form of Trafficking ($91.4 million since 2008)
- Assistance to Torture Victims ($114.7 million since 2008)
- Unaccompanied Alien Children ($5.5 billion since 2008)

In total, ORR provided $12.0 billion from 2008 to 2018, as shown in the chart. Note that this is substantially more than the $8.9 billion total from Tables 16 and 17, showing VOLAG and UAC contractor grants. Most of the difference is explained by the many affiliates and other independent organizations that feed off the refugee and UAC programs, in addition to funding provided to VOLAGs.

In Massachusetts alone, which brags that one of every six residents and one in five workers is foreign-born, there are 130 organizations that comprise the Massachusetts Immigrant and Refugee Advocacy Coalition (MIRA).[290] Other states have similar networks based on the size of their refugee/UAC programs and the level of non-profit engagement in the state.

Measuring refugee-related expenditures of these various other NGOs is beyond the scope of this book because some receive no government funding, relying only on private donations. But Table 22 offers a small sample of the many organizations that have taken advantage of ORR grants. ACCESS (the Arab Community Center for Economic and Social Services), AALV (the Association of Africans Living in Vermont), Jannus, Somali Bantu Community of Houston (SBCH), and Welcoming America are not affiliated with any VOLAG. IRSA, RST (Refugee Services of Texas), Opening Doors and the YMCA are. Friends of Youth (FOY) deals only with UACs.

Table 22

Selected HHS Refugee Resettlement/UAC Grants ($ Millions)									
	ACCESS	AALV	FOY	IRSA	Jannus	Opening Doors	RST	SBCH	Welcoming America	YMCA
2008	$0.3	$0.2	$0.0	$12.3	$0.8	$0.3	$2.2	$0.6	$0.0	$0.0
2009	$0.2	$0.3	$0.0	$12.8	$1.2	$0.3	$4.7	$0.6	$0.0	$0.0
2010	$0.3	$0.2	$2.2	$12.5	$2.7	$0.3	$12.5	$0.1	$0.0	$0.0
2011	$0.8	$0.2	$2.3	$12.5	$2.9	$0.3	$36.1	$0.2	$0.0	$0.0
2012	$0.9	$0.1	$2.2	$0.1	$2.5	$0.1	$32.7	$0.2	$0.1	$0.0
2013	$1.6	$0.3	$2.3	$0.2	$2.5	$0.3	$52.7	$0.4	$0.2	$0.0
2014	$2.0	$0.3	$2.3	$0.2	$2.6	$0.5	$53.8	$0.4	$0.2	$0.0
2015	$2.6	$0.3	$2.3	$0.1	$2.5	$0.7	$65.5	$0.6	$0.3	$0.0
2016	$1.8	$0.1	$3.3	$2.0	$2.6	$0.5	$68.9	$0.2	$0.2	$0.0
2017	$1.2	$0.1	$2.4	$32.2	$2.8	$0.4	$37.6	$0.2	$0.2	$15.7
2018	$1.1	$0.1	$6.5	$19.6	$3.9	$1.8	$6.8	$0.2	$0.0	$13.6
Total	$13.0	$2.2	$24.8	$104.6	$27.1	$5.2	$373.7	$3.6	$1.2	$29.3

Source: Department of Health and Human Services, Tracking Accountability in Government Grants System

Dearborn, Michigan-based ACCESS (the Arab Community Center for Economic and Social Services) describes itself as "the largest Arab-American community nonprofit in the United States."[291] According to its latest tax-exempt IRS filing, ACCESS took in $26.7 million in Fiscal Year 2016, $15.2

million of which was from government grants. [292] Funding for refugee resettlement was only a small part of its government-funded activity, but an important part nonetheless, providing yet another incentive to support the refugee resettlement program, in this case specifically for Muslim refugees.

Washington State-based FOY shows how the UAC program has exploded in 2018, as UACs flood the border in increasing numbers, and ever more are being housed.

AALV and SBCH are good examples of how government grants support refugees once they become established. Instead of finding regular employment, they create tax-exempt charities that provide services to the refugee community, while employing the more enterprising ones. All at taxpayer expense. This is a natural development, given the common languages and cultures, but it tends to further draw refugees into their own separate communities, where they are less likely to assimilate.

AALV has taken in a relatively small amount of its total revenues with special refugee grants, down to under $100k for the last three years, but its overall take from the government is much larger. In 2016, AALV received a total of $683,628 in government grants, 46 percent of its $1.5 million in revenues. The rest was service fees, mostly for interpreters. This was almost certainly paid for by some government entity—courts, schools, and the like. AALV's mission is to "Provide integration services to African refugees and immigrants." Its director, Yacouba Jacob Bogra, received $60,000 compensation in 2016. Other employee costs totaled about $450,000. [293] Many VOLAG affiliates are similarly run by former refugees, creating more natural advocates for the program.

SBCH has received under $200k for the past three years for refugee resettlement; however, its FY 2015 tax return shows revenues of $405k, of which $255k went to salaries and benefits. SBCH states its mission to be to "Provide education and acclimation of Somali refugees." SBCH received 90 percent of its revenues from government grants that year. [294] Table 22 however, lists over $600k for 2015. This could simply be a consequence of timing, but it points again to the need for auditing and better oversight of this program, which receives virtually none.

IRSA, the mysterious affiliate of USCRI, is listed in Table 22 as receiving $104.6 million since FY 2008. It has received matching grants for VOLAGs, HHS funding for State Administered Programs and Discretionary Grants, so it has been receiving grants independent of USCRI. With no apparently operative public office, and no record in USCRI files of providing funding to IRSA, this affiliate poses a very big question mark.

Jannus, Opening Doors, and RST are all VOLAG affiliates, receiving prime grants for some of HHS's various refugee programs and grants for State and Local Programs, which is pass-through money provided to the states by HHS.

Many organizations not normally associated with immigration issues have also jumped on board. Who could imagine, for example, that the YMCA of Greater Houston could take in almost $30 million for refugee resettlement over the last two years? The Y works as an affiliate for USCRI.

As described in its own section further on, Welcoming America is an influence operation, a propaganda mill with offices nationwide, created solely to build the "welcoming" narrative for refugees, immigrants, and illegal aliens, and vilify anyone who disagrees. It gets private donations from the usual suspects. Under the Obama administration, it also received taxpayer money. That has ended under Trump.

Wilson-Fish States

What happens when a state wants to leave the refugee resettlement program? Currently, sixteen states and San Diego County, California, have done just that. Recent state dropouts include Maine, Kansas, New Jersey, and Texas. These states dropped out in protest over the federal government's unresponsiveness to terrorism concerns. This did not help the states, however, because it does not end the program; it just means that the state now has lost whatever control over the program it ever had.

A controversial alternative program appoints a VOLAG to take over management when the state drops out. Such states are referred to as Wilson-Fish states, based on a 1984 law named for the legislation's congressional authors, Pete Wilson and Hamilton Fish. The original law called for alternative methods to providing welfare to refugees, but never anticipated assigning VOLAGs oversight of state programs. The regulation authorizing this was manufactured from whole cloth by HHS during the Clinton administration.

When State Department, ORR, and USCIS monies are counted, VOLAGs are paid up to $5,000 or more for each refugee they resettle, so they seek to maximize refugee numbers, and find it much easier to do so in states with no oversight. The numbers make the case.

Between FY 2002 (the earliest state-by-state refugee resettlement data available) and FY 2017,* Alabama, Alaska, Kansas, Kentucky, Maine, Nevada, New Jersey, North Dakota, Tennessee, and Texas dropped out. Of these, five have been run by VOLAGs long enough to compare resettlement data before the state left the program and after.

---

* FY 2018 was not included because the lowest recorded number of refugees were resettled that year, an involuntary reduction imposed by the Trump administration. Including FY 2018, then, would bias the results down.

Table 23

Average Annual Resettlement Numbers Before and After State Dropped Out				
	Before	After	1st Yr. % chg	Avg Annual % chg
Alaska (2004)	30	91	86%	203%
Kentucky (2006)	561	1,645	28%	193%
Nevada (2011)	336	572	45%	70%
North Dakota (2011)	268	508	53%	90%
Tennessee (2008)	684	1,459	76%	113%
Total	1,880	4,276	53%	127%

Source: Refugee Processing Center, www.WRAPSNET.org

Table 23 shows the results. Note that even in just the first year, refugee resettlement in those states shot up an average of over 50 percent. In total, these states have seen an average annual increase of 127 percent in refugee numbers since they relinquished program oversight. As refugee resettlement is a federal program, states have little recourse.

The refugee resettlement program thus becomes an unconstitutional unfunded mandate on the states, because state and local governments remain liable for state and local costs of any programs all legal permanent residents are eligible for, never mind the costs to schools, law enforcement, and the courts. Additionally, the Wilson-Fish program was never legislated, so should not have the force of law, but so far, it seems to. It has been challenged, unsuccessfully to this point, in court.[295]

Private Funding

Private foundations support the refugee resettlement agenda. Much of that money is spent on advocacy groups like Welcoming America as described earlier, but VOLAGs and affiliates receive substantial foundation funding in addition to taxpayer-funded government grants.

For example, HIAS has received at least $13.3 million from numerous, mostly Jewish foundations, since 1999.[296] CWS has received at least $106.4 million since 2000 from numerous foundations, including Open Society, Unbound Philanthropy, Ford, Schwab and others.[297] Open Society's 2017 Church World Service grant included $100,000 for affiliates in North Carolina and Ohio to "empower refugee and Muslim communities through trainings in leadership development, community organizing, Know Your Rights, de-escalation techniques, and civic participation."[298]

The International Rescue Committee has received over $325 million from private foundations since 1999, including Open Society ($2.3 million), Novo Foundation ($58.7 million), Buffett ($31.4 million), Vanguard ($23.4 million), Tides ($8.0 million), Newman's Own ($6.5 million), Unbound Philanthropy ($2.2 million), even Google ($2.8 million), and many others.[299] One hundred thousand dollars of Open Society's money was slated "to provide support for the executive transition" at IRC.[300] There is no further explanation of this grant, but this was the year Socialist former British MP David Miliband took the helm at IRC. Miliband made a cool $671,749 as CEO that year.[301] Did he need a fancy office makeover to go with his exorbitant salary? How they love to spend other people's money! A similar story could be told for the rest of the VOLAGs and their 300 plus affiliates.

THE RED-GREEN AXIS

W hen analysts warn that Muslims are intent on imposing Islamic Law (sharia) in defiance of the U.S. Constitution, Islamic apologists snicker that Muslims represent only 1 percent of the U.S. population, so how could they be a threat to anyone? There are numerous reasons to be concerned. Some have claimed there is a "tipping point" when Muslim populations migrate to non-Muslim countries. This usually occurs when Muslim populations reach about 5 percent of the total. They begin to demand special privileges, like blocking off streets for prayer, special prayer times and worship rooms at work and public facilities and insisting on the non-interference of host law enforcement for the imposition of sharia within Muslim population enclaves. At higher percentages, this civil disobedience turns to violence and terrorism.[302]

But in the U.S., this is already happening. The Islamic agenda, pursued by Islam's ambitious political and religious leaders and broadly supported by Muslim populations, is aggressively defended and promoted by the institutional Left, the legal Left, the education Left, the political Left, the media Left, the Hollywood Left, the religious Left, and now even the violent Left. These groups collectively represent a much larger percent of the U.S. population.

As a result of the Left's successful penetration of our cultural institutions, the Islamic vanguard in this country now enjoys the commanding heights of popular culture. With the Left's help they can cajole, indoctrinate, threaten, and punish anyone who opposes them—virtually dictating terms to the rest of us. And as Islam gains political power under the tutelage of its leftist advocates, the entire Muslim population begins to feel empowered and justified in its demands for special treatment and entitled in its flagrant antisemitism and hatred for Christianity. These combined factors make Islam the perfect weapon for leftist subversion to take advantage of what is, in fact, a temporarily symbiotic relationship.

The Left has used a very similar process to weaponize minority and other "marginalized" populations. So now for example, the Black Lives Matter (BLM) movement—whose leadership is comprised entirely of hardcore Communists and Socialists [303] —has been elevated to the presumptive role of spokesman for all American blacks, even though many American blacks recognize and detest BLM for the virulently anti-American organization it is. The gay rights agenda has similarly metastasized into a tyrannical, extreme Left movement intent on forcing acceptance of transgender bathrooms, pedophilia/pederasty, and even bestiality.

It is baffling to some, but really no coincidence, that CAIR has now publicly allied itself with BLM, and claims to champion gay rights—while its

Islamic brethren in the Middle East throw gays to their deaths from high-rise buildings and peddle in slavery of every kind.

Prominent members of CAIR have joined Democratic Socialists of America (DSA), the largest communist organization in America, with an estimated 44,000 members.[304] Linda Sarsour, the new model spokesperson for Islam, joined DSA in 2018. Newly-elected Michigan Democratic Rep. Rashida Tlaib bragged about her DSA membership during her campaign, while failed Michigan Democratic gubernatorial candidate Abdul El Sayed was christened "the Muslim Bernie."

Somali refugee and former CAIR-Iowa director Abshir Omar makes no effort to hide his DSA credentials either.[305] Many Islamic leaders, including senior Iranian clerical figures, were educated at Moscow's Patrice Lumumba University (now called The Peoples' Friendship University of Russia), a prominent training and KGB recruitment center for promising Third World students. While he denounced Saddam Hussein's socialist Ba'ath Party as infidels, even Osama bin Laden said that an alliance with Socialists against America, their common enemy, was justifiable.[306]

At a 2018 event in Des Moines, Iowa, speaker John Guandolo, president of Understanding the Threat, engaged in a conversation with Abshir Omar.

He asked Omar, "Is there a version of Islam that doesn't mandate killing apostates and homosexuals?"

According to Guandolo, Omar answered, "No, all Islam agrees that apostates and homosexuals must be killed."[307]

Given Islam's command to murder gays and apostates, the irony of devout Muslims allying with LGBTQ activists and blatant atheists, even becoming prominent members of such infidel organizations, cannot be ignored. Are these people really Muslims? Or does the objective of undermining Western civilization simply take precedence at this time?

John Guandolo speaks with Abshir Omar

The Left has been seeking to undermine our Constitutional form of government and the rule-of-law for a century. For if the rule-of-law becomes unreliable, the rule of the fist takes over, and the Left is good at that.

The American Civil Liberties Union (ACLU) has relentlessly chipped away at our Constitution for decades, most recently challenging Trump administration immigration policies by forum shopping to courts that the ACLU knows to be friendly to the Left. The open borders crowd challenges the rule-of-law by claiming "social justice" for illegal aliens is more important than law.

It is all part of a strategy to sow chaos in our society and make it ungovernable by anyone except the Left. With the Islamic vanguard, the Left can really ramp up its game. Leading activists of the Islamic Movement are particularly useful because they sow discord and disunity by refusing to assimilate, and engage in practices lawful under sharia, but that violate U.S. law, like domestic abuse against women and girls, female genital mutilation (FGM), polygamy, pedophilia/pederasty, and honor killing. They challenge American culture, traditions, and laws, and some courts are willing to side with them. Hiding behind the misapplication of the First Amendment's religious protections, they seek to undermine U.S. rule-of-law standards by demanding adoption of their own legal system, sharia. It is, rather, Article VI of the U.S. Constitution that should apply as the standard for lawful compliance in the U.S.

As this author has argued almost since Barack Obama broke on the national scene, Obama is a hardcore communist. He was born to a Muslim Kenyan father, which according to Islamic Law, makes him legally a Muslim. He also has Muslim connections through his stepfather, the Indonesian Lolo Soetoro Mangunharjo, and studied Qur'an and other subjects during elementary school years in an Indonesian madrassa. His middle name Hussein refers to Mohammed's grandson.[308] There is no record of Obama's having apostatized from Islam at any point in his life or being baptized into the Christian faith.

But Obama was mentored for eight years by a card-carrying Communist Party USA member, Frank Marshall Davis, and during his presidency surrounded himself with offspring and associates of Davis' Chicago Communist colleagues. His parents and grandparents were Communists, and the bizarre Islamic cult, Subud, that both his mother and stepfather joined, has communist—even Soviet—connections.[309] Obama's love for Islam, like that of most leftists, seems to be both cultural and strategic, because the Left has found Muslims to be the perfect wrecking ball for its subversive war against America.

The unholy alliance of VOLAGs, their affiliates, and self-interested politicians serves the axis—knowingly or otherwise. The relentless effort to resettle refugees and other very needy, and too often unassimilable, groups from across the globe, is changing the political, economic, and cultural dynamic all over the U.S., especially in smaller communities that often escape the public eye. Meanwhile a bipartisan congressional cabal seeking cheap labor and new voters resists efforts to rein in legal immigration or even reduce illegal immigration. The Obama administration's dangerous support for all things Islamic facilitated unprecedented numbers of refugees and other immigrant classes from Muslim-majority nations to flood into the country.

We have already witnessed the deadly consequences of these policies, as criminality and terrorist attacks committed by refugees and those resettled under other special immigrant categories begin to mirror the out-of-control situation in Western Europe. As refugee numbers grow, however, national organizations like the Council on American-Islamic Relations (CAIR) organize them, working hand-in-glove with American leftists to build power and subvert the rule of law, while attacking anyone who associates Muslim immigration with terrorism as Islamophobic.

Organizing for Action

Since the 2016 election, a nonstop, unprecedented, nationwide effort has been ongoing to undermine virtually every aspect of Trump's rule. Coming from many diverse quarters, all unified in opposition to different aspects of the Trump agenda, these offenses are actually the public face of the Red-Green Axis at work.

Most prominent among these actors, though only occasionally making public appearances, is former president Obama. Unlike most past presidents, he has not been content to sit on the sidelines and instead has worked incessantly to undermine his successor. He has overseen and orchestrated many of the larger public street protests through OFA, the organization he founded in 2007 as *Obama for America* to launch his presidential campaign.

Now known as *Organizing for Action*, OFA has gone through numerous phases. Following Obama's election, it was rebranded as *Organizing for America* to help promote his various agendas, especially Obamacare. It was dubbed "Obama 2.0" and benefited from a donor email list of over 13 million.[310] Then, during the 2012 election, it reverted to *Obama for America* as a grassroots campaign organization. Its current iteration was created in 2013 to once again promote Obama policies. During this process, a substantial organizational infrastructure was developed, and that infrastructure remains largely intact. Despite its "non-partisan" 501.c.4 designation, OFA is a radically partisan group.

Obama is able to remain at arm's length from the day-to-day operations of OFA, which he has delegated to a troop of trusted former Obama administration officials, many of whom have been involved off and on with OFA, some going back to its 2007 founding.[311] Instead, he oversees the Obama Foundation (OF). The Foundation's most prominent role is creation of the Obama Presidential Center—note that it is not referred to merely as a "library"—but its web description reveals greater ambitions:

> Founded in January 2014, the Obama Foundation is a living, working center for citizenship in the 21st century aimed at identifying, training, and connecting the next generation of leaders and engaged citizens. The Foundation is developing the Obama Presidential Center on the South Side of Chicago to

serve as headquarters for the projects it will undertake across the city, the nation, and around the world.

Therefore, there is doubtless much interaction between OF and OFA. A noteworthy aspect of OFA funding is its continued broad base of support, doubtless built on the network of donors created since the organization's inception in 2009. According to Open Secrets, the group received a total of $9 million from 3,179 individuals over 2013 and 2014.[312] Donations ranged from a low of $250, to $1 million. Between 2015 and 2016, OFA took in another $16 million.[313]

Funding for OFA includes donations from the following Obama Foundation Donors: David Shaw, $1 million, Mark Gallogly, $200,000, and Tom Campion, $100,000. But there were other noteworthy wealthy donors. Amy Goldman Fowler contributed $750,000 over two years. Fowler is the daughter of deceased billionaire New York developer Sol Goldman[314]. She is a well-known horticulturalist and is married to Cary Fowler, another famed horticulturalist and former executive director of the Global Crop Diversity Trust. Now called the Crop Trust, (net assets $167 million)[315], it was formed of a partnership with the UN and other international organizations dedicated to preserving "agricultural diversity"—UN control over world food supplies in other words.[316]

Ryan Smith, the founding manager of Variance Ventures, a Salt Lake City venture capitalist, contributed $476,260. He is a member of "Patriotic Millionaires," a group of wealthy Americans "committed to building a more prosperous, stable and inclusive nation."[317] Smith is described on its "Who We Are" page:

> Ryan became involved in progressive political issues via the Obama campaign and has continued to work with groups such as Democracy For America, Organizing For Action and Mew Media Ventures to name a few.[318]

Marcy Carsey contributed $250,000 to OFA over the 2013-2014 timeframe. She is a Hollywood-based TV producer. Her husband, Tom Werner, is also a producer and chairman of the Boston Red Sox. In 2014 he was a finalist for Commissioner of Major League Baseball, but the job ultimately went to Rob Manfred.[319] Between them, they have produced such TV shows as Mork & Mindy, Happy Days, Soap, Taxi, Roseanne, and Third Rock from the Sun. Werner and Carsey were friends and advisers to Bill Clinton during his tenure. Werner was inducted into the Television Hall of Fame in 1996.

Kenneth Levine is a former McAfee vice president. He is the co-founder of Brookline Venture Partners LLC and is also General Partner of Terawatt Ventures.[320]

Architect Jon Stryker contributed $100,000. Stryker is a New York based billionaire, worth $3.2 billion, and listed #251 on Forbes 400 wealthiest Americans. [321] He founded Arcus Foundation, a philanthropy dedicated to LGTB issues and conservation of great apes. Its mission statement:

> Arcus believes that respect for diversity among peoples and in nature is essential to a positive future for our planet and all its inhabitants. We work with experts and advocates for change to ensure that LGBT people and our fellow apes thrive in a world where social and environmental justice are a reality.[322]

With $5.6 billion, Stryker's sister, Ronda, is even wealthier, ranked #114 of the Forbes 400 wealthiest Americans.[323] She did not contribute to OFA, and says "I don't have a passion for politics ... I don't like what it does to people. I'm always disappointed." She and her siblings, however, are "are on the same page" politically.[324]

This is certainly true. While brother Jon devotes himself to gays and gorillas, sister Pat Stryker is yet another billionaire member of the Stryker clan (real time net worth $2.3 billion). [325] She and fellow Coloradan, gay activist and Obama Foundation donor, Tim Gill, were the big money behind the Democrats' successful effort to "turn Colorado blue." Their effort was the focus of a 2010 book, *The Blueprint: How the Democrats Won Colorado (and Why Republicans Everywhere Should Care).*[326] The "Blueprint" strategy has since been applied in numerous other states.[327]

There are many more like this among the 3,000 odd contributors, and doubtless more in the wings. Table 24, updated with the most recent data, lists the largest donors.[328]

Table 24
2013-2014 OFA Donations

Donor	Total Donations to OFA	Affiliation
David Shaw	$1,000,000	DE Shaw Research
Amy Goldman Fowler	$750,000	Sol Goldman Investments
Ryan Smith	$476,260	Variance Ventures
Marcy Carsey	$250,000	Carsey-Werner LLC
John Goldman	$225,000	John and Marcia Goldman Foundation
Mark Gallogly	$200,000	Centerbridge Partners
Kenneth Levine	$200,000	Venture Capitalist
Jon Stryker	$200,000	Jon Stryker Architecture
Laure Woods	$190,550	Philanthropist
Barbara Stiefel	$175,000	Stiefel Medicinal Soap Co. heir
Barbara Grasseschi	$165,000	Puma Springs Vineyards

Donor	Total Donations to OFA	Affiliation
William H. Freeman	$160,000	Freeman Webb Co.
Evan Goldberg	$150,000	Netsuite Inc.
Sandra McNeil-Rogers	$125,100	NJ Powerball sweepstakes winner
Anthony P. Crabb	$120,000	Puma Springs Vineyards
Paul Boskind	$105,000	Deer Oaks Mental Health
Francoise Haasch	$100,500	Law Offices of Francoise M Haasch
Tom Campion	$100,000	Zumiez
Paul Egerman	$100,000	New Israel Fund
Wayne Jordan	$100,000	Jordan Real Estate Investments
Marcia Goldman	$100,000	John and Marcia Goldman Foundation
Michael Cartwright	$100,000	American Addiction Centers

Source: OpenSecrets.org

OFA has partnered with the Indivisible Project, a 501.c.4 tax exempt activist group formed of former high-level Democratic congressional staff members. [329] Its first project was to publish the Indivisible Guide, a comprehensive blueprint for activists that rapidly gained popularity among the radical Left. Subsequently, Indivisible groups were the prime movers behind much of the early post-election, anti-Trump protests.[330] For all we know, Obama could have ordered its creation. Like so many other radical Left organizations, it gets funding from George Soros and others.

Its laundry list of goals includes getting rid of Trump & Co.:

- Impeach Them for Crimes and Misdemeanors
- Force Their Resignation Through Protest
- Expose Their Lies and Defend Truth

It is difficult to square this with Indivisible's supposed commitment to "legal, non-violent protest and political action," and other declared goals of defending and strengthening civil rights. What about the civil rights of Trump supporters? What about the legal authority of a democratically elected president? Indivisible claims to borrow its methods from the Tea Party. Former Trump press secretary, Sean Spicer, however, rejected that comparison. The Tea Party was a spontaneous, "very organic movement," he said, while Indivisible is "a very paid, Astroturf-type movement."[331] A hyper-partisan Organizing for Action clone.

Council On American-Islamic Relations (CAIR)

CAIR is probably the most prominent Islamic face of the Red-Green Axis. It was founded as a front for the Palestinian terrorist group HAMAS and was named by the Department of Justice (DOJ) as an unindicted co-conspirator in the Holy Land Foundation terrorism financing trial, the largest of its kind in U.S. history. It and hundreds of other named unindicted co-conspirators with demonstrated links to the Muslim Brotherhood, avoided indictment because, following his election, President Obama terminated the investigation.

CAIR Executive Director Nihad Awad is and has always been a devout, practicing Muslim. By his own admission, he became a member of HAMAS in 1994.[332] Prior to that, again by his own admission, he was a student leader of America's branch of the Palestine Liberation Organization (PLO), the Communist, terrorist organization founded by Yasser Arafat under the auspices of the Soviet KGB.[333]

CAIR has state chapters and is at the forefront of efforts to introduce some form of blasphemy laws in the U.S. to criminalize any effort to investigate and publicize what the group is doing. Like practically every other major Muslim organization in the U.S., CAIR is a front group of the Muslim Brotherhood (MB). The MB first began infiltrating the U.S. in the 1960s, but its strategic plan for America was not discovered until 2004, when a suspicious traffic stop led the FBI to search a residence in Annandale, Virginia. The homeowner turned out to be the archivist for the U.S. Muslim Brotherhood, whose entire home and garage held thousands of official MB documents. Among the most notable was the MB's "Explanatory Memorandum: On the General Strategic Goal for the Group in North America" It stated in part:

> The process of settlement is a 'Civilization-Jihadist Process' with all the word means. The Ikhwan [Muslim Brotherhood] must understand that their work in America is a kind of grand jihad in eliminating and destroying the Western civilization from within and "sabotaging" its miserable house by their hands and the hands of the believers so that it is eliminated and God's religion is made victorious over all other religions.[334]

CAIR pursues "litigation jihad," among other forms, though none is overtly violent *yet*. CAIR Chicago, for example, has launched 5,500 lawsuits over its 15-year history.[335] Jaylani Hussein, director of CAIR Minnesota, recently bragged of 360 lawsuits in 2017 alone (but quickly removed the YouTube video of his boast). Lawfare is one of CAIR's favorite tactics, along with threatening speakers—like yours truly—who expose its underbelly.

Last year, CAIR national jumped on the bandwagon with extreme Left groups in suing the FBI, Customs and Border Protection and other agencies charged with homeland security. It challenged, among other things, the DHS terrorist watch list, which allows DHS to catch terrorists attempting to enter the US[336] At least one state legislature has some sense. The Arkansas House just passed a resolution demanding state law enforcement suspend interactions with CAIR.[337] We'll see if it has wings.

Despite its roots in terrorism and direct connection to the Muslim Brotherhood, however, today CAIR is welcomed in the halls of power by both Republicans and Democrats. Texas GOP Rep. Michael McCaul chaired the U.S. House Committee on Homeland Security until Democrats took the majority following the 2018 election. On this photo of himself with CAIR Houston director Mustafa Carroll,

Texas GOP Rep. Michael McCaul, at right.

McCaul signed his name with the words, "To Mustafa and the Council on American-Islamic Relations, the moderate Muslim is our most effective weapon." At a "Muslim Capitol Day" event in Texas, McCaul said that American Muslims were, "above the law of the land."[338]

Facebook and Twitter now take advice from CAIR in their campaign to silence conservatives. Outspoken conservative activist Laura Loomer was banned from Facebook following complaints by CAIR that Loomer had called newly elected Rep. Ilhan Omar an antisemite. Meanwhile, Omar's blatant antisemitism has been on full display for a while. Loomer was also permanently banned from Twitter.[339]

Instead of being allowed to make inflammatory statements in Congress, Omar rshould be under investigation for document and financial fraud surrounding the allegation that she married her brother to obtain legal permanent residence for him while already married to someone else.[340] She has also defended terrorists, has possible ties to terrorists through her brother-in-law—whom she helped become executive secretary to Somali Prime Minister Hassan Ali Khayre. Ali Khayre is suspected of illegal activities as director of a Russian-controlled oil company in Somalia and is under investigation for links to terrorists, including al-Shabaab.[341] Ilhan Omar is a poster child for the Red-Green Axis.

US Council of Muslim Organizations

The Muslim Brotherhood agenda for the U.S. includes the subversive infiltration of every sphere of American society and co-option of unwitting Americans themselves in its cause. Less than two years before the official establishment of the United States Council of Muslim Organizations in March 2014, a clarion directive was issued by Tariq Ramadan, a quintessential leader of the Islamic Movement.[342] At the 11th Annual Muslim American Society-Islamic Circle of North America (MAS-ICNA) convention in Chicago, Illinois on December 21, 2012, Ramadan said:

> So this is why Muslims when they say we are at home should institutionalize the presence in the country... We are at home, show it! Not show it with what you say, show it with the institutions you have in this country — institutionalize the Muslim presence as Americans. This is home; this is where we can say 'that's where we are'...I think we are reconciling the West with the very essence of our universal principles — if we understand Islam the right way, if we understand why we are experiencing this historical moment of the Muslim presence in the West.[343]

Tariq Ramadan, the grandson of Muslim Brotherhood founder Hassan al-Banna, is no stranger to the USCMO agenda. In January 2010, Secretary of State Hillary Clinton gifted the U.S. Muslim Brotherhood with a key opportunity when she signed an order that lifted the ban that had prohibited Ramadan from entering the U.S.[344] Ramadan now could finally enter the United States for the first time since the Department of Homeland Security revoked his visa in July 2004 during the administration of President George W. Bush.

Almost immediately upon reentry, Ramadan spoke at two Muslim Brotherhood-sponsored events in April 2010, articulating the need for Muslim participation in US politics. It is not a coincidence that one month later, the USCMO's precursor, Project Mobilize, was formed.[345] Its objectives included:

- "To Develop the political capital existing within the Muslim American community;
- "To Organize the Muslim American community around issues determined relevant; and
- "To Advocate on behalf of the Muslim American community to elected officials and persons with political clout so that they act upon the concerns and desires of their Muslim American constituents."[346]

The Muslim Brotherhood understands that success of its plan to subvert the West from within depends on what it calls *the settlement process*: "In order for Islam and its Movement" to become "a part of the homeland" in which it lives, "stable" in its land, "rooted" in the spirits and minds of people, "enabled" in the life of its society and firmly established within organizations through which the Islamic structure is to be built, the Movement must work to obtain "the keys and tools of this "Civilization Jihadist" project that is the responsibility of the U.S. Muslim Brotherhood.[347]

Weeks following the March 2014 announcement of USCMO's creation in Washington, D.C. by leaders from some of the most prominent American Muslim organizations, the USCMO began preparing for its inaugural banquet to be held at the Hilton Crystal City (Virginia) Hotel on Tuesday, 10 June 2014.[348]

While limited information exists regarding the actual content of speeches and proceedings from the USCMO inaugural banquet, the Muslim Link Paper reported nearly "250 guests of the member organizations, leaders and imams of *masajid*, elected and government officials, dignitaries, civic and interfaith partners attended the banquet."[349] Two members of the U.S. Congress, Representatives André Carson (Democrat, IN-7th District), Keith Ellison (Democrat, MN-5th District), as well as Hassan El-Amin, Associate Judge, Prince George's County Circuit Court, 7th Judicial Circuit (Maryland) joined together on the speaker's dais with Muslim Brotherhood leadership to address the attendees. [350]

The June 2014 USCMO inaugural banquet was sponsored[351] by Helping Hand USA[352] (also known as Helping Hand for Relief and Development), ICNA Relief USA,[353] and Guidance Residential,[354] the largest U.S. provider of sharia-compliant home financing. The only Muslim charity invited to speak at the formation of USCMO in March 2014 was ICNA Relief USA.

The USCMO is described as an umbrella organization—and CAIR Executive Director Nihad Awad inferred that and more, with his assertion regarding the USCMO that "This is the dream of every American Muslim, to unify the approach, agenda and vision of the Muslim community. In the past, many people have tried to unite on a limited agenda, but this is a broad agenda for the American Muslim community." Awad stressed the need for a "platform to coordinate, to communicate, and unify the vision on critical issues both to the Muslim community and the society at large," because he believed that "Muslim voters can be swing voters in key elections, especially 2016." [355] The formation of the USCMO marks the first U.S. Muslim Brotherhood political party, and indeed the first religious identity political party in the history of this country.[356]

The USCMO was developed over a number of years under different names and was accommodated by then Secretary of State Hillary Clinton in early 2010 when she altered regulations banning US entry by terrorism-tied individuals. The USCMO includes CAIR, the Islamic Circle of North America (ICNA) , Muslim Alliance in North America (MANA), Muslim American Society (MAS), the Muslim Ummah of North America (MUNA), Muslim Legal Fund of America (MFA), the American Muslim Alliance (AMA), and many others, virtually all Muslim Brotherhood fronts.

Earlier efforts at such unity had not been successful. In December 1997, for example, seven national Islamic organizations met in Sunnyvale, CA to create a national Coordination Committee, whose goal would be to unify and provide "coordinated advice to America's six million Muslims on political issues and candidates." [357] Those organizations included the American Muslim Alliance (AMA), American Muslim Caucus (AMC), American Muslim Council (AMC), CAIR, National Council on Islamic Affairs, the Muslim Public Affairs Council (MPAC), and the Islamic Society of North America (ISNA). The effort failed.

The failed efforts to unify leadership for political ends underlines the importance of the current and apparently more successful USCMO initiative. The current political climate offers an opportunity not previously available to achieve the long-time Brotherhood goal of advancing its civilization jihad plans. These were laid out originally by influential Muslim Brotherhood theoretician Sayyid Qutb in his seminal 1964 monograph *Milestones*.[358]

Another figure prominent in USCMO's creation was Sabri Samirah, a Muslim Brotherhood leader in Jordan and former chairman of the Islamic Association for Palestine (IAP) in North America, a direct HAMAS off-shoot and the parent organization of CAIR. [359] Samirah was also banned from the US in 2004 by the Bush administration for his ties to terrorism but benefited from the Obama administration's loosened procedures. He returned to Chicago, Illinois in 2014 after 11 years in exile abroad. Samirah is no stranger to the Illinois political arena and quickly assumed leadership of several organizations. [360] Samirah worked with USCMO to begin implementing its political agenda through mobilization of Muslim voters in Illinois and led efforts to get out the vote in November of that year. [361]

In his efforts to mobilize voters, Samirah urged formation of a "Grassroots Unified Voting Bloc" that would energize Muslim voters to unify and collectively participate in those elections. The Gaza and Palestinian focus was an initial wedge issue—but as would become increasingly evident, the USCMO had its sights set on a much broader political agenda than that. [362]

It is not what most would consider a "moderate" agenda. In addition to CAIR Director Nihad Awad, USCMO's board of directors includes Imam Siraj Wahhaj, an alleged co-conspirator in the 1993 World Trade Center bombing.[363] Wahhaj's son currently faces prosecution in New Mexico for starving and abusing 11 children and allowing his own three-year-old son to die at an Islamic cult compound he ran.[364]

In August 2014, USCMO leadership met with U.S. Department of Homeland Security officials. Topics covered included civil rights and countering so-called 'violent extremism.' As reported by the USCMO on August 5, 2014, "The delegations also discussed future cooperation between the Council members and DHS with a focus on increasing engagements on a local level."[365] The USCMO leadership delegation included Secretary General Oussama Jammal, Nihad Awad and Robert McCaw of CAIR; Naeem Baig and Rameez Abed of ICNA; Osama Abu Irshaid of the American Muslims for Palestine (AMP) and Imam Talib Shareef of The Mosque Cares-Ministry of Imam W.D. Mohammed. DHS participation included: the Office of Civil Rights and Civil Liberty (CRCL), Countering Violent Extremism (CVE),

Counterterrorism, TSA, the Homeland Security Advisory Council and the Faith-based Security and Communications Advisory Subcommittee (FBAC).366

This meeting evidently established the parameters for the USCMO to plan a 10 February 2015 "Community Forum on Countering Violent Extremism" in Washington, DC that was sponsored by the Zakat Foundation of America. The USCMO event took place one week in advance of the Obama administration's own widely-touted CVE summit to address "violent extremism," held on February 18, 2015. 367

On April 13, 2014, in the early lead-up to the 2016 presidential election, the USCMO and Secretary General Jammal organized an unprecedented "First National Muslim Advocacy Day on Capitol Hill." The USCMO described this advocacy day on its website as "one of the next steps in growing the American Muslim community's political capacity and ability to move the needle" in Washington, D.C.368 The USCMO wraps itself in the American flag, to appear moderate and pro-American. This has earned the organization the title "Star Spangled Shariah."369

In view of just how far Muslim Brotherhood influence operations already have succeeded in "moving the needle" of U.S. foreign and domestic policy on critical issues involving Islamic terror and the Muslim Brotherhood, the continued development of the USCMO as a U.S. political movement requires close attention from citizens, law enforcement, security agencies, and political leaders. Sophisticated operations directed by the Muslim Brotherhood and cloaked in red, white, and blue but fixed steadfastly on the advancement of sharia in America must be recognized as the "Star Spangled Shariah" deception it is. 370

The USCMO ran 276 candidates nationwide at all levels in the 2016 and 2018 election cycles; 131 were elected. A report by CAIR, JetPac and MPower Change stated, "This new political class is aggressively non-institutional and represents a broader trend in American politics of an engaged political insurgency..."371 Ilhan Omar, Rashida Tlaib, and other Muslim politicians have benefited from the support of USCMO, which has become the leading edge of the civilization jihad movement in the US.

The USCMO was developed in close collaboration with the Turkish government of President Recep Tayyip Erdogan and has been described as "in effect, the U.S. branch of Erdogan's pro-Muslim Brotherhood Justice and Development Party (AKP)."372 Notably, Erdogan held closed-door meeting in New York City in September 2017, where he with prominent leaders of the foremost U.S. Muslim Brotherhood groups, including Nihad Awad of CAIR, Osama Abu Irshaid of American Muslims for Palestine, Mazen Mokhtar of the Muslim American Society, and the USCMO's Jammal. 373 Interestingly, Erdogan also met there with a then-little known Minnesota state legislator, now the increasingly-notorious Rep. Ilhan Omar (D-MN), who was later elected to Congress in the 2018 elections.

Omar was likely instrumental in bringing the Minnesota-based Islamic Association of North America (IANA), a large Somali group, into the USCMO. Formerly called the North American Council of Somali Imams (NACSI), the IANA has been around since 2001. The IANA joined USCMO in 2018, just months after Ilhan Omar met with Erdogan in New York.[374]

Today, the Muslim Brotherhood organizations which make up the USCMO pose a clear and compelling threat to U.S. national security and the U.S. Constitution. Evidence acquired by American and foreign security agencies documents that the Muslim Brotherhood engages in hostile intelligence collection against U.S. law enforcement and intelligence agencies.[*] It conducts influence operations against law enforcement and American policymakers and directly attacks and attempts to silence any citizen willing to speak up as a "hater," "bigot," or "Islamophobe." Such activities on the part of these groups constitute a direct threat to the security of the nation as well as the independence of its domestic and foreign policy.

The United States of America faces a clear and present danger from the USCMO because of its sharia-compliant agenda that supports and advocates jihad to achieve the re-establishment of a global Caliphate under rule of Islamic Law. The supremacist, totalitarian aspects of sharia are incompatible with our Constitution, our Republic, and natural law itself. The USCMO's "Star Spangled Shariah" narrative, combined with an agenda to manipulate the U.S. political system and co-opt disaffected and uninformed non-Muslim segments of society, requires immediate action by citizens, faith leaders, law enforcement, and legislators.[375]

Countering Violent Extremism

Obama and his fellow leftists weaponized Islam to their benefit in the same way they have weaponized all other groups: by declaring Muslims to be an oppressed minority. Obama expressed his sympathies early on in his infamous 2009 Cairo, Egypt speech "to the Muslim World." This sentiment was turned into official policy in the 2010 Presidential Study Directive-11 (PSD-11), which although still classified, is understood to outline the Obama administration's decision to promote the agenda of the Muslim Brotherhood both domestically and abroad. It was this document, PSD-11, that paved the way for the Obama administration's backing and support for the Islamic

---

[*] Documents entered into evidence in the 2008 Holy Land Foundation HAMAS terror funding trial are available at the website of the U.S. District Court, Northern District of Texas, http://www.txnd.uscourts.gov/judges/hlf2.html. See Appendix 1 of "Star Spangled Shariah" for a description of the "Global Project for Palestine" prepared by the Muslim Brotherhood in Amman, Jordan. The document instructs the MB to establish intelligence capabilities that include counterintelligence, intelligence collection, and surveillance. Appendix 1 also includes citations from the Charter of the Center of the Studies, the Intelligence and the Information, a document uncovered by Federal Law enforcement at the home of convicted Palestinian Islamic Jihad organizer and Muslim Brotherhood member Sami al-Arian.

Uprising of 2010-2011. Additionally, a 2011 memorandum stated that his administration would take a "civil rights" approach to law enforcement.[376] Using that as pretext, President Obama redirected federal law enforcement focus away from national security and toward "civil rights" and "civil liberties." Instead of focusing on Islamic jihad terrorism, the administration highlighted an agenda it called Countering Violent Extremism (CVE).

As the Congressional Research Service described it, CVE was designed to "address the forces that influence some people living in the United States to acquire and hold radical or extremist beliefs that may eventually compel them to commit terrorism."[377] Taken at face value, this sounds at least somewhat reasonable, *i.e.*, a proactive effort to prevent so-called 'violent extremism' from developing. The actual definition of 'violent extremism', however, was purposefully absent.

The Obama administration, the most hardcore leftist presidency in American history, had a completely different thing in mind. For that crowd, 'extremism' is in the eye of the beholder, and true 'extremists' were anyone who held differing political beliefs. Thus, we suddenly discovered that elderly Tea Partiers in wheelchairs and people who put Ron Paul stickers on their automobiles were in fact potential "domestic terrorists."[378] But when Nidal Hassan murdered 13 soldiers at Fort Hood in 2009, a clear and premeditated act of Islamic terrorism, the Obama administration labeled it "workplace violence."

CVE was actually the result of an influence operation conducted by Muslim Brotherhood and other similarly disposed Islamic supremacists that successfully infiltrated presidential administrations from Bill Clinton's, through George W. Bush's, to Obama's own. This subtle shift reoriented law enforcement priorities away from Islamic terrorism, seeking to prioritize "rightwing extremism," and succeeded in ending training, investigations, and intelligence gathering regarding Islamic terrorism, restricted the military rules of engagement overseas, and censored language deemed offensive to Muslims—even making it verboten to identify Islamic terrorist attacks as such.[379]

Consider the following list, that the U.S. Extremist Crime Database (ECDB) claims motivates "rightwing extremist" attacks:

- Fiercely nationalistic (as opposed to universal and international in orientation);
- Anti-global;
- Suspicious of centralized federal authority;
- Reverent of individual liberty (especially right to own guns; be free of taxes);
- Belief in conspiracy theories that involve a grave threat to national sovereignty and/or personal liberty;

- Belief that one's personal and/or national "way of life" is under attack and is either already lost or that the threat is imminent; and
- Belief in the need to be prepared for an attack either by participating in or supporting the need for paramilitary preparations and training or survivalism.[380]

Most readers will agree that this list characterizes the views of many Americans, virtually all patriots and constitutionalists, and anyone who identifies as a "prepper." What is happening in the U.S. is not a "conspiracy theory" but a well-documented fact. The existence of such a list is *prima facie* evidence that the government considers ordinary Americans as potentially dangerous.

The ECDB adds as an afterthought that "many persons having violent extreme far right views express support for some version of white supremacy, the Ku Klux Klan, and neo-Nazism."[381]

Do you see what they just did? This creates an official paper trail equating patriots, conservatives, constitutionalists, and preppers with the KKK and Nazis. And they have 106 fatal attacks in their database that ascribe those attacks to such common American beliefs.[382] But in most cases the attacks came from fringe groups and individuals like the Skinheads. Most target one person, and in many cases the motive was personal.

For example, the worst case of "rightwing extremism" involved a deranged individual who killed six and wounded eight of his co-workers at a Lockheed Martin plant in Meridian, Mississippi in 2003. It was clearly a case of *genuine* workplace violence involving revenge against co-workers from a man who committed suicide afterward. Some reports claim the attack was racially motivated, but the local sheriff noted that four blacks and five whites were wounded. He stated, "'There was no indication it involved race or gender as far as his targets were concerned.'"[383]

The ECDB goes further in attempting to equate "rightwing extremism" with Islamic terrorism, by noting that while more people have been killed by Islamic terrorists, there have been fewer total attacks. So according to CVE, 10 attacks by "rightwing extremists" where one person has been killed each time means more than one terrorist attack like Omar Mateen's mass murder of 49 in Orlando, Florida. But this is because the Islamic attacks are *genuine terrorist acts* that have sought to kill as many people as possible.

Department of Homeland Security intelligence officer Philip Haney went on the record as a whistleblower to describe how very effective counterterrorism research was halted by the Obama administration. The hundreds of records he painstakingly inputted on *genuine* terrorists operating in the U.S. were deleted from government databases, and Haney himself was investigated by multiple agencies, *for doing the job he was assigned to do.*[384] Haney asserts that had the administration allowed the program to continue, they may have been able to stop the Boston Marathon bombing, and the San Bernardino, California and Orlando, Florida terrorist attacks.[385]

Immigration Crisis Strategy

U.S. immigration policies, including but not limited to refugee resettlement, and our unwillingness to effectively protect our borders from mass incursions, have brought our nation to a crisis point. To paraphrase John P. Roche, presidential advisor to JFK and Lyndon Johnson, "it is less than a conspiracy, but more than an accident"[386] that we find ourselves in the position we're in today. For the hard Left and the Islamic Movement, fomenting crisis is an essential component of "eliminating and destroying the Western civilization from within and 'sabotaging' its miserable house by their hands and the hands of the believers..."[387]

The Left's goals, and strategies for effecting those goals, have not changed for over a century. The first object is to destroy the existing order. Karl Marx and Friedrich Engels both called for "the destruction of everything existing." One of their most adept followers was Sergey Nechayev, a 22-year-old Russian anarchist who in 1869 penned "The Revolutionary Catechism."[388] He said, "Our task is terrible, total, universal, and merciless destruction," and in that short document he laid out a strategy that became the blueprint for Communist revolutions worldwide. Points included:

- Penetrating all segments of society, pretending to fit in while plotting destruction.
- Attacking property rights, traditional society and morality.
- Executing entire classes of society.

Nechayev's method was to create so much chaos that the society would declare war on itself:

> The Society [of revolutionaries] has no aim other than the complete liberation and happiness of the masses — *i.e.*, of the people who live by manual labor. Convinced that their emancipation and the achievement of this happiness can only come about as a result of an all-destroying popular revolt, the Society will use all its resources and energy toward *increasing and intensifying the evils and miseries of the people until at last their patience is exhausted and they are driven to a general uprising*. (Emphasis added).

Does that not sound like where our society is today? While most people have never heard of him, it was Nechayev who popularized the Left's favorite mantra, "The ends justify the means." Nechayev was also the basis for one of Fyodor Dostoyevsky's main characters in his novel, *Demons*.

Nechayev said, "The object is perpetually the same: the surest and quickest way of destroying the whole filthy order," by its own hands. This statement echoes the Muslim Brotherhood's Explanatory Memorandum, which could well have taken some of its cues from Nechayev.

Elements of Nechayev's *Catechism* have been applied by many American leftists. Following are two of the most important. In 1966, a married pair of Columbia University sociology professors, Richard Cloward and Frances Fox Piven, penned a now notorious article for *Nation* magazine titled "The Weight of the Poor; A Strategy to End Poverty."[389] Cloward and Piven, both radical Socialists, opined that forcing as many people as possible onto the welfare rolls would create "a profound financial and political crisis," that would drive state and local governments to financial ruin. It came to be known as the Cloward-Piven Crisis Strategy, or simply the Crisis strategy.

The pair hoped that in the ashes of the crisis, they could then offer their radical solution: a guaranteed annual income for all citizens. It seems obvious to any rational thinker that a strategy calling for unprecedented increases in welfare spending would also eventually break the bank of federal government. It is coming close to that now.

The first test came in the late 1960s, using the National Welfare Rights Organization (NWRO). The strategy worked in New York City, where in the early 1970s, one person was on the dole for every two working in the private sector, and welfare consumed 23 percent of the city budget. New York was brought to insolvency in 1975. Mayor Rudy Giuliani subsequently called it deliberate economic sabotage and cited the pair as responsible.[390]

NWRO dissolved in 1975 but was quickly replaced by the Association of Community Organizations for Reform Now (ACORN). Cloward and Piven again selected a protégé to run ACORN: Wade Rathke, a veteran NWRO organizer. Rathke and other leftists sought back door methods to increasingly burden government with ever more demands for welfare. Over time they have achieved the equivalent of the guaranteed income by simply expanding the menu of welfare benefits and the qualifications for them. (The call for a $15/hour minimum wage is part of this effort.)

So, for example, according to a study by the Illinois Policy Institute, in Chicago, a single parent of two earning $8.50 per hour at some menial job, can collect benefits that will add up to the equivalent of a $65,000 per year income.[391] This recipient would have to earn $38/hour to achieve that annual income.

This explains why, as welfare programs become more generous, they kill incentives for achievement and guarantee that most people receiving them will remain reliant on the dole for life. It explains partially why employers seek immigrants to replace American workers. Welfare benefits are so generous, there is little incentive to work for low wages.

Immigrants from poor countries, however, find the wages very attractive. They go to work and apply for benefits as well. As a result, *we the taxpayer are effectively subsidizing low-wage foreign labor*, while immigrants take our jobs, and according to the law of supply and demand, depress wages.

Virulently anti-American radicals, Cloward and Piven were very happy with their creation. The massive welfare establishment created its own dynamic that would ultimately lead to fiscal collapse. As they wrote, "...this kind of mass influence is cumulative because benefits are continuous. Once eligibility for basic food and rent grants is established, the drain on local resources persists indefinitely."[392]

Next time you travel through a blighted ghetto neighborhood, with failing schools, drugs, crime, abandoned homes and understaffed, overworked first-responders, remember Cloward and Piven's triumphant claim, "the drain on local resources persists indefinitely."

But Cloward and Piven weren't nearly done. ACORN later gained notoriety as one of the groups behind the subprime mortgage crisis—another evolution of the Crisis Strategy.[393] The Clinton administration piled on, forcing banks to issue bad mortgages, but then having taxpayer-backed Fannie Mae (Federal National Mortgage Association) and Freddie Mac (Federal Home Loan Mortgage Corporation) underwrite the risk to the tune of $3 trillion.[394] The easily predictable real-estate bubble and subsequent crash assisted Obama in defeating Sen. John McCain in the 2008 presidential election.

Cloward and Piven also researched and promoted for ten years what ultimately became the National Voter Registration Act (also known as "Motor Voter"), signed by President Clinton in 1993, with the pair standing behind him at the signing ceremony (pictured above). It called for, among other things, automatic voter registration with license and motor vehicle registration, welfare, and other public benefits administered by state and local government.

ACORN also became involved in this issue, creating hundreds of thousands of fraudulent voter registrations prior to the 2008 election.

Today's massive problems with voter rolls, especially non-citizen voter registration, are another direct result of Cloward and Piven's handiwork.[395]

In every case, Cloward and Piven's strategy relies on the false mantra of "compassion." The poor "need" welfare, they "need help" registering to vote, they "deserve" to own a house, even if they can't afford it. Discover The Networks describes the Crisis strategy as a form of Trojan Horse:

> [The] outward purpose seems to be providing material help to the downtrodden, but whose real objective is to draft poor people into service as revolutionary foot soldiers; to mobilize poor people *en masse* to overwhelm government agencies with a flood of demands beyond the capacity of those agencies to meet. The flood of demands was calculated to break the budget, jam the bureaucratic gears into gridlock, and bring the system crashing down. Fear, turmoil, violence and economic collapse would accompany such a breakdown — providing perfect conditions for fostering radical change.[396]

President Obama was very familiar with Cloward, Piven and their strategy, having worked alongside ACORN, "my entire life." Then Chief of Staff Rahm Emanuel famously said, "You never want a serious crisis to go to waste. ... It's an opportunity to do things you think you could not do before."[397] Obama's entire eight years in the presidency were one big crisis strategy.[398]

Most people have never heard of Cloward and Piven, but among the hard Left, they are legends. It should be apparent as we watch illegal aliens flood the border while facing a tidal wave of third-world immigration through refugee resettlement and other programs—all sold as "compassion"—why and how their "Crisis" strategy applies to immigration as well.

It is in fact the most dangerous Crisis strategy devised yet—Cloward Piven on steroids. Waves of illegal aliens, refugees, and legal aliens are taking jobs and driving down wages, while utilizing welfare at astronomical rates, despite having access to multiple special grants allegedly designed to help them achieve "self-sufficiency," something that many never do. Other costs like terrorism, crime, disease, language, and cultural barriers, are existential threats to local communities and the nation at large.

All immigration, especially illegal immigration, is now being aggressively defended on the streets by violent Antifa mobs, while radicals in the courts block all efforts for relief. Anyone who objects is attacked as a bigot, racist, xenophobe, Islamophobe, Nazi, fascist, or just their favorite, "hater." And the final straw is the full-throated effort to criminalize speech, to prevent people from even *identifying* the problems, let alone discuss them.

More than any other single issue, mass immigration is "increasing and intensifying the evils and miseries of the people," as Nechayev prophesied, drawing us to the brink of anarchy.

NETWORKING, PROPAGANDA AND CULTURE SHAPING

T he first edition of the Red-Green Axis introduced you to the notion of "culture shaping," the Left's slimy term for manipulating public opinion. The idea is once again to use the mantle of "compassion" to arm twist the public into not merely supporting, but actually promoting the Red-Green Axis's immigration agenda.

Weaponized Civil Rights

The generally accepted definition of "refugee" was established at the 1951 UN Convention Relating to the Status of Refugees, since augmented by the 1967 Protocol Relating to the Status of Refugees. According to the official UN definition, a "refugee" is someone who is unwilling to return to his home country due to a "well-founded fear of being persecuted for reasons of race, religion, nationality, membership of a particular social group or political opinion."[399] The U.S. was a signatory to both of these accords and its refugee definition is essentially the same.

It sounds innocent enough, but what if membership in a particular social or religious group meant that one practiced cannibalism? What if one's politics, for example communism or enforcement of Islamic Law, advocated the overthrow of the United States? The law is silent on that. You are only ineligible as a refugee if you yourself, "ordered, incited, assisted, or otherwise participated in the persecution of any person on account of race, religion, nationality, membership in a particular social group, or political opinion."[400]

But even that exception is often overlooked. For example, the Cambodian refugee camps housed both refugees fleeing the murderous Khmer Rouge and actual Khmer Rouge members. We took both. Prior to the 1980 Refugee Act, refugees were granted entry to the U.S. by the attorney general through something called humanitarian parole. It was official U.S. policy to focus primarily on refugees fleeing communism.[401] The Refugee Act ended, and I would argue, reversed this focus. Now we get the communists.

It is important to note here that under these definitions, "individuals who have crossed an international border fleeing generalized violence are not considered refugees." [402] If taken literally, this would exclude large numbers of people who are regularly resettled anyway, for example many of the Syrians fleeing that country's conflict, most, if not all, Somalis, and even the above-mentioned Khmer Rouge, who should have been excluded for being the murderous monsters they were. It is as absurd as allowing Islamic State fighters from Europe to return home, which many countries do!

Similar language guides our anti-discrimination and "hate" crime laws, first articulated in the Civil Rights Act of 1964, which banned discrimination on the basis of race, sex, color, religion, or national origin. That definition has expanded over time by either new legislation or regulatory fiat. The Equal Employment Opportunity Commission (EEOC) now prohibits discrimination on the basis of race, color, sex, sexual orientation, gender identity, marital status, political affiliation, religion, national origin, age, disability, parental status, and genetic information.[403]

In practice, this has resulted in hiring quotas and other preferences for the target group. It facilitates anti-discrimination lawsuits and other legal action, protests, boycotts, and so forth. Activists are seeking the same kind of legal protection now for Muslims to protect them against "Islamophobia," including the passage of blasphemy laws. This has already occurred in Europe. And whereas these protections legally only extend to U.S. citizens, the Left has constantly sought to expand these "rights" to cover practically anyone, including illegal aliens.

The Left has multiple goals in pursuing this strategy: 1. to cultivate votes by finding ever more groups that can be singled out for preferential treatment by the government, 2. creating ever more divisions of competing groups, *e.g.*, straight vs gay, black vs white, old vs young, citizen vs immigrant, etc., and most importantly, 3. isolating, marginalizing, and ultimately criminalizing those Americans who uphold the Constitution, the rule of law, traditions, and traditional morality.

The sum total of this effort has been to tie our courts in knots and facilitate the Left's relentless war against the Trump administration. The latest insanity finds an Obama-appointed, San Francisco district court judge claiming that denying illegal aliens the right to request asylum violates their civil rights.[404]

The Language of Hate

The Left presents its immigration agenda as one of generous, even biblical "compassion." We are to "welcome the stranger," and open our doors to migrants "fleeing war and oppression," when frequently their goal is to simply circumvent immigration laws to enjoy the freedom, employment opportunities and generous welfare programs America provides.

Should you point out this obvious ploy, question its dangerous challenge to the rule of law, criticize the heavy costs it imposes on the community, or raise any other red flags, you are immediately characterized as a "racist," a "bigot," a "xenophobe", or "Islamophobe." The Left forces you into a box. You either capitulate and accept its agenda or are symbolically (for now) exiled from the human race.

Operators in the Red-Green Axis are aggressively seeking to weaponize "hate crime" laws to include any language that offends them. It has already occurred in Europe and Canada, where speaking truthfully about some of the very anti-Western beliefs and practices of Islam, pointing to rising Islamic terrorism in Europe, or identifying the growing gang rape and grooming gang phenomena as attributable to Middle Eastern men, can get you thrown in jail as a "hater." This "hate crimes" strategy is now being extended to any criticism of the open borders agenda. It has been codified in the UN migration compact, as described earlier.

More and more frequently, the Red-Green Axis has been successfully silencing critics. CAIR's Nihad Awad and his allies scored a high-profile victory recently by getting Judge Jeannine Pirro suspended by Fox News for comments regarding Rep. Ilhan Omar. Her crime? Islamophobia. Pirro reasonably asked if Rep. Ilhan Omar would put Islamic law (sharia) above her duty to the U.S. Constitution: "Is her adherence to this Islamic doctrine [wearing a hijab] indicative of her adherence to sharia law, which in itself is antithetical to the United States Constitution?"

That is a perfectly valid question, borne out by Omar's behavior. She casually violated longstanding House rules against wearing religious headgear, unlike 170 Jewish representatives[405] who have respected the 181-year-old ban, and no one called her on it. Instead, the newly-elected Democrat House removed the ban.[406] That in itself was at once a bow to sharia supremacy and a demonstration of Democrats' antisemitic bias. And Omar's frequently outrageous statements and behavior already reveal a contempt for the Constitution.

Today, we can see the "hate" tactic in operation every day when left-wing professors, journalists, performers, and politicians ridicule, misrepresent, threaten, or just suppress statements by anyone with an opposing view, or facts that might upset the leftist narrative. The Southern Poverty Law Center, Media Matters for America, and even the Anti-Defamation League, are assisting in this effort today. Social media does the same by "deplatforming," "shadow-banning," and other forms of censorship, while online payment processors discriminate against those with a politically incorrect mission or message, sometimes financially crippling them.

It is an unscrupulous, mean-spirited, self-serving, and dangerous form of psychological manipulation that has reduced our political discourse to infantile, elementary school playground name-calling. It is a national disgrace, delivered to us entirely from the Islamic Movement and its willing partners on the left. But because it is so effective at marginalizing opponents, the targets can lose friends, jobs, access to major communications platforms, and standing in the community, *permanently*. It is a form of psychological warfare and political terrorism.

Given its pedigree, this is not surprising. The strategy was conjured up by early big thinkers of the Left and was designed specifically to discredit its enemies and destroy our first and most important freedom: that of free speech. It is frequently misunderstood as a spontaneous, visceral reaction to beliefs the Left finds unacceptable. Those with more political savvy suggest it is an application of Saul Alinsky's Rule #13: Pick the target, freeze it, personalize it, and polarize it.[407] But it is actually a very specific tactic formulated 100 years ago by the Soviet Communist Party.

Vladimir Lenin, the Soviet Union's first leader, articulated this idea when he said, "We must be ready to employ trickery, deceit, law-breaking, withholding and concealing truth... We can and must write in a language which sows among the masses hate, revulsion, and scorn toward those who disagree with us."[408]

In the Soviet Union under Lenin and Stalin, individuals so vilified could face a death sentence.[409] But the tactic was urged on party members worldwide as suggested by this 1943 message from the Soviet Communist Party to the communist parties of the world:

> "Members and front organizations must continually embarrass, discredit and degrade our critics. When obstructionists become too irritating, label them as fascist or Nazi or anti-Semitic... constantly associate those who oppose us with those names that already have a bad smell. The association will, after enough repetition, become `fact' in the public mind."[410]

Lenin and his Bolsheviks believed that stifling speech was essential to their cause. He said:

> Why should freedom of speech and freedom of the press be allowed? Why should a government which is doing what it believes is right allow itself to be criticized? It would not allow opposition by lethal weapons. Ideas are much more fatal things than guns.[411]

Repressive Tolerance

The German Communist Herbert Marcuse developed the idea of suppressing conservative speech in America in his 1965 essay "Repressive Tolerance." Marcuse was one of the better-known members of the so-called Frankfurt School. Founded in Frankfurt, Germany in 1923 as the Institute for Social Research, the school was disbanded when Hitler rose to power, and its professors—all Jewish Communists—fled. Most came to America.

The Frankfurt School was reinstituted at Columbia University. Marcuse taught there before heading to Harvard, Brandeis, and finally the University of California, San Diego. He mentored Angela Davis, the black American Communist involved at the time with the Black Panthers, first at Brandeis, then at UC San Diego, which she attended specifically because he was there.[412]

Marcuse and his fellow Frankfurt School Marxists created Critical Theory, an intellectual tool to deconstruct the West through constant criticism. Echoing the Soviets, their teaching relentlessly accused Western societies of being "the world's greatest repositories of racism, sexism, xenophobia, homophobia, anti-Semitism, fascism, and Nazism."[413]

In order to correct the oppressive imbalance Marcuse claimed exists in Western societies, he suggested that—again recalling Lenin—those oppressed by the society had a special right to conceal and suppress truth, engage in violence, law-breaking, and other civil disobedience to get their way:

> Under the conditions prevailing in this country, tolerance does not, and cannot, fulfill the civilizing function attributed to it by the liberal protagonists of democracy, namely, protection of dissent... I believe that there is a 'natural right' of resistance for oppressed and overpowered minorities to use extralegal means if the legal ones have proved to be inadequate... If they use violence, they do not start a new chain of violence but try to break an established one.[414]

In the sphere of public debate this meant:

> Not "equal" but more representation of the Left would be equalization of the prevailing inequality... Given this situation, I suggested in "Repressive Tolerance" the practice of discriminating tolerance in an inverse direction, as a means of shifting the balance between Right and Left by restraining the liberty of the Right, thus counteracting the pervasive inequality of freedom (unequal opportunity of access to the means of democratic persuasion) and strengthening the oppressed against the oppressors ...[415]

Marcuse further described the types of people who needed to have their freedom curtailed:

> [It] would include the withdrawal of toleration of speech and assembly from groups and movements which promote aggressive policies, armament, chauvinism, discrimination on the grounds of race and religion, or which oppose the extension of public services, social security, medical care, etc. Moreover, the restoration of freedom of thought may necessitate new and rigid restrictions on teachings and practices in the educational institutions which, by their very methods and concepts, serve to enclose the mind within the established universe of discourse and behavior--thereby precluding a priori a rational evaluation of the alternatives.[416]

In Marcuse's formulation, anyone who opposes, for example, programs like social security or Medicaid, is by definition a racist, sexist, etc. and should have his/her voice and activities silenced.

The Role of the Southern Poverty Law Center

Marcuse's Repressive Tolerance was read widely and his tactics readily adopted by the Left, but Marcuse also had a direct connection to the Southern Poverty Law Center. SPLC co-founder Julian Bond and Herbert Marcuse were close associates. They got to know each other through their membership in the National Conference for New Politics, an organization Bond co-founded. Late Senator James Eastland described the NCNP as "working hand-in-glove with the Communist Party" to foment "revolution in the United States." In 1976 Bond and Marcuse also helped found the radical journal In These Times.[417]

In 1970, Bond joined the Democratic Socialist Organizing Committee which ultimately became Democratic Socialists of America.[418] He co-founded the Student Nonviolent Coordinating Committee, [419] later led by black separatists Stokely Carmichael and H. Rap Brown, who advocated guerrilla warfare in the U.S. Though Bond was elected to the Georgia legislature, the body refused to seat Bond three times because of his agitation against the Vietnam War. Bond called on communist lawyer Leonard Boudin to represent him. Boudin's other clients included the government of Fidel Castro, Soviet agent of influence Paul Robeson, and Pentagon Papers leaker Daniel Ellsberg. Boudin's daughter, Kathie, was a Weather Underground terrorist, who served 25 years for her participation in the 1981 Brinks robbery that left two policemen and one Brinks guard dead.[420]

Bond and Marcuse also shared an interest in Marcuse's protégé Angela Davis. When she was jailed for her alleged role in the Black Panther murder of a California Judge, she recruited attorney Howard Moore, Bond's brother-in-law, who had also helped represent Bond in his battle to be seated with the Georgia legislature.[421] Davis was also a member of Bond's SNCC.[422] Bond later wrote the foreword to Davis' book, *If They Come in the Morning: Voices of Resistance.*[423]

The SPLC uses the "hate" tactic invented by Lenin and further developed by Marcuse and Saul Alinsky, to spear political opponents. It does so by lumping mainstream conservative organizations like the Family Research Council, ACT for America, and the Center for Security Policy in with Skinheads, Neo-Nazis, and other extremist groups. Having thus conflated all their political enemies, SPLC spokesman Mark Potok has said, "our aim in life is to destroy these groups, completely destroy them."[424]

As Lenin predicted, when repeated enough publicly, the lie becomes the truth. It saves the Left from actually having to argue any issue on the basis of facts, because they would lose every time. Instead, their political and intellectual opponents are simply discredited. It is a shameless, unscrupulous tactic that has reduced the national dialogue to infantile, elementary school name-calling, all brought to us courtesy the radical Left, and now used by the radical Islamists. But they have been very successful.

The SPLC is regularly cited by news outlets anytime they want to discredit someone as a "racist," "bigot," or "Islamophobe." The refugee resettlement industry now advocates publicly shaming anyone who questions the program and has recruited the SPLC in its efforts to identify and discredit critics. Amazon, Facebook, Google, and others follow SPLC guidance in identifying "haters." But recently, the SPLC has run into some problems of its own regarding widespread abuse alleged by employees, including charges of racism and sexual harassment. Co-founder Morris Dees has been fired and two other top SPLC executives have resigned. More good news followed with the 17 April 2019 report that Twitter had severed ties with the SPLC, which was no longer a member of Twitter's Trust and Safety Council.[425]

It remains to be seen whether SPLC will retain its current level of influence. SPLC has received much criticism from both the left and right over the years and has survived and prospered. This author believes it will continue to do so. The people who use SPLC's "hate" list are well-aware of its fraudulent, defamatory nature, but being from the Left, those clients are less interested in the truth than in having a pretext to conduct their own war on traditional America. It would not be surprising to see SPLC hire people even more radical than those who left.

Shutting Down Free Speech

They have worked for years to "culture shape" our society. But some of us just refuse to be reeducated like the commissars would have us. So. the Red-Green Axis is now aggressively pushing to both define and criminalize "hate" speech. It is the most sophisticated version of the Leninist tactic yet. CAIR has been at it for years and lobbies the government to amend hate crimes law to included hate speech—as defined by CAIR and the Left, of course. SPLC provides the ammunition.

In 2017, this author and DHS Whistleblower Philip Haney were prevented from giving a presentation in Sioux Falls, South Dakota, following complaints by a former CAIR Minnesota attorney.[426] In 2018, author and talk show host Brannon Howse was forced to cancel four of five Midwest counter-jihad conferences at a very heavy cost due to threats from Antifa and similar groups that had heard of the events from a posting on the SPLC website.[427] Antifa and violent student protests against conservative speakers on college campuses and throughout the U.S. have become a regular feature on the news. Meanwhile, the Red-Green Axis continues its aggressive efforts to criminalize speech.

They seek to achieve what has already happened in Europe, where it is now a crime to speak negatively about the problems created by an overwhelming influx of mostly young male Muslim migrants. Austrian native Elisabeth Sabaditsch-Wolff was prosecuted after giving a series of speeches articulating the dangers Islam poses to Western Civilization. Her crime? She reportedly said of the marriage between Mohammed and his six-year-old bride, Aisha "... A 56-year-old and a six-year-old? ... What do we call it, if it is not paedophilia?"[428]

Now the Swamp has jumped in. A brand-new group bolstered by two related websites has announced itself. The group is called *Change the Terms* and calls on technology companies to shut down anyone saying things they define as "hateful."

Its website states:[429]

> WE ARE A COALITION OF CIVIL RIGHTS, HUMAN RIGHTS, TECHNOLOGY POLICY, AND CONSUMER PROTECTION ORGANIZATIONS.
>
> WE BELIEVE THAT TECH COMPANIES NEED TO DO MORE TO COMBAT HATEFUL CONDUCT ON THEIR PLATFORMS.

This is an agenda that has become all too familiar at this point. Who are the "haters?" Of course, according to *Change the Terms*, they are:

> For example, white supremacist and other organizations inciting hate are using online platforms to organize, fund, recruit supporters for, and normalize racism, sexism, xenophobia, religious bigotry, homophobia and transphobia, among others...
>
> This chills the online speech of the targeted groups, curbs democratic participation, and threatens people's safety and freedom in real life...
>
> Change the Terms uses the term "hateful activities" to mean activities that incite or engage in violence, intimidation, harassment, threats, or defamation targeting an individual or group based on their actual or perceived race, color, religion, national origin, ethnicity, immigration status, gender, gender identity, sexual orientation, or disability.

According to the Left, conservatives are all white supremacists, even when they aren't white. Conservatives don't normally "engage in violence, intimidation, harassment, threats, or defamation" either. Unlike the Left, we believe in the rule of law. Those who actually do engage in these kinds of activities are this group and the people affiliated with it.

In fact, the very creation of this group is a form of threat and harassment because it telegraphs their intentions to us. It is in essence a declaration of war. The Left controls most media and they know it. The few less regulated media sources still available to non-leftists are social media and internet news sites. So, their overt goal is to shut us out of those as well.

The way they will succeed is to do what they always do: turn reality on its head. They will lie by calling the truth "defamation," and label any message that they don't like "harassment." Black is white, good is bad and you *will* comply. By their definition, this book is defamation. As we have already seen earlier, the UN has already been successful at declaring such literature as a crime.

The list of founders and supporters tells you everything you need to know:

Center for American Progress—Leftist think tank founded by Clinton insider John Podesta

Color of Change—Activist organization co-founded by self-described communist, Van Jones

Free Press—A "progressive" news outlet founded by hardcore Socialist Robert McChesney

Southern Poverty Law Center—Communist inspired institutional hate group

Lawyers Committee for Civil Rights Under Law—Extreme Left legal organization.

Council on American-Islamic Relations—Muslim Brotherhood front

Church World Service—Yes, that CWS

And the following:

- 18 Million Rising
- Advocates for Youth
- African American Ministers in Action
- Arab American Association of NY
- Arkansas United
- Athlete Ally
- Benton Foundation
- CASA de Maryland
- Center for Community Change
- Center for Media Justice
- Center for Victims of Torture
- Coalition for Humane Immigrant Rights (CHIRLA)
- Consumer Action
- Define American
- Deplatform Hate
- Emgage Action
- Equality California
- Faith in Public Life
- Franciscan Action Network (FAN)
- Hollaback

- Illinois Coalition of Immigrant and Refugee Rights (ICIRR)
- Massachusetts Immigrant and Refugee Advocacy Coalition (MIRA)
- Media Mobilizing Project
- MPower Change
- Muslim Advocates
- National Hispanic Media Coalition
- National Immigrant Justice Center
- National Immigration Law Center (NILC)
- National Urban League
- OneAmerica
- Progressive Leadership Alliance of Nevada (PLAN)
- The Revolutionary Love Project
- Services, Immigrant Rights, and Education Network (SIREN)
- South Asian Americans Leading Together (SAALT)
- The Arc of the United States
- United Church of Christ, Office of Communication, Inc.
- United We Dream
- Western States Center
- Yemeni Student Association

Another recently created website with the same goal is *Reject White Nationalism*, (https://rejectwhitenationalism.org.) Many of the same actors listed above are affiliates, along with some new ones. But the objective is the same: to use Leninist tactics to discredit anyone who cares about our nation as "racists," "bigots," etc. It is so tiresome. The site provides Facebook and Twitter links to every member of the U.S. Congress, a very handy tool that they will no doubt use to demand the criminalization of free speech and shut us down as Herbert Marcuse advocated. CAP receives millions from Soros and other well-heeled leftists.

Welcoming America: An Influence Operation

There are thousands of organizations working the propaganda angle. Only with immigration they have added a "religious" twist. The most prominent of these is Welcoming America, a nationwide organization that has grown substantially since the first edition of this book. The Welcoming network includes over 93 local government "partners" and 117 non-profits, including numerous VOLAG affiliates, 10 YMCA branches and even some governmental entities, like the Atlanta Regional Commission.[430]

Amazing whom you can bring to the table when enough money is involved. But many of these organizations have been infiltrated by the Left. Welcoming America now includes the Southern Poverty Law Center and other similarly extremist organizations in its membership as well.[431]

Welcoming America exploits a Bible theme, "welcoming the stranger", which appears in a few places in the Old and New Testaments. Probably the most useful for the open borders crowd is Matthew 25:35, which states, "for I was hungry and you gave Me food; I was thirsty and you gave Me drink; I was a stranger and you took Me in."

First, when he says "I was a stranger and you took ME in," Christ is talking about *himself*, not just any run-of-the-mill stranger off the street, and certainly not teeming crowds of immigrants, legal or otherwise. That is why Me is capitalized.

But those who have bothered to actually read the Bible, unfortunately including many members of liberal churches involved in the "welcoming" agenda, who misrepresent Biblical teachings every day, will protest, quoting some of the following verses: "Then the righteous will answer Him saying... When did we see You a stranger and take You in, or naked and clothe You?" (25:37-38). Jesus explains, "Assuredly, I say to you, inasmuch as you did it to one of the least of these My brethren, you did *it* to Me." (35:40) Further along Jesus says, "Assuredly I say to you, inasmuch as you did not do *it* to one of the least of these, you did not do *it* to Me. And these will go into everlasting punishment, but the righteous into eternal life." (35:45-46).

In each case *Jesus is referring to his BRETHREN, that is, his Christian followers*. Of course, newcomers to a community are always welcomed. That is a matter of traditional American courtesy. We don't need to be taught to be "welcoming."

In no part of the Bible does "Welcoming the stranger" refer to welcoming masses of illegal aliens flooding the border, or teeming hordes brought to the U.S. by financially motivated federal contractors working with politically motivated organizations looking to exploit these people either for low wages, votes or both. We are not required to take them in, nor are we required to clothe, feed or support them! In fact, *the opposite is true*.

Another good one is Hebrews 13:2: "Do not forget to entertain strangers, for by so *doing* some have unwittingly entertained angels." So, denying access to millions of people exploiting our borders in one way or another may be rejecting angels? You have to hand it to them for their chutzpah. There are more, but in every case, it is a deliberate perversion of biblical doctrine to serve the Left's radical agenda.

Most of the people pushing this narrative are virulently anti-Christian atheists —for example the communist sympathizers of the Southern Poverty Law Center, or the stridently anti-Christian ACLU. Those who claim to be Christians and push this narrative are committing gross apostasy, and demonstrate their utter unbelief, because true Christians know that to mislead believers justifies a punishment worse than death. As Matthew 18:6 says, "it would be better for him if a large millstone were hung around his neck and he were drowned at the bottom of the sea."

Prominent evangelical Christian leader Kelly Kullberg says that the open borders, leftwing activists, "demand that Americans 'welcome the stranger,' but rarely do they teach, or likely even know, the whole counsel of biblical teaching on migration and citizenship."[432]

> You'll likely never hear them talking about the story of Nehemiah and Ezra, helping Israel rebuild its faith, culture and walls—with both weapons of protection and tools of construction. They won't quote Isaiah 1:7, in which aggressive migration is seen as a curse, 'Your country is desolate, your cities burned with fire; your fields are being stripped by foreigners right before you, laid waste as when overthrown by strangers,'[433]

That's a pretty apt description of what is happening in Europe and here as well. Kelly goes on:

> In the Bible, we do not find the teaching of open borders, sanctuary cities as currently defined and illegal migration. In the Bible, we find respect of borders, nations, laws and customs—we find wise welcome...
>
> In cities where foreign law and customs are valued over American laws, we naturally see escalating crime, overwhelmed healthcare and welfare systems, domestic abuse and political chaos.[434]

Here's another apropos biblical analogy. At the house of Lazarus, Mary anointed Jesus with expensive oil, rubbing it on his feet with her hair. But one of his disciples objected saying, "Why was this fragrant oil not sold for three hundred denarii and given to the poor?" John 12:5. (Note: three hundred denarii equated to a worker's annual wage at that time.) The disciple was Judas Iscariot, who, as explained in John 12:6, could care less about the poor, but was intent on stealing the money.

Is that not exactly what is happening here? The Left wails about compassion, then waits, hands out, to take government money to "help" illegal aliens, refugees and other assorted "poor and downtrodden," while engorging themselves on taxpayer dollars and building capacity for a reliable voter base. At the same time resettlement organizations capitalize on well-meaning but gullible, ignorant Christian groups that provide volunteers, clothing, food, transportation and whatever else is needed to show they are "welcoming."

Welcoming America, the preeminent culture shaping organization, is a major leftist influence operation. Here's the con: you *must* be welcoming, it is your *Christian duty*, and if you really step up, there might even be money in it for you too. If you are *not welcoming*, then you can't possibly be Christian, much less a *good* Christian. You must be a "hater," "bigot," "racist,"

"Islamophobe," etc.; "greedy," and "selfish;" or the latest, a "white nationalist," even if you aren't white.

David Lubell, the founder of Welcoming America, created it in 2009, probably not coincidentally, following the election of Barack Obama as president. His goal was to "build a robust *good receiving communities movement* and create an *enabling environment* for more people and institutions to **recognize the role everyone must play in furthering the integration of recent immigrants** in the fabric of the U.S. (Emphasis added).[435]

Welcoming America's goal is to force Americans to accept mass immigration. Instead of addressing the problems created by immigrant populations that have no concept of our constitutional republic and no interest in assimilating, it engages organizations with a vested interest in immigration to improve messaging:

> David has identified a number of critical levers that, with low activation energy, can spark deep, scalable change. He is drawing in natural allies such as other organizations working on immigrant integration across the country and building a network of " welcoming " affiliates as implementing partners... In addition, he is working with municipal officials and influencing several federal government bodies to require that grantees working with immigrants engage receiving communities as part of their strategies. Understanding that media and advertising play a critical role in informing public opinion, he is also targeting these industries. Among other critical actors, David is beginning to work with corporations who have a vested business interest in making their communities more welcoming.[436]

Much of the Welcoming America agenda can be traced back to the Building New American Communities (BNAC) initiative, a three-year project funded by the Office of Refugee Resettlement around the turn of the 21st century. [437] ORR drove the effort to accommodate refugees and other immigrants and get them involved in the political process as soon as possible. Four principles guided this agenda:

1. New Americans should be involved significantly in decision-making processes;
2. Integration is a two-way process that implicates and benefits both new Americans and receiving community members;
3. Coalitions are among the vehicles that can foster effective and meaningful collaborations in order to tackle the numerous challenges and opportunities associated with socio-economic, cultural, and demographic change. These involve public-private partnerships that reach across levels of government and include a

broad array of non-governmental organizations, as well as institutions and individuals from many different segments of society; and

4. Resources should be devoted to integration-focused interventions, as well as coalition building and training opportunities, which lead to systemic change.[438]

Note that this was all initiated with our tax dollars. ORR has long been the home of embedded leftists. Unfortunately, the same can be said for much of the federal government.

Lubell uses the Delphi technique, a very manipulative method of putting people on two sides of an issue into the room and encourage "dialogue", with the end already predetermined. The bad guys, us, can express all our concerns over mass immigration, and they will listen patiently, with the expectation that you will listen patiently to their side. Having done that, the game is over, and they've won. This is made perfectly plain in their explanation:

> David and his team engage members from both groups to participate in and lead good welcoming events: Spaces where they can openly discuss their fears and build trust-based relationships with foreign-born U.S. residents. *These carefully crafted interventions lead to significant shifts in the attitudes* and actions of these two population groups. (Emphasis added).[439]

Of course, the only change in attitude that matters is ours. The "foreign-born U.S. residents," are handpicked and know exactly how to behave. If you object, everyone in the room frowns on you, for after all, you aren't being "fair." So, you sit still and fume, while everyone else seeks to be more "open-minded" to avoid the group's cold shoulder. In the end, we're all friends, and see, swamping your community with needy, unassimilable hordes really isn't so bad after all. Their side hasn't budged an inch, but your objections have been effectively defanged.

But Lubell and the "Welcoming" team haven't stopped there. They recruit media to push their message, and seek support from corporations that may benefit from low wage immigrant labor:

> Understanding that media and advertising play a critical role in informing public opinion, he is also targeting these industries. Among other critical actors, David is beginning to work with corporations who have a vested business interest in making their communities more welcoming.[440]

Welcoming America has been very successful in its efforts. Many politicians support the refugee program specifically so they can be considered "welcoming," because to be "unwelcoming" is just another code word for "racist, bigot, xenophobe, etc."

Public officials have been lambasted as "bigots" simply for questioning the program's cost. In one case, an effort was launched to recall a city commissioner in Fargo, North Dakota for merely posing this question.[441] The effort failed, but how do responsible government leaders function in such an environment? Weaker politicians abdicate their responsibilities to their electorate to avoid negative press attacks.

In February 2018, the author testified at a South Dakota state senate hearing on a proposed bill to limit refugee resettlement in the state. One state senator raised objections to the bill *that she had supported*, saying she didn't want the state to appear "unwelcoming." Meanwhile, the state was facing substantial fiscal burdens from a large and growing refugee community in Sioux Falls and other cities.

She was clearly reacting to Welcoming America's narrative. But it is not a legislator's job to base decisions on whether her state appears "welcoming" or not, just so she can preserve her cherished "welcoming" image. It is her job to serve the citizens who elected her, citizens who will be on the hook for the myriad state and local costs associated with refugee resettlement.

According to Table 22, Welcoming America has received $1.2 million from the federal government, all during the Obama years. The Trump administration zeroed out its federal support—a welcome change—but Welcoming America gets much more from private donors. Between 2011 and 2016, Welcoming America received almost $10 million from open borders foundations like Open Society ($450,000), Unbound Philanthropy ($984,450), Kellogg ($200,000), Kaplan, ($595,000), the Einhorn Family Trust ($1.5 million), Carnegie, ($325,000), and others.[442]

Welcoming America and other similarly oriented propaganda shops are diabolical, corrupt, conspicuously disingenuous and self-serving—a malevolent cog in the agenda to erase America.

WHAT IS TO BE DONE

America is in crisis. The Red-Green Axis immigration agenda is one dimension of the deliberate crisis being foisted on our nation. It cannot be separated from the others as they are all dedicated in one way or another to our nation's downfall. The target is national sovereignty and rule-of-law, to be replaced with a totalitarian one, whether of the secular or Islamic variety.

The current immigration agenda, however, *guarantees* victory for our enemies because demographics *is* destiny. . On March 8, 2019, House Democrats made that goal explicit with a vote to defend municipalities that gave voting rights to illegal aliens. Rep. John Lewis, (D-GA) announced, "We are prepared to open up the political process and let all of the people come in..."[443]

This was included as a part of HR 1, the Democrats' first proposal under the new Democrat-controlled House. It included numerous radical changes to election law, such as automatic voter registration, prohibitions on cleaning voter rolls (currently a requirement under the National Voter Registration Act), same day voter registration and other onerous provisions that would open the door to massive voter fraud.[444] HR 1 is unlikely to pass in the US Senate, but reveals clearly the brad Democrat effort to manipulate vote laws in its favor.

There have been some positive developments, however. The #WalkAway and #BLEXIT movements, comprised of former leftists and minorities who have seen the light, could blunt the effect of mass immigration somewhat. But unless strongly encouraged and supported by the rest of us concerned Americans, it will not be adequate. The numbers are just too stark.

Building the wall will reduce illegal immigration and discourage the mass migrations exemplified by the caravans. It is a critical first step. But with legal immigration allowing over 1 million immigrants annually, the numbers will eventually dictate a leftwing majority in Congress, most state legislatures and the presidency, as these future voters obtain citizenship.

The organized, institutional Left, including media, the courts, schools and colleges and our political classes, have proven themselves utterly corrupt, unethical and contemptuous of our constitutional republican framework. Once they obtain enough power, avenues for legitimate democratic elections increasingly will be snuffed out. These compulsively despotic people will take power and use the levels of power to keep it at all costs.

On the evening of November 7, 2018, members of Antifa protested in front of Fox News host Tucker Carlson's house and attempted to break down his front door.[445] Tucker's wife was home alone and hid herself in a closet. One of the protesters suggested using a pipe bomb. Antifa published his home address and that of other Carlson colleagues online. Tucker asked "How can you go out for dinner and leave the kids at home at this point? If they're talking about pipe bombs ... how do you live like that?"[446]

In this case, the police defended Carlson, but that has not always happened. Increasingly, local jurisdictions are controlled by leftists perfectly happy to order police to stand down, as they did in Charlottesville, Virginia, resulting ultimately in the death of one protester, or at Berkeley, where rioters torched the campus in protesting conservative speaker, Milo Yiannopoulos. If the Left is able to obtain its oft-stated desire for a "permanent progressive majority", these types of occurrences will seem tame by comparison.

The Left does not seek answers to pressing social problems: it seeks power, and all it needs to exercise that power is a pretext. Its chants of "racism," "fascism," "white privilege", and the like are merely that: pretexts for violent confrontation. Given free rein it will lead to murder.

Legal immigration *must* be reduced to only those who can fill a perceived need—for example, high tech employment in areas where there is a domestic deficiency—and legal residence should only be granted to those who want to assimilate, learn the language, and strengthen our constitutional republic. At present, this means not more than 150,000 per year.

Most immigrants obtaining Legal Permanent Resident (LPR) status today are the consequence of chain migration, the Diversity Visa, refugee resettlement, and other programs. They seek the benefits America offers, but are not generally compelled by a desire to assimilate as were immigrants from earlier times. Muslim immigrants are being told specifically not to assimilate.

Laws and regulations must be changed to effect these results. The open spigot of taxpayer and private foundation money feeding this growing anti-Americanism must be curtailed.

The current refugee resettlement system, which incentivizes endless resettlement and widespread fraud, must be abolished. Refugee resettlement and asylum must be reduced to only those who clearly meet the standard after a process of intensive vetting. Most today do not. Immigration regulations that allow virtually anyone who crosses our border to claim asylum must be changed.

Unethical judges, as so many have revealed themselves to be since the 2016 election, need to be shown the door. The activities of politicians and activists willing to prevent a duly elected president from carrying out the policies he was elected for need to be resoundingly rejected in the court of public opinion and at the ballot box.

The Red-Green Axis's increasingly aggressive efforts to criminalize speech under the "hate speech" banner must be extinguished completely.

Given our First Amendment, it is astonishing that this even needs to be mentioned, but it does. The corrupt establishment has made clear that its prerogatives are much more important than dealing with inconvenient truths, even if it means disabling the Bill of Rights. If they are successful, all our freedoms will be lost.

This is where we find ourselves today. These critical changes will not be made as long as Democrats and establishment Republicans beholden to corporate interests rule Washington. For the long term, the education establishment must begin the long, hard task of reeducating our young, who have been led down the garden path of Socialism for over a generation.

Ironically, the Red-Green Axis agenda is ultimately self-defeating. If they achieve their objectives, the golden goose of American prosperity will be killed. Because the world economy is dependent on American markets and is buoyed by American productivity and affluence, the entire world will be plunged into an unprecedented depression that few will survive.

Dire predictions? Yes, but not far off if we ignore them. Americans dedicated to the cause of freedom must unite and throw off the shackles being tightened by the Red-Green Axis. Our nation is at a tipping point. Will we return sanity to our immigration policies and ethics to government? Will the increasingly aggressive socialists and Islamists impose their will on American society? These questions go beyond the answer to any one policy but are key to finding our way forward with *all* policies.

References

1. "Speech by Prime Minister Viktor Orbán on 15 March," Website of the Hungarian Government, March 16, 2016, accessed November 12, 2018, http://www.kormany.hu/en/the-prime-minister/the-prime-minister-s-speeches/speech-by-prime-minister-viktor-orban-on-15-march.

2. Carly Read, "Prince Charles pays tribute to Nice terror attack victims with flowers from Highgrove," *Sunday Express*, May 7, 2018, accessed November 12, 2018, https://www.express.co.uk/news/royal/956384/prince-charles-camilla-parker-bowles-nice-france-visit.

3. Ashley Collman, Ben Ashford, Will Stewart and Regina F. Graham, "Uzbek terrorist appears shackled in court in a wheelchair after it emerges he had thousands of ISIS videos on his phone, asked to fly terror flag in his hospital room and chose Halloween because he thought more people would be on the streets," *U.K. Daily Mail*, November 2, 2017, https://www.dailymail.co.uk/news/article-5038871/Who-Uzbek-driver-mowed-innocents-NYC.html.

4. Brian Skoloff, AP, "Ariz. bomb suspect charged with previous murder," *USA Today*, July 22, 2013, accessed August 12, 2018, https://www.usatoday.com/story/news/nation/2013/07/22/arizona-bomb-suspect-charges/2575815/.

5. Paul Farrell, "Abdul Razak Ali Artan: 5 Fast Facts You Need to Know," *Heavy.com*, Nov 29, 2016, accessed November 5, 2018, https://heavy.com/news/2016/11/abdul-razak-ali-artan-ohio-state-university-osu-stabbing-suspect-terrorist-somalia-refugee-isis/.

6. Marc Santora and Adam Goldman, "Ahmad Khan Rahami Was Inspired by Bin Laden, Charges Say," *The New York Times*, Sept. 20, 2016, accessed October 12, 2018, https://www.nytimes.com/2016/09/21/nyregion/ahmad-khan-rahami-suspect.html.

7. "Officer, suspect ID'd in Crossroads stabbings," *SC Times*, Sept. 19, 2016, accessed October 12, 2018, https://www.sctimes.com/story/news/local/2016/09/17/reports-several-hurt-crossroads-center-incident/90607870/.

8. David Inserra, " Terror Plot 104 Targets the Fourth of July," *Heritage Foundation*, July 3, 2018, accessed August 5, 2018, https://www.heritage.org/terrorism/commentary/terror-plot-104-targets-the-fourth-july.

9. Paul Beard, "FBI: 300 refugees probed as terrorists, 'truly alarming'," *Washington Examiner*, March 06, 2017, accessed November 12, 2017, https://www.washingtonexaminer.com/fbi-300-refugees-probed-as-terrorists-truly-alarming.

10. James Simpson, "Reds Exploiting Blacks: The Roots of Black Lives Matter, Accuracy in Media, January 12, 2016, accessed July 6, 2018, https://www.aim.org/special-report/reds-exploiting-blacks-the-roots-of-black-lives-matter/.

11. "Drexel Professor Under Fire For 'White Genocide' Tweet," *CBS Philly*, December 26, 2016, accessed November 10, 2018, https://www.onenewspage.us/video/20161226/6386262/Drexel-Professor-Under-Fire-For-White-Genocide-Tweet.htm.

12. Kristen Bialik, Alissa Scheller and Kristi Walker, "6 facts about English language learners in U.S. public schools," *Pew Research Center*, October 25, 2018, accessed November 5, 2018, http://www.pewresearch.org/fact-tank/2018/10/25/6-facts-about-english-language-learners-in-u-s-public-schools/.

13. Ron Schachter, "Are Schools Getting Tongue-Tied? ESL programs face new challenges," District Administration, March 22, 2013, accessed November 10, 2018, https://www.districtadministration.com/article/are-schools-getting-tongue-tied.

14. "How to file a Complaint," Wage and Hour Division, U.S. Department of Labor, accessed November 5, 2018, https://www.dol.gov/whd/workers.htm.

15. "Portland Public Schools EL Local Plan 2015-17," *Oregon Department of Education*, June 5, 2015, accessed November 10, 2018, https://www.pps.net/cms/lib/OR01913224/Centricity/Domain/181/PPS_EL_Plan_-_June_5_2015.pdf.

16. John Fensterwald, "Feds back English learner lawsuit against state, *EdSource*, July 24, 2014, accessed July 25, 2018, https://edsource.org/2014/feds-back-english-learner-lawsuit-against-state/65759.

17. Analysis of city education budgets conducted by author in 2015 and published Lewiston School budgets.

18. "2017-2018 Draft Budget Report," *Lewiston Public Schools*, March 1, 2017. accessed November 10, 2018, https://drive.google.com/file/d/0B0SPmQZG3fwtc29rQ19sYWRHanM/view.

19. 2018-2019 Draft Budget Report, Lewiston Public Schools, March 2, 2018, accessed November 5, 2018, https://drive.google.com/file/d/12sAFyHVzKbYfPvU30tNr2EPGt4mbQbR8/view.

20. "Portland Public Schools EL Local Plan 2015-17,: *Portland Public Schools*, June 5, 2015, accessed November 10, 2018, https://www.pps.net/cms/lib/OR01913224/Centricity/Domain/181/PPS_EL_Plan_-_June_5_2015.pdf.

21. Ibid.

22. "Demographics," *Minneapolis Public Schools*, accessed November 10, 2018, http://multilingual.mpls.k12.mn.us/demographics.

23. Rachel Slama, Ed.D., Erin Haynes, Ph.D., Lynne Sacks, Ed.D., Dong Hoon Lee, Diane August, Ph.D, "Massachusetts English Language Learners' Profiles and Progress: A Report for the Massachusetts Department of Elementary and Secondary Education," *American Institutes for Research*, October 2015, accessed August 12, 2018, http://www.doe.mass.edu/research/reports/2015/10MA-ELLStudyReport.pdf, pp. 10, 13, 14.

24. "English Language Learners in Public Schools," *National Center for Education Statistics*, April 2018, accessed June 12, 2018, https://nces.ed.gov/programs/coe/indicator_cgf.asp.

25. "Mayor of Lynn, Massachusetts, on influx of illegal immigrants," *Fox News*, July 16, 2014, accessed August 14, 2018, https://www.foxnews.com/transcript/mayor-of-lynn-massachusetts-on-influx-of-illegal-immigrants.

26. Lynn officials: Illegal immigrant children are stressing city services, *Boston 25 News*, July 14, 2014, accessed July 12, 2018, https://www.boston25news.com/news/lynn-officials-illegal-immigrant-children-are-stressing-city-services/142063086.

27. "New Hampshire High School Rankings," *School Digger*, 2017-2018, accessed November 5, 2018, https://www.schooldigger.com/go/NH/schoolrank.aspx?level=3.

28. "New Hampshire Middle School Rankings," *School Digger*, 2017-2018, accessed November 5, 2018, https://www.schooldigger.com/go/NH/schoolrank.aspx?level=2.

29. "Worst 10 New Hampshire Elementary Schools," *School Digger*, 2017-2018, accessed November 5, 2018, https://www.schooldigger.com/go/NH/schoolrank.aspx?pagetype=bottom10.

30. Olivia Anderson-Blythe, "Safety concerns arise as violence continues to escalate at Minneapolis Southwest High School," *AlphaNews*, March 13, 2018, accessed November 10, 2018, http://alphanewsmn.com/safety-concerns-arise-as-violence-continues-to-escalate-at-minneapolis-southwest-high-school/.

31. Neil Munro, "Muslim Immigrants Must Not Assimilate, Says Progressive Ally Linda Sarsour," *Breitbart News*, July 7, 2017, accessed August 10, 2018, https://www.breitbart.com/politics/2017/07/07/muslim-immigrants-must-not-assimilate-says-progressive-ally-linda-sarsour/.

32. "Ayaan Hirsi Ali says controversial Women's March organizer is a 'fake feminist'," Women In The World, February 2, 2017, accessed November 5, 2018, https://womenintheworld.com/2017/02/02/ayaan-hirsi-ali-says-controversial-womens-march-organizer-is-a-fake-feminist/.

33. "Ideology and Terror: Understanding the Tools, Tactics, and Techniques of Violent Extremism: Full Committee Hearing," *U.S. Senate Committee on Homeland Security & Governmental Affairs*, June 14, 2017, accessed July 12, 2018, https://www.hsgac.senate.gov/hearings/ideology-and-terror-understanding-the-tools-tactics-and-techniques-of-violent-extremism.

34. Brent Scher and Joe Schoffstall, "Secretive Liberal Donor Network Plots 2020 Strategy in DC," *Washington Free Beacon*, November 16, 2018, accessed November 22, 2018, https://freebeacon.com/politics/secretive-liberal-donor-network-plots-2020-strategy-d-c/.

35. "Memo: Strategic Outlook for the 2008 Elections," *Scribd,* September 27, 2007, accessed May 21, 2018, https://www.scribd.com/document/329671653/NYC-Meeting-2007-Final-Draft-4#from_embed.

36. "SEIU's Eliseo Medina wants immigration reform for 8 million new progressive voters," *YouTube*, Jan 31, 2013, accessed July 25, 2018, https://youtu.be/pSCG8TVgfh8.

37. Mohammad M. Fazel-Zarandi, Jonathan S. Feinstein and Edward H. Kaplan, "The number of undocumented immigrants in the United States: Estimates based on demographic modeling with data from 1990 to 2016," *PLOS One*, September 21, 2018, accessed November 12, 2018. https://doi.org/10.1371/journal.pone.0201193.

38. "Table 1. Persons Obtaining Lawful Permanent Resident Status: Fiscal Years 1820 to 2017," *Yearbook of Immigration Statistics 2017*, November 6, 2018, accessed November 20, 2018, https://www.dhs.gov/immigration-statistics/yearbook/2017/table1.

39. Roy Maurer, "U.S. Family-Based Immigration Policy Is the Exception," *SHRM*, June 15, 2018, accessed August 12, 2018, https://www.shrm.org/resourcesandtools/hr-topics/talent-acquisition/pages/us-immigration-policy-is-the-exception.aspx.

40. Zach Dorfman, "How Silicon Valley Became a Den of Spies: The West Coast is a growing target of foreign espionage. And it's not ready to fight back," *Politico*, July 27, 2018, accessed November 12, 2018, https://www.politico.com/magazine/story/2018/07/27/silicon-valley-spies-china-russia-219071.

41. Bill Gertz, "China's Intelligence Networks in United States Include 25,000 Spies: Dissident reveals up to 18,000 Americans recruited as Chinese agents," *Washington Free Beacon*, July 11, 2017, accessed November 5, 2018, https://freebeacon.com/national-security/chinas-spy-network-united-states-includes-25000-intelligence-officers/.

42. Dorfman, *op. cit.*

43. Steven A. Camarotta and Karen Zeigler, "1.8 Million Immigrants Likely Arrived in 2016, Matching Highest Level in U.S. History," *Center for Immigration Studies*, December 28,

2017, accessed January 21, 2018, https://cis.org/Report/18-Million-Immigrants-Likely-Arrived-2016-Matching-Highest-Level-US-History.

44. Obama Administration Awarded Contracts Worth Over $310 Million for Legal Representation of Unaccompanied Alien Minors, *Immigration Reform Law Institute*, December 6, 2018, accessed December 6, 2018, http://www.irli.org/single-post/2018/12/06/Obama-Administration-Awarded-Contracts-Worth-Over-310-Million-for-Legal-Representation-of-Unaccompanied-Alien-Minors.

45. "Vera Institute of Justice, Inc.," *IRS Form 990: Return of Organization Exempt from Taxation*, May 12, 2017, accessed December 6, 2018, https://www.guidestar.org/FinDocuments/2016/131/941/2016-131941627-0e32fc49-9.pdf.

46. "Vera Institute of Justice, Inc.," *Foundation Search*, accessed December 10, 2018, http://foundationsearch.com/FindFunders/GrantVisualizer.aspx?searchid=4189153.

47. Neil Munro, "Washington Post: Border Rush May Hit 100,000 Migrants in March," *Breitbart News*, March 4, 2019, accessed March 6, 2019, https://www.breitbart.com/politics/2019/03/04/washington-post-border-rush-may-hit-100000-migrants-in-march/.

48. "Illegal Aliens Quietly Being Relocated Throughout US on Commercial Flights," *Judicial Watch*, January 19, 2018, Accessed January 21, 2018, https://www.judicialwatch.org/blog/2018/01/illegal-aliens-quietly-relocated-throughout-u-s-commercial-flights/.

49. Ibid.

50. "Department of Homeland Security Border Security Metrics Report: Table 1. Model-Based and Observational Apprehension Rates, FY 2003 – FY 2016," *Department of Homeland Security*, May 1, 2018, accessed November 5, 2018, https://www.dhs.gov/sites/default/files/publications/BSMR_OIS_2016.pdf, 11.

51. BRYAN BAKER, "Estimates of the Unauthorized Immigrant Population Residing in the United States: January 2014," *Office of Immigration Statistics, Department of Homeland Security*, July 2017, accessed November 12, 2018, https://www.dhs.gov/sites/default/files/publications/Unauthorized%20Immigrant%20Population%20Estimates%20in%20the%20US%20January%202014_1.pdf.

52. Robert Justich and Betty Ng, CFA, "The Underground Labor Force is Rising to the Surface," *Bear Stearns*, January 3, 2005, accessed April 14, 2015, http://www.steinreport.com/BearStearnsStudy.pdf.

53. Fazel-Zarandi, Feinstein, and Kaplan, *op. cit.*

54. David Martosko, "Up to 34 MILLION blank 'green cards' and work permits to be ordered ahead of Obama illegal immigrant 'amnesty'," *Daily Mail.com*, October 28, 2014, accessed April 13, 2015, http://www.dailymail.co.uk/news/article-2800356/us-immigration-authorities-prep-order-34-million-blank-green-cards-work-authorization-papers-obama-readies-executive-order-illegal-aliens.html.

55. Alan Gomez, "There are 3.6M 'DREAMers' — a number far greater than commonly known," *USA TODAY*, January 18, 2018, accessed November 13, 2018, https://www.usatoday.com/story/news/nation/2018/01/18/there-3-5-m-dreamers-and-most-may-face-nightmare/1042134001/.

56. James G. Gimpel, "Immigration's Impact on Republican Political Prospects, 1980 to 2012," *Center for Immigration Studies*, April 15, 2014, accessed October 5, 2018, https://cis.org/Immigrations-Impact-Republican-Political-Prospects-1980-2012.

57. "Exit Polls," *CNN*, accessed November 12, 2018, https://www.cnn.com/election/2018/exit-polls.

58. Ryan Saavedra, "Texas Democrats Ask Non-Citizens To Register To Vote, Pre-Checked Citizenship Box On Applications, Report Says," *Daily Signal*, October 18, 2018, accessed November 12, 2018, https://www.dailywire.com/news/37334/texas-democrats-ask-non-citizens-register-vote-ryan-saavedra.

59. Bill Fletcher and Marc Joffe, "California's Total State and Local Debt Totals $1.3 Trillion," *California Policy Center*, January 10, 2017, accessed November 10, 2018, https://californiapolicycenter.org/californias-total-state-local-debt-totals-1-3-trillion/.

60. Joel B. Pollak, "Jerry Brown Blames 'Low-Life Politicians' for 'Sanctuary State' Backlash," *Breitbart.com*, April 17, 2018, accessed August 20, 2018, https://www.breitbart.com/politics/2018/04/17/jerry-brown-blames-low-life-politicians-sanctuary-state-backlash/.

61. George Skelton, "Governors' tough talk can't block refugees," *Los Angeles Times*, Nov 23, 2015, accessed August 15, 2018, https://www.latimes.com/local/politics/la-me-pol-sac-cap-brown-refugees-20151123-column.html.

62. Debbie Elliot, "A Lesson in History: Resettling Refugees of Vietnam," *NPR*, January 14, 2007, accessed August 209, 2018, https://www.npr.org/templates/story/story.php?storyId=6855407.

63. Tiffany Gabbay, "Founder of Judge Curiel's La Raza Group: Whites Go Back to Europe, CA to Be 'Hispanic State': 'California is going to become a Hispanic state, and if anyone doesn't like it, they should leave,'" *truth Revolt*, June 10, 2016, accessed August 8, 2018, https://www.truthrevolt.org/news/founder-judge-curiels-la-raza-group-whites-go-back-europe-ca-be-hispanic-state.

64. Richard Pollock, "FLASHBACK: Democrats Tried To Block Thousands Of Vietnam War Refugees, Including Orphans," *Daily Caller News Foundation*, January 29, 2017, accessed August 20, 2018, https://dailycaller.com/2017/01/29/flashback-when-liberal-democrats-opposed-refugees-and-even-orphans/.

65. Javier Panzar and Javier Panzar, "It's official: Latinos now outnumber whites in California," *LA Times*, Jul 08, 2015, accessed July 28, 2018, https://www.latimes.com/local/california/la-me-census-latinos-20150708-story.html

66. "Pueblo Sin Fronteras," *Influence Watch*, accessed November 25, 2018, https://www.influencewatch.org/non-profit/pueblo-sin-fronteras/.

67. "On Watch: Exposing Mainstream Media Lies About the Illegal Alien Invasion: Judicial Watch Interview with Ami Horowitz," *Judicial Watch*, November 21, 2018, accessed November 28, 2018, https://youtu.be/lfP2UJP0hJE.

68. "Emma Lozano," *Influence Watch*, accessed November 25, 2018, https://www.influencewatch.org/person/emma-lozano/.

69. "Elvira Arellano," *Influence Watch*, accessed November 25, 2018, https://www.influencewatch.org/person/elvira-arellano/.

70. Teo Reyes, "Chicago Immigrant Workers 'Get on the Bus' For Freedom Rides," *LaborNotes*, September 30, 2003, accessed November 10, 2018, http://labornotes.org/2003/09/chicago-immigrant-workers-%E2%80%98get-bus%E2%80%99-freedom-rides.

71. "Emma Lozano," *Op. Cit.*

72. "Pueblo Sin Fronteras," *Op. Cit.*

73. Stephen Wynne, "Soros Funding Catholic Open Borders Push Millions funneled to pro-amnesty Catholic Legal Immigration Network," *Church Militant*, April 6, 2018, accessed November 28, 2018, https://www.churchmilitant.com/news/article/catholic-group-colludes-with-soros-on-open-borders.

74. "Catholic Legal Immigration Network, Inc.," *IRS Form 990 Return of Organization Exempt from Income Tax 2016*, May 22, 2017, accessed November 29, 2018, https://www.guidestar.org/FinDocuments/2016/521/584/2016-521584951-0e15e4c7-9.pdf, 36-48.

75. "Grant Visualizer: Catholic Legal Immigration Services," *Foundation Search*, accessed November 29, 2018, http://www.foundationsearch.com.

76. "Search the Nonprofit Network: Centro Sin Fronteras," *The Center for Public Integrity*, August 3, 2016, accessed November 10, 2018, https://www.publicintegrity.org/2016/08/02/20030/search-nonprofit-network.

77. Illinois Coalition for Immigrant and Refugee Rights, *IRS Form 990 Return of Organization Exempt from Income Tax*, tax years 2015-2017, accessed November 25, 2018.
2017:
http://990s.foundationcenter.org/990_pdf_archive/363/363783551/363783551_201706_990.pdf;
2016:
http://990s.foundationcenter.org/990_pdf_archive/363/363783551/363783551_201606_990.pdf;
2015:
http://990s.foundationcenter.org/990_pdf_archive/363/363783551/363783551_201506_990.pdf.

78. "Award Search: Refugee and Entrant Assistance State Administered Programs, FY 2015-2017," *Tracking Accountability in Government Grants, Department of Health and Human Services*, accessed November 30, 2018, https://taggs.hhs.gov/SearchAward.

79. "Illinois Coalition 2017 990, *op. cit.* http://990s.foundationcenter.org/990_pdf_archive/363/363783551/363783551_201706_990.pdf, 39-67.

80. "Illinois Coalition 2015 990, *op. cit.* http://990s.foundationcenter.org/990_pdf_archive/363/363783551/363783551_201606_990.pdf, 2.

81. "National Lawyers Guild," July 14, 2017, accessed December 5, 2018, *Keywiki.org*, https://keywiki.org/National_Lawyers_Guild#cite_ref-warcalledpeace_4-4.

82. John Bonder, "Soros-Backed Attorneys Helping Caravan Migrants Get Asylum in U.S.," *Breitbart*, November 20, 2018, accessed November 25, 2018, https://www.breitbart.com/politics/2018/11/20/soros-backed-attorneys-helping-caravan-migrants-get-asylum-in-u-s/.

83. "National Lawyers Guild National Immigration Project," *Foundation Search*, accessed December 31, 2018, www.foundationsearch.org.

84. "On Watch," *op. cit.*

85. Ibid.

86. Ibid.

87. "Agency Revenue by Government Donor 2016: UNHCR" *United Nations System: Chief Executive Board for Coordination*, accessed December 5, 2018, https://www.unsceb.org/content/FS-D00-01?agency=UNHCR.

88. "Agency Revenue by Government Donor2016: UNICEF," *United Nations System: Chief Executive Board for Coordination*, accessed December 5, 2018, https://www.unsceb.org/content/FS-D00-01?agency=UNICEF.

89. Ben Marquis, "Report: Migrant Caravan Members Pushed Women, Children to Front of Line To Avoid Tear Gas," *Conservative Tribune*, November 26, 2018, accessed November 28,

2018, https://www.westernjournal.com/ct/report-migrant-caravan-members-pushed-women-children-front-line-avoid-tear-gas/.

90. Naaz Modan, "CAIR Chapter Reps to Join National Faith Leaders at San Diego Border Action in Support of Asylum Seekers," *CAIR*, December 7, 2018, accessed December 8, 2018, https://www.cair.com/cair_chapter_reps_to_join_national_faith_leaders_at_san_diego_bord er_action_in_support_of_asylum_seekers.

91. "American Friends Service Committee (AFSC)," *Discover the Networks*, December 12, 2018, accessed December 12, 2018, https://www.discoverthenetworks.org/organizations/american-friends-service-committee-afsc/.

92. Melanie Arter, "DHS Predicts 1 Million Illegal Aliens Will Try to Cross the Border This Year," *CNS News*, March 6, 2019, accessed March 10, 2019, https://www.cnsnews.com/news/article/melanie-arter/dhs-predicts-one-million-illegal-aliens-will-try-cross-border-year.

93. J.R. Nyquist and Dr. Anca-Maria Cernea, "Russian Strategy and Europe's Refugee Crisis," *Center for Security Policy*, May 29, 2018, accessed June 5, 2018, https://www.centerforsecuritypolicy.org/wp-content/uploads/2018/05/Russia_Refugee_05-28-18.pdf.

94. Ian Drury, "Four out of five migrants are NOT from Syria: EU figures expose the 'lie' that the majority of refugees are fleeing war zone," *U.K. Daily Mail*, September 18, 2015, accessed June 5, 2018, https://www.dailymail.co.uk/news/article-3240010/Number-refugees-arriving-Europe-soars-85-year-just-one-five-war-torn-Syria.html.

95. Valerie Hudson, "Europe's Man Problem: Migrants to Europe skew heavily male—and that's dangerous," *Politico*, January 05, 2016, accessed June 5, 2018, https://www.politico.com/magazine/story/2016/01/europe-refugees-migrant-crisis-men-213500.

96. "How Close Was Merkel to the Communist System?" *Spiegel Online*, May 14, 2013, accessed June 5, 2018, http://www.spiegel.de/international/germany/new-book-suggests-angela-merkel-was-closer-to-communism-than-thought-a-899768.html.

97. "Definition of Terms: Alien," *Department of Homeland Security*, March 16, 2018, accessed November 10, 2018, https://www.dhs.gov/immigration-statistics/data-standards-and-definitions/definition-terms.

98. "Alien," *Dictionary.com*, accessed December 12, 2017, http://www.dictionary.com/browse/alien.

99. Matthew O'Brien, Spencer Raley and Jack Martin, "The Fiscal Burden of Illegal Aliens on U.S. Taxpayers," *Federation for American Immigration Reform*, 2017, accessed July 12 2018, http://www.fairus.org/sites/default/files/2017-09/Fiscal-Burden-of-Illegal-Immigration-2017.pdf.

100. Steven A. Camarota and Karen Zeigler, "63% of Non-Citizen Households Access Welfare Programs Compared to 35% of native households," Center for Immigration Studies, December 2, 2018, accessed December 2, 2018, https://www.cis.org/Report/63-NonCitizen-Households-Access-Welfare-Programs.

101. "English Language Learners in Public Schools," *op. cit.*

102. Matthew O'Brien and Spencer Raley, "The Fiscal Cost of Resettling Refugees in the United States," *Federation for American Immigration Reform*, February 5, 2018, accessed August 2, 2018, https://www.fairus.org/issue/legal-immigration/fiscal-cost-resettling-refugees-united-states.

103. Steven A. Camarota, Karen Zeigler, and Jason Richwine, "Births to Legal and Illegal Immigrants in the U.S.," *Center for Immigration Studies*, October 9, 2018, accessed

November 12, 2018, https://www.cis.org/Report/Births-Legal-and-Illegal-Immigrants-US.

104. Lukas Mikelionis, Griff Jenkins, "One-third of migrants in caravan are being treated for health issues, Tijuana health official says," *Fox News*, November 29, 2018, accessed November 30, 2018, https://www.foxnews.com/world/caravan-migrants-suffer-from-respiratory-infections-tuberculosis-chickenpox-other-health-issues-tijuana-government-says.

105. James Simpson, "How an Obama Administration Policy is Destroying Lives," *Accuracy in Media*, October 16, 2014, accessed July 12, 2018, https://www.aim.org/aim-column/how-an-obama-administration-policy-is-destroying-lives/#comments.

106. Bryan Nelson, "Outbreak of mysterious polio-like disease plagues residents in 22 states," *Mother Nature Network*, October 16, 2018, accessed November 12, 2018, https://www.mnn.com/health/fitness-well-being/stories/outbreak-mysterious-polio-disease-plagues-residents-22-states.

107. Judy Stone, "Chagas: An Emerging Infectious Disease Threat In U.S.," *Forbes*, October 1, 2016, accessed November 5, 2018, https://www.forbes.com/sites/judystone/2015/10/01/chagas-an-emerging-infectious-disease-threat-in-u-s/#4cabe8a16530.

108. "Chagas Disease Spreading to US, Death Rate Higher Than Expected," *Nutrition Review*, May 19, 2017, August 12, 2018, https://nutritionreview.org/2017/05/death-rate-from-chagas-disease-higher-than-expected/.

109. "Kissing Bugs and Chagas Disease in the United States," *Texas A&M Veterinary Medicine and Biomedical Sciences*, 2018, accessed November 5, 2018, https://kissingbug.tamu.edu/.

110. Stone, *op. cit.*

111. "Fiscal Year 2018 ICE Enforcement and Removal Operations Report," *U.S. Immigration and Customs Enforcement*, accessed December 20, 2018, https://www.ice.gov/doclib/about/offices/ero/pdf/eroFY2018Report.pdf.

112. "Alien Incarceration Report: Fiscal Year 2018, Quarter 1," *U.S. Departments of Homeland Security, & Justice*, June 6, 2018, accessed July 12, 2018, https://www.justice.gov/opa/press-release/file/1069281/download.

113. "Texas Criminal Illegal Alien Data," *Texas Department of Public Safety*, December 5, 2018, accessed December 6, 2018, https://www.dps.texas.gov/administration/crime_records/pages/txCriminalAlienStatistics.htm.

114. CRIMINAL ALIEN STATISTICS: Information on Incarcerations, Arrests, Costs and Removals," *Government Accountability Office*, July 2018, accessed November 17, 2018, https://www.gao.gov/assets/700/693162.pdf.

115. Daryl R. Fischer, Ph.D., "PRISONERS IN ARIZONA: A Profile of the Inmate Population," *ARIZONA PROSECUTING ATTORNEYS' ADVISORY COUNCIL*, March 2010, accessed July 12, 2018, http://apaac.az.gov/images/stories/prisoners_in_arizona-033010.pdf, p. 54.

116. John R. Lott, "Undocumented Immigrants, U.S. Citizens, and Convicted Criminals in Arizona," Crime Prevention Research Center, February 18, 2018, accessed November 12, 2018, https://papers.ssrn.com/sol3/papers.cfm?abstract_id=3099992.

117. "Criminal Alien Statistics," *op cit.*

118. Stephen Dinan, "'Sanctuary' refuses to take blame after triple homicide, says ICE responsible for illegal immigrant," *The Washington Times*, November 9, 2018, accessed November 10, 2018, https://www.washingtontimes.com/news/2018/nov/9/ice-illegal-immigrant-sanctuary-charged-3-murders/.

119. Andrea Estes and Maria Cramer, "ICE agent was in courthouse. Did judge and others help man flee?" *Boston Globe*, December 2, 2018, accessed December 4, 2018, https://www.bostonglobe.com/metro/2018/12/01/newton-judge-role-reportedly-examined-after-immigrant-evades-ice/Mshdn3gllPZhVA7mZ9fa3M/story.html?camp=breakingnews:newsletter.

120. John Binder, "Americans to Court: Stop Giving Taxpayer Money to Illegal Alien Accused of Killing Mollie Tibbetts," *Breitbart*, October 16, 2018, accessed October 20, 2018, https://www.breitbart.com/politics/2018/10/16/americans-to-court-stop-giving-taxpayer-money-to-illegal-alien-accused-of-killing-mollie-tibbetts/.

121. "Demographics of Immigrants in the United States Illegally," *ProCon.org*, August 19, 2014, accessed December 12, 2017, https://immigration.procon.org/view.resource.php?resourceID=000845.

122. "Statistical Portrait of the Foreign-born Population in the United States, 2015," *Pew Research Center* tabulations of 2015 American Community Survey (1% IPUMS), May 3, 2017, accessed December 12, 2017, http://www.pewhispanic.org/2017/05/03/facts-on-u-s-immigrants-current-data/.

123. "Table 41D. Aliens Removed by Criminal Status and Region and Country of Nationality: Fiscal Years 2007 to 2016," *Department of Homeland Security, Yearbook of Immigration Statistics,* November 30, 2017, accessed December 12, 2017, https://www.dhs.gov/immigration-statistics.

124. *Ibid.*

125. "Table 3. Persons Obtaining Lawful Permanent Resident Status by Region and Country of Birth: Fiscal Years 2007 to 2016," *Department of Homeland Security, Yearbook of Immigration Statistics,* July 18, 2017, accessed December 12, 2017, https://www.dhs.gov/immigration-statistics/yearbook/2016.

126. Criminal Alien Statistics, *op. cit.*

127. Declaring a National Emergency Concerning the Southern Border of the United States, *Federal Register*, 20 February 2019, https://www.federalregister.gov/documents/2019/02/20/2019-03011/declaring-a-national-emergency-concerning-the-southern-border-of-the-united-states

128. "NEW REPORT ON REPLACEMENT MIGRATION ISSUED BY UN POPULATION DIVISION," *United Nations*, March 17, 2000, accessed November 12, 2018, https://www.un.org/press/en/2000/20000317.dev2234.doc.html.

129. Douglas O. Linder, "Testimony of Alger Hiss before the House Committee on Un-American Activities" *Famous Trials*, August 5, 1948, accessed December 29, 2017, http://www.famous-trials.com/algerhiss/655-8-5testimony.

130. James S. Sutterlin, "The Founding of the United Nations : an Interview with Alger Hiss," *United Nations Dag Hammarskjöld Library*, 1990, accessed March 4, 2018, http://dag.un.org/handle/11176/89612.

131. William F. Jasper, Global Tyranny ... Step by Step: The United Nations and the Emerging New World Order (Appleton, Wisconsin: Western Islands, 1992), 48.

132. *Ibid.*, 36.

133. *Ibid.*, 45.

134. *Ibid.*, 48.

135. Robert D. Novak, "BETRAYAL AT YALTA," *Washington Post*, August 18, 1997, accessed March 5, 2018, https://www.washingtonpost.com/archive/opinions/1997/08/18/betrayal-at-yalta/eb3e17d5-d685-4867-9c66-90efcf875c5b.

136. Jasper, *op. cit.*, 48.

137. "Secrets, Lies and Atomic Spies: Alger Hiss," *NOVA Online*, January 2002, accessed March 5, 2018, http://www.pbs.org/wgbh/nova/venona/dece_hiss.html.

138. "SI congratulates António Guterres on nomination as UN Secretary-General," *Socialist International*, October 6, 2016, accessed March 11, 2018, http://www.socialistinternational.org/viewArticle.cfm?ArticleID=2476.

139. Juliana Geran, "The Many Ways the U.N. Serves the USSR," *Heritage Foundation*, May 3, 1984, accessed December 29, 2017, http://www.heritage.org/homeland-security/report/the-many-ways-the-un-serves-the-ussr.

140. Jasper, *op. cit.*, 16.

141. Jasper, *op. cit.*, 17.

142. "This Day in History, January 13, 1950: Soviets boycott United Nations Security Council," *History*, accessed March 6, 2018, https://www.history.com/this-day-in-history/soviets-boycott-united-nations-security-council.

143. There goes Taipei, *Life*, November 5, 1971, accessed March 12, 2018, https://books.google.com/books?id=FkAEAAAAMBAJ&printsec=frontcover&dq=there+g oes+taipei+life+magazine&hl=en&sa=X&ved=0ahUKEwiewpaR7efZAhXK2lMKHZ3NCDs Q6AEIKTAA#v=onepage&q&f=false.

144. "12th Annual Immigration Law and Policy Conference," *Migration Policy Institute*, October 29, 2015, accessed March 5, 2018, https://www.migrationpolicy.org/events/12th-annual-immigration-law-and-policy-conference. See also: "Keynote Address: H.E. António Guterres – 2015 Immigration Law and Policy Conference," *Vimeo*, October 29, 2015, accessed March 5, 2018, https://vimeo.com/144524105.

145. Marc Thiessen, "How ISIS Smuggles Terrorists Among Syrian Refugees," *Newsweek*, April 27, 2016, accessed March 5, 2018, http://www.newsweek.com/how-isis-smuggles-terrorists-among-syrian-refugees-453039. Also see: Ann Corcoran, "Note to Antonio Guterres! Terrorists do use refugees as cover to get into Europe," *Refugee Resettlement Watch*, November 10, 2015, accessed March 5, 2018, https://refugeeresettlementwatch.wordpress.com/2015/11/10/note-to-antonio-guterres-terrorists-do-use-refugees-as-cover-to-get-into-europe/.

146. "UNHCR Statistical Yearbook 2016," *UNHCR*, February 2018, accessed March 5, 2018, p. 87, http://www.unhcr.org/en-us/statistics/country/5a8ee0387/unhcr-statistical-yearbook-2016-16th-edition.html.

147. Lara Jakes, "U.N. Refugee Chief: Western Leaders Stir Up 'Hatred for the Stranger, for the Immigrant'," *Foreign Policy*, March 15, 2016, accessed October 10, 2018, https://foreignpolicy.com/2016/03/15/u-n-refugee-chief-western-leaders-stir-up-hatred-for-the-stranger-for-the-immigrant/.

148. Rebecca Kaplan, "Hillary Clinton: U.S. should take 65,000 Syrian refugees," *CBS News: Face the Nation*, September 20, 2015, accessed August 18, 2018, https://www.cbsnews.com/news/hillary-clinton-u-s-should-take-65000-syrian-refugees/.

149. "The Vancouver Action Plan: 64 Recommendations for National Action", *Habitat, UN Conference on Human Settlements*, May 31 to June 11, 1976, accessed May 21, 2015, http://www.un-documents.net/van-plan.htm.

150. "Vancouver Plan of Action, Recommendation A.4 More equitable distribution," *Habitat, UN Conference on Human Settlements*, May 31 to June 11, 1976, accessed, May 21, 2015, http://habitat.igc.org/vancouver/vp-a.htm.

151. *Ibid.*

152. Ibid.

153. "Recommendations from the Vancouver Plan of Action, June 1976, Section D, Land," *Habitat, UN Conference on Human Settlements*, May 31 to June 11, 1976, accessed May 21, 2015, http://habitat.igc.org/vancouver/vp-d.htm.

154. See: http://www.climaterefugees.com/Home.html.

155. "GLOBAL COMPACT FOR SAFE, ORDERLY AND REGULAR MIGRATION," *United Nations*, July 11, 2018, accessed September 5, 2018, https://www.un.org/pga/72/wp-content/uploads/sites/51/2018/07/migration.pdf.

156. "Resolution adopted by the General Assembly on 19 September 2016 71/1. New York Declaration for Refugees and Migrants," *United Nations*, October 3, 2016, accessed October 5, 2018, http://www.un.org/en/ga/search/view_doc.asp?symbol=A/RES/71/1.

157. Michele Blood, "Criticism of Migration Could Become a Criminal Offense' Under UN's Global Pact," *Lifezette*, December 2, 2018, accessed December 4, 2018, https://www.lifezette.com/2018/12/criticism-of-migration-could-become-a-criminal-offense-under-u-n-s-global-pact/.

158. "Merkel admits that UN Global Compact on Migration is binding," *Free West Media*, December 17, 2018, accessed December 20, 2018, http://freewestmedia.com/2018/12/17/merkel-admits-that-un-global-compact-on-migration-is-binding/?fbclid=IwAR3qjTy7_5xx6B7WqRQ5vJGBcxBcYcfMCPVEyUF7I0gi2nphyBx3-6PQsSw.

159. Hege Storhaug, *Islam: Europe Invaded, America Warned*, Amazon Digital Services LLC, November 8, 2018, https://www.amazon.com/gp/product/B07KBXWP5D/ref=dbs_a_def_rwt_hsch_vapi_taft_p1_i0.

160. Bruce Bawer, "Targeting Hege Storhaug: Norway's government and "civil society" have now made it clear – they're out to get her," *FrontPage Magazine*, January 8, 2019, accessed January 8, 2019, https://www.frontpagemag.com/fpm/272477/targeting-hege-storhaug-bruce-bawer.

161. Sarah Mervosh, "Minneapolis, tackling housing crisis and inequity, votes to end single-family zoning," *SF Gate*, December 13, 2018, accessed December 13, 2018, https://www.sfgate.com/g00/news/article/Minneapolis-Tackling-Housing-Crisis-and-13463911.php.

162. David Bacon, "Should Labor Defend Undocumented Workers?" *Democratic Left*. Fall 2009, 14, https://d3n8a8pro7vhmx.cloudfront.net/dsausa/pages/265/attachments/original/1357940816/Fall_2009.pdf?1357940816.

163. John Krueger, "Ted Kennedy asks aid for Viet refugees," *Stars and Stripes*, May 10, 1966, accessed August 22, 2018, https://www.stripes.com/news/ted-kennedy-asks-aid-for-viet-refugees-1.15229.

164. "Refugee Act," *SenseAgent Dictionary*, accessed November 12, 2018, http://dictionary.sensagent.com/Refugee_Act/en-en/.

165. "Refugee Act of 1980," *National Archives Foundation*, accessed August 22, 2018, https://www.archivesfoundation.org/documents/refugee-act-1980/.

166. "Agency Revenue by Government Donor," *United Nations System Chief Executives Board for Coordination*, accessed December 28, 2017, https://www.unsceb.org/content/FS-D00-01?agency=UNHCR.

167. Organization of Islamic Cooperation (OIC) website: https://www.oic-oci.org/home/?lan=en

168. "CAIR and the Foreign Agents Registration Act," *Center for Security Policy*, March 1, 2010, accessed June 3, 2015, http://www.centerforsecuritypolicy.org/2010/03/01/cair-and-the-foreign-agents-registration-act/, p. 5.

169. "The Reception and Placement Program," *U.S. Department of State,* accessed August 12, 2018, https://www.state.gov/j/prm/ra/receptionplacement/index.htm.

170. "FY 2019 Notice of Funding Opportunity for Reception and Placement Program," *Bureau of Population, Refugees, and Migration*, March 15, 2018, accessed August 16, 2018, https://www.state.gov/j/prm/funding/fy2019/279289.htm.

171. Rowan Scarborough, "Obama vetting procedures allowed Iraqi terrorists into U.S.; Trump wants tougher system," *Washington Times*, January 31, 2017, accessed August 10, 2018, https://www.washingtontimes.com/news/2017/jan/31/obama-refugee-vetting-procedure-enabled-iraqi-terr/.

172. Melanie Arter, "FBI Director Admits U.S. Will Have No Basis to Vet Some Syrian Refugees," *CNS News*, October 21, 2015, accessed October 12, 2018, https://www.cnsnews.com/news/article/melanie-hunter/fbi-director-admits-us-will-have-no-basis-vet-some-syrian-refugees.

173. Niki Nicastro McCuistion, "Pros and Cons of Middle East Refugees Coming to America," *McCuistion*, May 8, 2016, accessed August 22, 2018, http://www.frtv.org/2016/05/pros-and-cons-of-middle-east-refugees-coming-to-america/.

174. "DHS Knew Illegal Aliens Falsely Claimed 'Credible Fear' to Stay in U.S.," *Judicial Watch*, November 23, 2015, accessed August 23, 2018, https://www.judicialwatch.org/blog/2015/11/dhs-knew-illegal-aliens-falsely-claimed-credible-fear-to-stay-in-u-s/.

175. "Potentially Ineligible Individuals Have Been Granted U.S. Citizenship Because of Incomplete Fingerprint Records," *Department of Homeland Security, Office of Inspector General*, September 8, 2016, accessed August 23, 2018, https://www.oig.dhs.gov/assets/Mgmt/2016/OIG-16-130-Sep16.pdf.

176. Cristina Marcos, "Internal memo: Refugee program vulnerable to fraud," *The Hill*, September 22, 2016, accessed September 7, 2018, https://thehill.com/policy/national-security/297359-ice-memo-refugee-program-vulnerable-to-fraud.

177. Paul Nachman, "Jan Ting: A U.S. Senate Candidate Who Doesn't Need Enlightenment on Immigration," September 16, 2006, accessed November 5, 2017, https://vdare.com/posts/jan-ting-a-u-s-senate-candidate-who-doesn-t-need-enlightenment-on-immigration.

178. Mary Doetsch, "Failures In Refugee Vetting Process Lead To Criminal Activity In Our Hometowns," *Daily Caller*, August 27, 2018, accessed October 5, 2018, https://dailycaller.com/2018/08/27/failures-in-refugee-vetting/.

179. Ibid.

180. Ann Corcoran, "State Department: Possibly tens of thousands of Somalis in the US illegally," *Refugee Resettlement Watch*, November 12, 2008, accessed November 10, 2018, https://refugeeresettlementwatch.wordpress.com/2008/11/12/state-department-possibly-tens-of-thousands-of-somalis-in-the-us-illegally/.

181. S Brandt, "Housing board grants rent relief to tenants on extended absences," *Star Tribune*, September 29, 2016, accessed August 5, 2017, http://www.startribune.com/housing-board-grants-rent-relief-to-tenants-on-extended-absences/395300741/.

182. Charles Thaddeus Fillinger, "A Decade of Policy Failure: The Impact of Mass Refugee Fraud on the U.S. Immigration System," *ILW.com*, July 30, 2018, accessed September 12, 2018, http://ilw.com/articles/Policy-Paper-A-Decade-of-Policy-Failure.

183. Mary Franson and Matt Dean, "Unacceptable foot-dragging at DHS on whistleblower claims," *StarTribune*, January 25, 2019, accessed March 8, 2019, http://www.startribune.com/unacceptable-foot-dragging-at-dhs-on-whistleblower-claims/504893362/.

184. Ann Corcoran, "Food Stamp Fraud," *Refugee Resettlement Watch*, accessed December 10, 2018, https://refugeeresettlementwatch.wordpress.com/?s=food+stamp+fraud.

185. EBTerrorism: How Fraud-Riddled SNAP Funds Terrorism, Fails at Enforcement, Wastes Taxpayer Money, *Government Accountability Institute*, October 23, 2018, accessed November 12, 2018, http://g-a-i.org/wp-content/uploads/2018/10/2018_GAI_SNAP_FRAUD_TERROR.pdf.

186. Jan Ting, "'Dreamers' and Social Security fraud," *The Washington Times*, March 27, 2018, accessed July 5, 2018, https://www.washingtontimes.com/news/2018/mar/27/how-obama-sacrificed-social-security-benefits-to-m/.

187. Ibid.

188. Bob Segall, "Secret IRS policy hides identity theft from victims," *13 WTHR*, October 29, 2015, accessed June 12, 2018, https://www.wthr.com/article/secret-irs-policy-hides-identity-theft-victims.

189. Ibid.

190. Terence P. Jeffrey, "IRS Gave $14 Billion in Refundable Tax Credits to Illegals, *CNS News*, July 17, 2013, accessed July 25, 2018, https://www.cnsnews.com/commentary/terence-p-jeffrey/irs-gave-14-billion-refundable-tax-credits-illegals.

191. Ronald W. Mortensen, "DACA Recipients Should Make Restitution to Their American Identity Theft Victims," October 26, 2017, accessed November 12, 2018, https://cis.org/Mortensen/DACA-Recipients-Should-Make-Restitution-Their-American-Identity-Theft-Victims.

192. Ibid.

193. Steven A. Camarota, "The High Cost of Resettling Middle Eastern Refugees," *Center for Immigration Studies*, November 4, 2015, accessed December 29, 2017, https://cis.org/Report/High-Cost-Resettling-Middle-Eastern-Refugees.

194. "Refugees and Asylum," *U.S. Citizenship and Immigration Service*, November 12, 2015, accessed August 10, 2018, https://www.uscis.gov/humanitarian/refugees-asylum.

195. "Haitian Boat People," *ImmigrationToUnitedStates.org*, accessed August 22, 2018, http://www.immigrationtounitedstates.org/536-haitian-boat-people.html.

196. "Moments in U.S. Diplomatic History: A Flood of Cuban Migrants — The Mariel Boatlift, April-October 1980," *Association for Diplomatic Studies and Training*, April, 2015, accessed November 10, 2018, https://adst.org/2015/04/a-flood-of-cuban-migrants-the-mariel-boatlift-april-october-1980/.

197. "Cuban Haitian Entrant Program (CHEP)," *U.S. Citizenship and Immigration Services*, accessed August 22, 2018, https://www.uscis.gov/humanitarian/humanitarian-parole/cuban-haitian-entrant-program-chep.

198. ANNUAL REPORT TO CONGRESS," *Office of Refugee Resettlement*, Fiscal Year 2016, accessed August 12, 2018, https://www.acf.hhs.gov/sites/default/files/orr/arc_16_508.pdf, p. 57.

199. Marc R. Rosenblum and Faye Hipsman, "Normalization of Relations with Cuba May Portend Changes to U.S. Immigration Policy," *Migration Policy Institute*, January 13, 2015, accessed November 5, 2018, https://www.migrationpolicy.org/article/normalization-relations-cuba-may-portend-changes-us-immigration-policy.

200. "FACT SHEET: CHANGES TO PAROLE AND EXPEDITED REMOVAL POLICIES AFFECTING CUBAN NATIONALS," *U.S. Department of Homeland Security*, January 12, 2017, accessed

August 10, 2018,
https://www.dhs.gov/sites/default/files/publications/DHS%20Fact%20Sheet%20FINA
L.pdf.

201. "PROPOSED REFUGEE ADMISSIONS FOR FISCAL YEAR 2019: REPORT TO CONGRESS," *U.S. Departments of State, Health and Human Services and Homeland Security*, September 24, 2018, accessed October 15, 2018, https://www.state.gov/documents/organization/286401.pdf, p. 4.

202. "Pending Cases," *Executive Office for Immigration Review*, October 24, 2018, accessed November 12, 2018, https://www.justice.gov/eoir/page/file/1060836/download.

203. "Fact Sheet: Asylum in the United States," *American Immigration Council*, May 14, 2018, accessed July 12, 2018, https://www.americanimmigrationcouncil.org/research/asylum-united-states.

204. "Asylum: Additional Actions Needed to Assess and Address Fraud Risks," *Government Accountability Office*, December 2, 2015, accessed August 28, 2018, https://www.gao.gov/products/GAO-16-50.

205. Jim Seida, "Feds Raid California 'Maternity Hotels' for Birth Tourists," *NBC News*, March 3, 2015, accessed November 20, 2018, https://www.nbcnews.com/news/us-news/feds-raid-l-maternity-hotel-birth-tourists-n315996.

206. David North, Just How Does an Anchor Baby Anchor the Illegal Alien Parent? *Center for Immigration Studies*, January 16, 2011, accessed November 12, 2018, https://cis.org/North/Just-How-Does-Anchor-Baby-Anchor-Illegal-Alien-Parent.

207. "Heartland Alliance International, LLC," Form 990, Return of Organization Exempt From Income Tax, 2017, *IRS*, April 17, 2018, accessed May 17, 2018, https://pdf.guidestar.org/PDF_Images/2017/300/739/2017-300739799-0f0465fa-9.pdf.

208. Daniel Horowitz, "3 reasons why the media's 'walls won't work to stop drugs' argument is wrong," *Conservative Review*, January 14, 2019, accessed January 14, 2019, https://www.conservativereview.com/news/3-reasons-why-the-medias-walls-wont-work-to-stop-drugs-argument-is-wrong/.

209. "Fact Sheet: Unaccompanied Alien Children, *ACF*, accessed December 12, 2018, https://www.acf.hhs.gov/sites/default/files/orr/orr_fact_sheet_on_unaccompanied_alien_childrens_services_0.pdf.

210. Cyrus Mehta, "Obama's Paradoxical Deportation Policies," *The Insightful Immigration Blog*, August 7, 2014, accessed November 12, 2018, http://blog.cyrusmehta.com/2014/04/obamas-paradoxical-deportation-policies.html.

211. Aaron Terrazas, "Salvadoran Immigrants in the United States," *Migration Policy Institute*, January 5, 2010, accessed November 12, 2018, https://www.migrationpolicy.org/article/salvadoran-immigrants-united-states/.

212. Jessica Vaughan, "Eroding the Law and Diverting Taxpayer Resources," *Center for Immigration Studies*, April 23, 2015, accessed May 10, 2015, http://cis.org/Testimony/Vaughan-Senate-Unaccompanied-Minors-042315.

213. "Temporary Protected Status: Overview and Current Issues", *Congressional Research Service*, October 10, 2018, accessed November 12, 2018, https://www.everycrsreport.com/files/20181010_RS20844_9fda549df539d8fcfb32f381133838fbb08cc46d.pdf.

214. Daniel Horowitz, "End the diversity visa lottery TODAY," *Conservative Review*, November 1, 2017, accessed August 12, 2018, https://www.conservativereview.com/news/end-the-diversity-visa-lottery-today/.

215. Vaughan, *op. cit.*

216. 45 CFR 400.2 - Definitions, https://www.law.cornell.edu/cfr/text/45/400.2.

217. Kirk Petersen, "Not a Beat Skipped," *The Living Church*, August 21, 2018, accessed September 29, 2018, https://livingchurch.org/2018/08/21/not-a-beat-skipped/.

218. "ANNUAL REPORT TO CONGRESS: Office of Refugee Resettlement, Fiscal Year 2016," *Administration for Children and Families*, June 14, 2018, accessed August 12, 2018, https://www.acf.hhs.gov/sites/default/files/orr/arc_16_508.pdf, p. 26.

219. "PROPOSED REFUGEE ADMISSIONS FOR FISCAL YEAR 2019," *U.S. Departments of State, Homeland Security and Health and Human Services*, accessed October 30, 2018, https://www.state.gov/documents/organization/286401.pdf, pp. 30-31.

220. Matthew O'Brien and Spencer Raley, "The Fiscal Cost of Resettling Refugees in the United States," *FAIR*, February 5, 2018, accessed August 16, 2018, https://www.fairus.org/issue/legal-immigration/fiscal-cost-resettling-refugees-united-states.

221. "The U.S. Refugee Admissions Program," *Refugee Council USA*, June 24, 2015, accessed August 22, 2018, p. 34.

222. Cordelia Zars, Peter Biello, Natasha Haverty & Jack Rodolico, "Eight Years Waiting for a Home: Public Housing Assistance in NH," *NHPR*, August 4, 2016, accessed August 22, 2018, http://www.nhpr.org/post/eight-years-waiting-home-public-housing-assistance-nh#stream/0.

223. "John Ogonowski and Doug Bereuter Farmer-to-Farmer Program," *USAID*, April 13, 2016, accessed August 16, 2018, https://www.usaid.gov/what-we-do/agriculture-and-food-security/supporting-agricultural-capacity-development/john-ogonowski.

224. USASpending.gov.

225. Ibid.

226. Ibid.

227. Ibid.

228. "Catholic Charities, 2018" *USASpending.gov*, accessed August 16, 2018.

229. "Southwest Border Migration FY2018," *U.S. Customs and Border Protection*, August 8, 2018, accessed August 15, 2018, https://www.cbp.gov/newsroom/stats/sw-border-migration.

230. Ion Mihai Pacepa, "The Secret Roots of Liberation Theology," *National Review*, April 23, 2015, accessed May 15, 2015, http://www.nationalreview.com/article/417383/secret-roots-liberation-theology-ion-mihai-pacepa.

231. Mark D. Tooley, "World Council of Churches: The KGB Connection," *FrontPage Magazine*, March 31, 2010, accessed May 5, 2015, http://www.frontpagemag.com/2010/mark-d-tooley/world-council-of-churches-the-kgb-connection/.

232. Ann Corcoran, *Refugee Resettlement and the Hijra to America (Civilization Jihad Reader Series) (Volume 2)*, Washington: Center for Security Policy, 2015, http://www.amazon.com/Refugee-Resettlement-America-Civilization-Reader/dp/1508820708.

233. "National Council of Churches," *DiscoverTheNetworks.com*, accessed May 10, 2015, http://www.discoverthenetworks.org/printgroupProfile.asp?grpid=6916.

234. "Some Frequently Asked Questions About The National Council of Churches and the Elian Gonzalez Case: How did the NCC become involved in the Elian Gonzalez case?" *NCCUSA.org*, accessed May 12, 2015, http://www.ncccusa.org/news/faq.html#qone.

235. "Muslims Building Bridges of Interfaith Among the Community," *Muslim American Magazine and Media*, December 31, 2014, accessed October 10, 2018, http://www.muslimamerican.com/building-bridges-of-interfaith/.

236. "'Bridge-Building' to Nowhere," *Center for Security Policy*, November 23, 2015, accessed October 15, 2018, https://www.centerforsecuritypolicy.org/2015/11/23/e-book-release-bridge-building-to-nowhere/.

237. "Quentin Young: The Quentin Young, Barack Obama Relationship", *Keywiki.org*, February 13, 2015, accessed May 12, 2015, http://keywiki.org/Quentin_Young#The_Quentin_Young.2C_Barack_Obama_relationship.

238. "The Catholic Charities Network," *Catholic Charities USA*, 2018, accessed January 14, 2018. https://catholiccharitiesusa.org/network.

239. Matthew Vadum, "Left-Wing Radicalism in the Church: CCHD and ACORN" *Human Events*, October 26, 2009, accessed May 2, 2015, http://humanevents.com/2009/10/26/leftwing-radicalism-in-the-church-cchd-and-acorn/.

240. Author unknown, "A Commentary on the Industrial Areas Foundation", *CatholicCulture.org*, accessed May 15, 2015, http://www.catholicculture.org/culture/library/view.cfm?id=2885.

241. "Catholic Social Teaching, *JusticeforImmigrants.org*, accessed May 2, 2015, http://www.justiceforimmigrants.org/social-teachings.shtml.

242. "Abstract: Chicago Religious Task Force on Central America Records, 1982-1992," *Wisconsin Historical Society*, accessed April 20, 2015, http://digital.library.wisc.edu/1711.dl/wiarchives.uw-whs-m93153.

243. "Mission and Values," *HIAS*, accessed November 12, 2018, https://www.hias.org/mission-and-values.

244. Sharon Samber and Bill Swersey, "Jewish Leaders on HIAS-ADL Trip Witness Border Crisis Up Close," HIAS, Aug 24, 2018, accessed November 12, 2018, https://www.hias.org/blog/jewish-leaders-hias-adl-trip-witness-border-crisis-close.

245. "ZOA Praises ADL's Greenblatt for Condemning Choice of Sarsour for Anti-Semitism Panel," *ZOA*, November 21, 2017, accessed July 12, 2018, https://zoa.org/2017/11/10377118-zoa-praises-adls-greenblatt-for-condemning-choice-of-sarsour-for-anti-semitism-panel/.

246. Paul Sperry, "To Russia With Love?" *WND*, May 19, 2000, accessed August 12, 2018, https://www.wnd.com/2000/05/7246/.

247. Form 990 - Return of Organization Exempt From Income Tax - 2016, *Internal Revenue Service*, September 21, 2017, accessed March 5, 2018, http://www.guidestar.org/FinDocuments/2016/135/633/2016-135633307-0e71bcd0-9.pdf.

248. Melanie Nezer, "Resettlement at Risk: Meeting Emerging Challenges to Refugee Resettlement in Local Communities," *HIAS.org*, February 2013, accessed May 5, 2015, http://www.hias.org/sites/default/files/resettlement_at_risk_1.pdf.

249. Scott Walker, "Guidestar Drops SPLC's Fake 'Hate Group' Label," *Capital Research Center*, June 26, 2017, accessed July 28, 2018, https://capitalresearch.org/article/guidestar-drops-splcs-fake-hate-group-label/.

250. James Simpson, "Rutland: How a Mayor Conspired in Secret to Resettle Syrians in Small Vermont Town," *Breitbart.com*, June 9, 2016, accessed October 12, 2018, https://www.breitbart.com/national-security/2016/06/09/emails-reveal-mayor-conspired-secret-resettle-syrians-town/.

251. Lola Duffort, "Author sees plot in refugee resettlement," *Rutland Herald*, May 25, 2016, accessed October 12, 2018, https://www.rutlandherald.com/news/author-sees-plot-in-refugee-resettlement/article_c0d7a657-b048-5f9f-b032-ff137d980a1d.html.

252. Kathleen Phalen Tomaselli, "Hate groups seen infiltrating Rutland," *Rutland Herald,* June 2, 2016, accessed October 12, 2018, https://www.rutlandherald.com/news/hate-groups-seen-infiltrating-rutland/article_39b29565-9061-5b90-ba5e-7e06691a27c8.html.

253. "Office of Inspector General Semiannual Report to the Congress, October 1, 2015 - March 31, 2016," *U.S. Agency for International Development,* March 31, 2016, accessed November 5, 2018, https://oig.usaid.gov/sites/default/files/2018-06/sarc_03312016.pdf, pp. 41-42.

254. "OIG Semiannual Report to the Congress: April 1, 2016 - September 30, 2016," *U.S. Agency for International Development,* September 30, 2016, accessed November 5, 2018, https://oig.usaid.gov/sites/default/files/2018-06/sarc_093016.pdf, p. 28.

255. This can be found at the website, https://worldrelief.org/welcoming-the-stranger.

256. Michael Patrick Leahy, "Source: Claims of Financial Mismanagement, Fraud, and Harassment at Lutheran Immigration and Refugee Service Spark External Investigation," *Breitbart News,* November 11, 2017, accessed August 8, 2018, https://www.breitbart.com/politics/2017/11/11/source-claims-financial-mismanagement-fraud-harassment-lutheran-immigration-refugee-service-spark-external-investigation/.

257. "People: Linda Hartke," *Center for Migration Studies,* accessed November 5, 2018, http://cmsny.org/people/linda-hartke/.

258. "Non-Lutheran, Michelle Obama adviser to lead Lutheran Immigration and Refugee Service (LIRS)," *AlphaNewsMN,* March 5, 2019, accessed March 6, 2019, https://alphanewsmn.com/non-lutheran-michelle-obama-adviser-to-lead-lutheran-immigration-and-refugee-service-lirs/.

259. "2016 Return of Organization Exempt from Income Taxes: Lutheran Immigration and Refugee Service," *IRS Form 990,* August 14, 2017, accessed August 16, 2018, https://pdf.guidestar.org/PDF_Images/2016/132/574/2016-132574854-0e638bdd-9.pdf.

260. "Central American Minors Program," USCRI, 2014, accessed May 10, 2015, http://www.refugees.org/our-work/refugee-resettlement/central-american-minors-program.html

261. "Eskinder Negash Appointed Chief Executive Officer of U.S. Committee for Refugees and Immigrants," *U.S. Committee for Refugees and Immigrants,* April 2018, accessed April 2, 2019, https://refugees.org/news/eskinder-negash-appointed-ceo/.

262. "Executive Profile: Eskinder Negash," *Bloomberg,* accessed September 5, 2018, https://www.bloomberg.com/research/stocks/private/person.asp?personId=11313430&privcapId=6877563.

263. "U.S. Committee for Refugees and Immigrants, Inc. Return of Organization Exempt from Income Tax 2016," *IRS Form* 990, July 11, 2017, accessed June 2, 2018, https://pdf.guidestar.org/PDF_Images/2016/131/878/2016-131878704-0e57e9c9-9.pdf.

264. Michael Patrick Leahy, "Mysterious Retirement of Lavinia Limon at U.S. Committee for Refugees and Immigrants Raises Questions About Federal Program," *Breitbart News,* January 19, 2018, accessed August 12, 2018, https://www.breitbart.com/politics/2018/01/19/mysterious-retirement-of-lavinia-limon-at-us-committee-for-refugees-and-immigrants-raises-questions-about-federal-program/.

265. "Affiliate Directory," *Department of State, Bureau of Population, Refugees, and Migration, Office of Admissions - Refugee Processing Center,* December 13, 2016, accessed August 20, 2018,

https://travel.state.gov/content/dam/visas/SIVs/Public%20Affiliate%20Directory.pdf. Pp. 9, 10, 27.

266. "Camba, Inc.: Form 990, Return of Organization Exempt From Taxation 2016," *Internal Revenue Service*, July 10, 2017, accessed August 18, 2018, https://pdf.guidestar.org/PDF_Images/2016/112/480/2016-112480339-0e54379d-9.pdf.

267. "U.S. Refugee Admissions and Resettlement Program," *U.S. Department of State*, April 1, 2001, accessed August 16, 2018, https://2001-2009.state.gov/g/prm/rls/fs/2001/3401.htm.

268. "Immigration and Refugee Services of America," *Bloomberg*, accessed August 15, 2018, https://www.bloomberg.com/research/stocks/private/snapshot.asp?privcapId=6877563

269. Melanie Nezer, RESETTLEMENT AT RISK: Meeting Emerging Challenges to Refugee Resettlement in Local Communities, *HIAS*, February 2013, accessed August 10, 2018, http://www.hias.org/sites/default/files/resettlement_at_risk_1.pdf.

270. Melanie Nezer, "Immigration and Refugee Services of America," *Frosina.org*, December 8, 2008, accessed August 16, 2018, https://www.frosina.org/immigration-and-refugee-services-of-america-irsa/.

271. "Eskinder Negash," *U.S. Committee for Refugees and Immigrants*, accessed August 12, 2018, http://refugees.org/about/.

272. "U.S. Committee for Refugees and Immigrants: Form 990, Return of Organization Exempt from Income Tax," *Internal Revenue Service*, July 11, 2017, accessed August 22, 2018, https://www.guidestar.org/FinDocuments/2016/131/878/2016-131878704-0e57e9c9-9.pdf.

273. Petersen, "Not a Beat Skipped," *op. cit.*

274. Ibid.

275. Ibid.

276. "About," *InterAction*, accessed November 205, 2018, https://www.interaction.org/about/board-directors.

277. "Champions of Change," *The Obama White House*," accessed December 5, 2018, https://obamawhitehouse.archives.gov/champions/american-diaspora-communities/tsehaye-teferra.

278. Southwest Key Programs, Inc., Form 990, Return of Organization Exempt From Taxation, 2016" *Internal Revenue Service*, March 31, 2017, accessed August 13, 2018, https://pdf.guidestar.org/PDF_Images/2016/742/481/2016-742481167-0dfdab8c-9.pdf.

279. Ibid.

280. "Refugee Resettlement Programs", *Department of Health and Human Services, Office of Refugee Resettlement*, accessed May 25, 2015, http://www.acf.hhs.gov/programs/orr/programs/.

281. Mica Rosenberg, "Exclusive: Dozens of refugee resettlement offices to close as Trump downsizes program," *Reuters*, February 14, 2018, accessed November 12, 2018, https://www.reuters.com/article/us-usa-immigration-refugees-exclusive-idUSKCN1FY1EJ.

282. "Affiliate Directory," *op. cit.*

283. "2016 Annual Report," *Catholic Charities of Onondaga County*, 2017, accessed August 15, 2018, https://issuu.com/catholiccharitiesofonondagacounty/docs/catholic_charities_annual_report, pp. 12-25.

284. James Simpson phone call to CCOC, August 15, 2018.

285. Marnie Eisenstadt, "Trump policies stop the flow of refugees to Syracuse, once a resettlement magnet," *Syracuse.com*, August 1, 2018, accessed August 12, 2018, https://www.syracuse.com/news/index.ssf/2018/08/trump_policies_stop_the_flow_of_r efugees_to_syracuse_once_a_resettlement_magnet.html.

286. *Ibid.*

287. "Catholic Charities of the Roman Catholic Diocese of Syracuse, NY, Form 990, Return of Organization Exempt From Taxation, 2016" *Internal Revenue Service*, June 27, 2017, accessed August 13, 2018, https://www.guidestar.org/FinDocuments/2016/150/532/2016-150532085-0e569ebb-9.pdf.

288. "HIAS Pennsylvania: Form 990, Return of Organization Exempt From Taxation," *Internal Revenue Service*, August 14, 2017, accessed August 18, 2018, https://pdf.guidestar.org/PDF_Images/2016/231/405/2016-231405597-0e00b181-9.pdf.

289. "Annual Report 2015-2016," *HIAS Pennsylvania*, accessed August 12, 2018, https://hiaspa.org/sites/hiaspa.org/files/attachments/hias_pa_2016_annual_report_digi tal.pdf.

290. "MIRA," *Massachusetts Immigrant and Refugee Advocacy Coalition*, accessed August 17, 2018, http://miracoalition.org/about-us.

291. "About ACCESS," *ACCESS*, accessed August 15, 2018, https://www.accesscommunity.org/about.

292. "Arab Community Center for Economic and Social Services, Form 990, Return of Organization Exempt From Taxation," *Internal Revenue Service*, March 9, 2017, accessed May 14, 2018, https://www.guidestar.org/FinDocuments/2016/237/444/2016-237444497-0e2c6053-9.pdf.

293. "Return of Organization Exempt from Taxation 2016: Association of Africans Living in Vermont, Inc." *IRS Form 990*, September 14, 2017, accessed November 20, 2018, https://pdf.guidestar.org/PDF_Images/2016/030/371/2016-030371003-0e741a3a-9.pdf.

294. "Return of Organization Exempt from Taxation 2016: Somali Bantu Community of Greater Houston, Inc." *IRS Form 990*, August 12, 2016, accessed November 20, 2018, https://pdf.guidestar.org/PDF_Images/2015/300/345/2015-300345773-0d165169-9.pdf.

295. James Simpson, "Judge To Tennessee: You'll Take Refugees Whether You Want To Or Not," *The Federalist*, April 2, 2018, accessed July 10, 2018, http://thefederalist.com/2018/04/02/judge-tennessee-youll-take-refugees-whether-want-not/.

296. "HIAS," *Foundation Search*, August 15, 2018.

297. "Church World Service," *Foundation Search*, August 15, 2018.

298. "Grants Database, Church World Service," *Open Society Foundations*, 2017, accessed August 12, 2018, https://www.opensocietyfoundations.org/grants-database/?filter_keyword=church%20world%20service#OR2016-32152.

299. "International Rescue Committee," *Foundation Search*, August 15, 2018.

300. "Grants Database, International Rescue Committee," *Open Society Foundations*, 2016, accessed August 12, 2018, https://www.opensocietyfoundations.org/grants-database/?filter_keyword=international%20rescue%20committee#OR2016-2.

301. "International Rescue Committee, Form 990, Return of Organization Exempt From Taxation," *Internal Revenue Service*, May 15, 2017, accessed August 18, 2018,

https://www.guidestar.org/FinDocuments/2016/135/660/2016-135660870-0e1beb3d-9.pdf

302. Tim Murray, "The Islamic Tipping Point: Does recognizing an extreme predicament make one an 'extremist'?" *Humanist Perspectives*, Issue 183, Winter 2012-2103, accessed May 30, 2018, https://www.humanistperspectives.org/issue183/05-FEATURE_TippingPoint-06_pp_12-15.pdf.

303. James Simpson, "Reds Exploiting Blacks: the Roots of Black Lives Matter," *Accuracy in Media*, January 12, 2016, accessed April 20, 2018, https://www.aim.org/special-report/reds-exploiting-blacks-the-roots-of-black-lives-matter/.

304. "Democratic Socialists of America," *KeyWiki.org*, July 6, 2018, accessed December 12, 2018, https://keywiki.org/Democratic_Socialists_of_America.

305. Kelly McGowan, "Abshir Omar, Somali refugee, joins Des Moines City Council race," *Des Moines Register*, June 28, 2017, accessed April 10, 2018, https://www.desmoinesregister.com/story/news/2017/06/28/abshir-omar-somali-refugee-joins-des-moines-city-council-race/435970001/.

306. "Alleged bin Laden tape a call to arms," *CNN*, February 14, 2003, accessed April 20, 2018, http://www.cnn.com/2003/WORLD/meast/02/11/sprj.irq.wrap/.

307. John Guandolo (President, Understanding the Threat), interviewed by James Simpson, phone, April 9, 2018. See also: https://www.understandingthethreat.com/marxists-jihadis-assault-truth/.

308. Andrew McCarthy, "Suborned in the U.S.A." *CBS News*, July 31. 2009, accessed December 26, 2017, https://www.cbsnews.com/news/suborned-in-the-usa/.

309. Alan Jones and Mary Fanning, "CLUES UNLOCK OBAMA I.D. MYSTERY: FBI Soviet spy files, SUBUD cult, and a dead body," *The American Report*, August 19, 2015, accessed November 5, 2018, http://theamericanreport.org/2015/08/19/clues-unlock-obama-id/.

310. Chris Cillizza, "Obama Announces 'Organizing for America'," *The Washington Post*, January 17, 2009, accessed March 16, 2017, http://voices.washingtonpost.com/thefix/white-house/obama-announces-organizing-for.html.

311. See, for example, LinkedIn entry for OFA Executive Director, Katie Hogan. "Katie Hogan," *LinkedIn*, accessed January 25, 2018, https://www.linkedin.com/in/katie-hogan-8716339/.

312. "Organizing for Action Committee," *Center for Responsive Politics*, accessed March 15, 2017, https://www.opensecrets.org/obama/ofa.php.

313. "Organizing for Action: Form 990, Return of Organization Exempt From Taxation 2016," *Internal Revenue Service*, September 15, 2017, accessed August 18, 2018, https://pdf.guidestar.org/PDF_Images/2016/461/827/2016-461827418-0e86e469-90.pdf.

314. Wolfgang Saxon, "Sol Goldman, Major Real-Estate Investor, Dies," *New York Times*, October 19, 1987, accessed March 16, 2017, http://www.nytimes.com/1987/10/19/obituaries/sol-goldman-major-real-estate-investor-dies.html.

315. https://www.croptrust.org/wp-content/uploads/2016/04/Crop-Trust-final-signed-FS-2015.pdf.

316. "Crop Trust to conserve plant diversity: Rich and poor nations sign on to save seeds worldwide," *Food and Agricultural Organization of the United Nations*, October 21, 2004, accessed March 16, 2017, http://www.fao.org/newsroom/en/news/2004/51211/index.html.

317. http://patrioticmillionaires.org/about/.

318. http://patrioticmillionaires.org/who-we-are/.

319. Peter Abraham, "Tom Werner a finalist to be MLB commissioner," *Boston Globe*, August 6, 2014, accessed March 16, 2017, https://www.bostonglobe.com/sports/2014/08/05/red-sox-chairman-tom-werner-among-finalists-mlb-commissioner/FoB9AFTReXppTYATC1wmFJ/story.html.

320. "Kenneth R. Levine," *Bloomberg*, accessed March 16, 2017, http://www.bloomberg.com/research/stocks/private/person.asp?personId=12505770&privcapId=7702248.

321. "#309 Jon Stryker, - Real Time Net Worth," *Forbes*, November 16, 2018, accessed November 16, 2018, https://www.forbes.com/profile/jon-stryker/.

322. "Who We Are," *Arcus Foundation*, accessed March 16, 2017, http://www.arcusfoundation.org/who-we-are/.

323. "#134 Ronda Stryker, - Real Time Net Worth," *Forbes*, November 16, 2018, accessed November 16, 2018, https://www.forbes.com/profile/ronda-stryker/.

324. Julie Mack, "Ronda Stryker's sense of passion and purpose make her recipient of 2013 YWCA Lifetime Woman of Achievement award," *Michigan Live*, May 19, 2013, accessed March 16, 2017, http://www.mlive.com/news/kalamazoo/index.ssf/2013/05/ronda_stryker_to_receive_ywca.html.

325. "#701 Pat Stryker, - Real Time Net Worth," *Forbes*, November 16, 2018, accessed November 16, 2018, https://www.forbes.com/profile/pat-stryker/?list=rtb.

326. Adam Schrager and Rob Witwer, *The Blueprint: How the Democrats Won Colorado (and Why Republicans Everywhere Should Care)* (Golden, Colorado: Fulcrum Publishing, 2010).

327. Matthew Vadum, "The Left's 'Blueprint' for Perpetual Power," *Capital Research Center*, May 23, 2010, https://capitalresearch.org/article/the-lefts-blueprint-for-perpetual-power/.

328. "Organizing for Action: Who's Giving to Obama-Linked Nonprofit?," *OpenSecrets.org*, June 17, 2014, accessed March 16, 2017, https://www.opensecrets.org/news/2014/06/organizing-for-action-whos-giving-to-obama-linked-nonprofit/#woods.

329. Aaron Klein, "Obama's Organizing for Action Partners with Soros-Linked 'Indivisible' to Disrupt Trump's Agenda," *Breitbart*, February 19, 2017, accessed May 15, 2018, http://www.breitbart.com/big-government/2017/02/19/obamas-organizing-action-partners-soros-linked-indivisible-disrupt-trumps-agenda/.

330. Elana Schor and Rachael Bade, "Inside the protest movement that has Republicans reeling," *Politico*, February 10, 2017, accessed May 14, 2018, https://www.politico.com/story/2017/02/protest-movement-republicans-234863.

331. Ibid.

332. "CAIR's Awad: In support of the Hamas Movement," *Investigative Project on Terrorism*, March 22, 1994, accessed April 10, 2018, https://www.investigativeproject.org/223/cairs-awad-in-support-of-the-hamas-movement.

333. *Ibid.* Also see: James Simpson, "Who Was Yasser Arafat?" *Front Page Magazine*, March 2005, accessed May 23, 2018, http://www.discoverthenetworks.org/Articles/Who%20Was%20Arafat.htm.

334. "An Explanatory Memorandum: From the Archives of the Muslim Brotherhood in America," *Center for Security Policy*, May 25, 2013, accessed December 29, 2017, https://www.centerforsecuritypolicy.org/2013/05/25/an-explanatory-memorandum-from-the-archives-of-the-muslim-brotherhood-in-america/.

335. "A Note from the Executive Director," *CAIR Chicago 2018 Annual Report*, accessed April 2, 2019, https://drive.google.com/file/d/1OK68mOlk39aj7HOvTymUVIVtAopZsbcE/view.

336. Naaz Modan, "CAIR Files Broad Challenge to Watchlisting System, Including TSA's Quiet Skies Program," *CAIR*, August 08, 2018, accessed November 12, 2018, https://www.cair.com/cair_files_broad_challenge_to_watchlisting_system_including_tsa_s_quiet_skies_program.

337. Christopher Holton, "Arkansas Legislature Takes a Stand Against CAIR," *Center for Security Policy*, February 19, 2019, accessed March 1, 2019, https://www.centerforsecuritypolicy.org/2019/02/19/arkansas-legislature-takes-a-stand-against-cair/.

338. Matthew Boyle, "McCaul Meets With Islamic Leader Who Says U.S. Muslims Are 'Above Law Of Land'," *Breitbart News*, February 18, 2015, accessed November 10, 2018, https://www.breitbart.com/politics/2015/02/18/mccaul-writes-on-photo-with-islamic-leader-who-says-u-s-muslims-above-law/.

339. Jordan Schachtel, "Report: Facebook and Twitter consult with terror-tied CAIR over who gets banned from platforms," *Conservative Review*, January 8, 2019, accessed January 9, 2019 https://www.conservativereview.com/news/report-facebook-and-twitter-consult-with-terror-tied-cair-over-who-gets-banned-from-platforms/.

340. "DFL candidate Ilhan Omar explains marital history in statement," *Fox 9*, August 18, 2016, accessed November 12, 2018, http://www.fox9.com/news/dlf-candidate-ilhan-omar-clarifies-marital-history-in-response-to-questions.

341. James Simpson, "Ilhan Omar: Poster Child for the Red-Green Axis," *PJ Media*, February 27, 2019, accessed February 27, 2019, https://pjmedia.com/homeland-security/ilhan-omar-poster-child-for-the-red-green-axis/.

342. Center for Security Policy, "Star Spangled Shariah: The Rise of America's First Muslim Brotherhood Political Party" (Center for Security Press, 2015), 14.

343. Notes from Muslim American Society-Islamic Circle of North America Annual Chicago Convention, December 2012.

344. "U.S. Government Lifts Ban on Tariq Ramadan," a blog entry posted by Tariq Ramadan to his website at http://tariqramadan.com/blog/2010/01/20/usgovernment-lifts-ban-on-tariq-ramadan/, accessed 17 March 2014.

345. "Genesis," *op. cit.*

346. Ibid.

347. "An Explanatory Memorandum on the General Strategic Goals for the Group in North America," as published by the Center for Security Policy. PDF available online at http://www.centerforsecuritypolicy.org/wpcontent/uploads/2014/05/Explanatory_Memoradum.pdf.

348. United States Council of Muslim Organizations, "USCMO Inauguration - June 10, 2014," http://www.uscmo.org/inauguration/, accessed 19 June 2014.

349. The Muslim Link, "New Umbrella Group Holds Inaugural Banquet," http://www.muslimlinkpaper.com/community-news/community-news/3679-newumbrella-group-holds-inaugural-banquet.html, accessed 19 June 2014.

350. Center for Security Policy, "Star Spangled Shariah: The Rise of America's First Muslim Brotherhood Political Party" (Center for Security Press, 2015), 34.

351. Muslim Link Paper, "New Umbrella Group Holds Inaugural Banquet," http://www.muslimlinkpaper.com/community-news/community-news/3679-newumbrella-group-holds-inaugural-banquet.html, accessed 23 June 2014.

352. Helping Hand for Relief and Development, https://www.hhrd.org/ and Helping Hand USA https://www.facebook.com/helpinghandusa, accessed 23 June 2014.

353. ICNA Relief USA, http://icnarelief.org/site2/index.php, accessed 24 June 2014.

354. Guidance Residential, http://www.guidanceresidential.com/about/, accessed 24 June 2014.

355. Center for Security Policy, "Star Spangled Shariah: The Rise of America's First Muslim Brotherhood Political Party" (Center for Security Press, 2015), 16.

356. "Genesis of the US Council of Muslim Organizations Muslim Brotherhood Political Party," *Center for Security Policy*, May 19, 2014, accessed March 5, 2019, https://www.centerforsecuritypolicy.org/2014/05/19/genesis-of-the-us-council-of-muslim-organizations-muslim-brotherhood-political-party/.

357. Washington Report on Middle East Affairs, "SEVEN MUSLIM ORGANIZATIONS ESTABLISH NATIONAL COORDINATION COUNCIL," March 1998, http://www.wrmea.org/wrmea-archives/192-washington-reportarchives-1994-1999/march-1998/11744-muslim-american-activism-seven-muslimorganizations-establish-national-coordination-council.html

358. "Milestones by Syed Qutb Shaheed," *HolyBooks.com*, January 17, 2015, accessed April 17, 2019, https://www.holybooks.com/milestones-by-syed-qutb-shaheed/.

359. Center for Security Policy, "Star Spangled Shariah: The Rise of America's First Muslim Brotherhood Political Party" (Center for Security Press, 2015), 63.

360. Ibid.

361. Center for Security Policy, "Star Spangled Shariah: The Rise of America's First Muslim Brotherhood Political Party" (Center for Security Press, 2015), 69.

362. Center for Security Policy, "Star Spangled Shariah: The Rise of America's First Muslim Brotherhood Political Party" (Center for Security Press, 2015), 84.

363. Alex VanNess, "Who Is Linda Sarsour's Mentor?," *The Clarion Project*, August 22, 2018, accessed March 1, 2019, https://clarionproject.org/linda-sarsour-mentor/.

364. Janon Fisher, "Children on New Mexico compound were forced to wash body of dead boy as punishment, prosecutors say," *New York Daily News*, August 27, 2018, accessed March 1, 2019, https://www.nydailynews.com/news/crime/ny-news-abdul-ghani-imam-siraj-wahhaj-new-mexico-abdul-ghani-20180827-story.html.

365. US Council of Muslim Organizations, "USCMO Leadership Meet With DHS Officials," 5 August 2014, accessed 27 January 2015, https://uscmo.org/index.php/2014/08/05/uscmo-leadership-meet-with-dhs-officials/.

366. Ibid.

367. Center for Security Policy, "Star Spangled Shariah: The Rise of America's First Muslim Brotherhood Political Party" (Center for Security Press, 2015), 120.

368. US Council of Muslim Organizations, "National Advocacy Day," http://www.uscmo.org/national-advocacy-day/, accessed 28 January 2015

369. *Star Spangled Shariah: The Rise of America's First Muslim Brotherhood Party*, Washington, DC: Center for Security Policy Press, September 15, 2015, https://www.centerforsecuritypolicy.org/2015/09/15/book-release-star-spangled-shariah-the-rise-of-americas-first-muslim-brotherhood-party/.

370. Center for Security Policy, "Star Spangled Shariah: The Rise of America's First Muslim Brotherhood Political Party" (Center for Security Press, 2015), 120.

371. "The Rise of American Muslim Changemakers: Political Organizing in the Trump Era," *CAIR, JetPac, MPower Change*, accessed April 2, 2019, https://d3n8a8pro7vhmx.cloudfront.net/cairhq/pages/15965/attachments/original/1542317535/Rise_of_the_changemakers_2.pdf?1542317535.

James Simpson

372. Clare M. Lopez, "Photos Surface Revealing 2017 'Closed-Door' Meeting Between Rep. Ilhan Omar and Turkish President Erdogan," *PJ Media*, April 11, 2019, accessed April 16, 2019, https://pjmedia.com/homeland-security/photos-surface-revealing-2017-closed-door-meeting-between-rep-ilhan-omar-and-turkish-president-erdogan/.

373. Lopez, *op. cit.*

374. Ibid.

375. Center for Security Policy, "Star Spangled Shariah: The Rise of America's First Muslim Brotherhood Political Party" (Center for Security Press, 2015), 121.

376. NATIONAL STRATEGY FOR COUNTERTERRORISM, The White House, June 28, 2011, accessed April 18, 2019, https://obamawhitehouse.archives.gov/sites/default/files/counterterrorism_strategy.pdf.

377. Jerome P. Bjelopera, "Countering Violent Extremism in the United States," *Congressional Research Service*, February 19, 2014, accessed December 5, 2018, https://fas.org/sgp/crs/homesec/R42553.pdf.

378. T.J. Greaney, "'Fusion center' data draws fire over assertions," *Columbia Daily Tribune*, Mar 14, 2009, accessed November 12, 2018, https://www.columbiatribune.com/article/20090314/News/303149835.

379. Frank J. Gaffney, Jr. and Clare M. Lopez, 2016, *See No Shariah 'Countering Violent Extremism' and the Disarming of America's First Line of Defense*, Vol. 9, Civilization Jihad Reader Series, Washington, DC: Center for Security Policy Press, pp. 11-15.

380. "COUNTERING VIOLENT EXTREMISM: Actions Needed to Define Strategy and Assess Progress of Federal Efforts," *Government Accountability Office*, April 2017, accessed November 12, 2018, https://www.gao.gov/assets/690/683984.pdf, pp. 28-29.

381. Ibid.

382. Ibid. pp 29-32.

383. David M. Halbfinger and Ariel Hart, "Man Kills 5 Co-Workers at Plant and Himself," *New York Times*, July 9, 2003, accessed November 12, 2018, https://www.nytimes.com/2003/07/09/us/man-kills-5-co-workers-at-plant-and-himself.html.

384. Philip Haney & Art Moore, See Something, Say Nothing: A Homeland Security Officer Exposes the Government's Submission to Jihad," (Washington: WND Books, 2016).

385. "Fmr DHS Official Philip Haney: Deleted Records Tying Muslims to Terrorism Might Have Stopped Attacks," *Breitbart*, June 15, 2016, accessed March 24, 2018, http://www.breitbart.com/video/2016/06/15/fmr-dhs-official-philip-haney-deleted-records-tying-muslims-terrorism-might-stopped-attacks/.

386. John P. Roche, *The History and Impact of Marxist-Leninist Organizational Theory*, Cambridge: Institute for Foreign Policy Analysis, Inc., 1984, p. x.

387. "Explanatory Memorandum," *op. cit.*

388. Sergey Nechayev, "The Revolutionary Catechism," *Marxists.org*, accessed November 12, 2017, https://www.marxists.org/subject/anarchism/nechayev/catechism.htm.

389. Richard Cloward and Frances Fox Piven, "The Weight of the Poor; A Strategy to End Poverty," *The Nation*, May 2, 1966, accessed January 25, 2018, https://www.commondreams.org/news/2010/03/24/weight-poor-strategy-end-poverty.

390. Cloward-Piven Strategy (CPS), *Discover The Networks*, accessed June 24, 2018, https://www.discoverthenetworks.org/organizations/clowardpiven-strategy-cps.

391. Erik Randolph, "Modeling Potential Income and Welfare-Assistance Benefits in Illinois: Findings and Recommendations," *Illinois Policy Institute*, June 22, 2015, accessed August 12, 2018, https://nebula.wsimg.com/92d8ac7d5aaf3b2df9d4dfaaddcde435?AccessKeyId=EEB98E648E3097DCA50D&disposition=0&alloworigin=1.

392. Cloward and Piven, *op. cit.*

393. James Simpson, "Barack Obama and the Strategy of Manufactured Crisis," *American Thinker*, September 28, 2008, accessed July 15, 2018, https://www.americanthinker.com/articles/2008/09/barack_obama_and_the_strategy.html.

394. Edward Pinto, "From the American dream to bailout America: How the government loosened credit standards and led to the mortgage meltdown," *American Enterprise Institute*, accessed November 12, 2018, https://www.aei.org/wp-content/uploads/2014/10/pinto-bailout-america-timeline-government-mortgage-complex_1305029805.pdf.

395. James Simpson, "The Left's National Vote Fraud Strategy Exposed," *Accuracy in Media*, May 8, 2012, accessed July 12, 2018, https://www.aim.org/special-report/the-lefts-national-vote-fraud-strategy-exposed/.

396. Ibid.

397. Rahm Emanuel, " Rahm Emanuel on the Opportunities of Crisis," *YouTube*, November 19, 2008, accessed November 10, 2018, https://youtu.be/_mzcbXi1Tkk.

398. James Simpson, "Cloward Piven Government," *American Thinker*, November 23, 2009, accessed November 10, 2018, https://www.americanthinker.com/articles/2009/11/clowardpiven_government.html.

399. "Text of the 1951 Convention Relating to the Status of Refugees: Convention and Protocol Relating to the Status of Refugees," *United Nations*, July 28, 1951, http://www.unhcr.org/3b66c2aa10.pdf.

400. "Refugee," Immigration and Nationalities Act, section 101(a)(42).

401. Chan, Sucheng, "Cambodians in the United States: Refugees, Immigrants, American Ethnic Minority," Oxford Research Encyclopedia, September 2015, accessed April 1, 2018, http://americanhistory.oxfordre.com/view/10.1093/acrefore/9780199329175.001.0001/acrefore-9780199329175-e-317.

402. "Asylum and the Rights of Refugees," *International Justice Resource* Center, accessed August 22, 2018, https://ijrcenter.org/refugee-law/.

403. Facts about Discrimination in Federal Government Employment Based on Marital Status, Political Affiliation, Status as a Parent, Sexual Orientation, and Gender Identity, *EEOC*, accessed November 5, 2018, https://www.eeoc.gov/federal/otherprotections.cfm.

404. Kevin Daley, "Judge Stops Trump Asylum Ban as Migrant Caravan Nears," *Daily Signal*, November 20, 2018, accessed November 20, 2018, https://www.dailysignal.com/2018/11/20/judge-stops-trump-asylum-ban-as-migrant-caravan-nears/.

405. "Jewish Members of U.S. Congress: House of Representatives (1845 - Present)," *Jewish Virtual Library*, accessed March 12, 2019, https://www.jewishvirtuallibrary.org/jewish-representatives-in-the-united-states.

406. "Democrats change House rules to allow lawmakers to wear Muslim headwear," *Supreme Insider*, January 5, 2019, accessed April 2, 2019, https://www.supremeinsider.com/democrats-change-house-rules-to-allow-lawmakers-to-wear-muslim-headwear/.

407. Alinsky, Saul D. *Rules for Radicals: A Pragmatic Primer for Realistic Radicals*. Vintage Books ed. New York, NY: Vintage Books, 1989. 130.

408. Reese, Charlie. "An Interview With Lenin Through The Magic Of Historical Record." Orlando Sentinel. April 12, 1985. Accessed July 15, 2017. http://articles.orlandosentinel.com/1985-04-12/news/0290120030_1_lenin-morality-communist.

409. Kenez, Peter. *Cinema and Soviet Society: From the Revolution to the Death of Stalin*. London and New York: I.B. Tauris, 2001. 139.

410. Goode, Stephen. "Radical Leftovers." Insight on the News. November 22, 1999. Accessed July 14, 2017. https://www.questia.com/read/1G1-57800502/radical-leftovers.

411. Reese, Charlie. "An Interview With Lenin Through The Magic Of Historical Record." Orlando Sentinel. April 12, 1985. Accessed July 15, 2017. http://articles.orlandosentinel.com/1985-04-12/news/0290120030_1_lenin-morality-communist.

412. Rockefeller, Terry and Louis Massiah. "Interview with Angela Davis." Washington University Digital Gateway Texts. May 24, 1989. Accessed July 20, 2017. http://digital.wustl.edu/e/eii/eiiweb/dav5427.0115.036marc_record_interviewer_proce ss.html.

413. Buchanan, Patrick. The Death of the West: How Dying Populations and Immigrant Invasions Imperil Our Country and Civilization. New York, NY: St. Martin's Griffin, 2002, 80.

414. Marcuse, Herbert. "Repressive Tolerance." In Wolff, Robert Paul, Barrington Moore, Jr. and Herbert Marcuse, *A Critique of Pure Tolerance*. Boston, MA: Beacon Press, 1965. Accessed July 15, 2017. 117. http://www.marcuse.org/herbert/pubs/60spubs/1965MarcuseRepressiveToleranceEng 1969edOcr.pdf.

415. Marcuse, Herbert. "Repressive Tolerance." In Wolff, Robert Paul, Barrington Moore, Jr. and Herbert Marcuse, *A Critique of Pure Tolerance*. Boston, MA: Beacon Press, 1965. Accessed July 15, 2017. 119, 120. http://www.marcuse.org/herbert/pubs/60spubs/1965MarcuseRepressiveToleranceEng 1969edOcr.pdf.

416. Marcuse, Herbert. "Repressive Tolerance." In Wolff, Robert Paul, Barrington Moore, Jr. and Herbert Marcuse, *A Critique of Pure Tolerance*. Boston, MA: Beacon Press, 1965. Accessed July 15, 2017. 100, 101. http://www.marcuse.org/herbert/pubs/60spubs/1965MarcuseRepressiveToleranceEng 1969edOcr.pdf.

417. "About Us." In These Times. Accessed July 19, 2017. http://inthesetimes.com/about/.

418. "In Memory of Julian Bond (1940-2015)." Democratic Socialists of America. August 18, 2015. Accessed July 20, 2017, http://www.dsausa.org/julian_bond_dl.

419. Bond, Julian. "SNCC: What We Did." Monthly Review. October 2000. Accessed July 20, 2017, https://monthlyreview.org/2000/10/01/sncc-what-we-did/.

420. Simpson, James. "Southern Poverty Law Center: Institution of Weaponized Hate." *Social Contract*. Spring 2018. Accessed August 17, 2018, https://www.thesocialcontract.com/artman2/publish/tsc_28_3/tsc-28-3-simpson.shtml.

421. Stern, Sol. "The Campaign to Free Angela Davis and Ruchell Magee." The New York Times. March 8, 1998. Accessed July 20, 2017, http://www.nytimes.com/books/98/03/08/home/davis-campaign.html.

422. Rockefeller, Terry and Louis Massiah. "Interview with Angela Davis." Washington University Digital Gateway Texts. May 24, 1989. Accessed July 20, 2017,

http://digital.wustl.edu/e/eii/eiiweb/dav5427.0115.036marc_record_interviewer_process.html.

423. Davis, Angela. *If They Come in the Morning: Voices of Resistance*. Kindle Edition. London, New York: Verso: 2016, https://www.amazon.com/dp/0893880221/ref=rdr_ext_sb_ti_hist_1.

424. Tyler O'Neil, "Southern Poverty Law Center: 'Our Aim in Life Is to Destroy These Groups, Completely'," PJ Media, September 1, 2017, accessed August 12, 2018, https://pjmedia.com/trending/2017/09/01/southern-poverty-law-center-our-aim-in-life-is-to-destroy-these-groups-completely/.

425. Nolan, Lucas, "Report: Twitter Drops Far-Left SPLC as 'Safety Partner', *Breitbart*, 17 April 2019, https://www.breitbart.com/tech/2019/04/17/report-twitter-drops-far-left-splc-as-safety-partner/

426. James Simpson, "CAIR Shutting Down Free Speech," *Bombthrowers.com*, October 31, 2017, accessed November 12, 2018, https://www.bombthrowers.com/article/cair-shutting-down-free-speech/.

427. James Simpson, "Antifa And The SPLC Successfully Shut Down Four Anti-Islam Conferences," *Daily Caller*, April 12, 2018, accessed November 12, 2018, https://dailycaller.com/2018/04/12/anti-islam-events-wisconsin-minnesota-shut-down-antifa-splc/.

428. George Martin, "Woman's conviction in Austria for calling the Prophet Mohammed a paedophile did not breach her right to free speech, European Court of Human Rights rules," *U.K. Daily Mail*, October 25, 2018, accessed November 12, 2018, https://www.dailymail.co.uk/news/article-6316567/Woman-correctly-convicted-Austria-calling-Prophet-Mohammed-paedophile-ECHR-rules.html.

429. https://www.changetheterms.org/terms.

430. "Our Network," *Welcoming America*, accessed August 15, 2018, https://www.welcomingamerica.org/programs/our-network.

431. "Our Network", *Welcoming America*, accessed October 12, 2018, https://www.welcomingamerica.org/programs/our-network.

432. "Evangelical Leader: St. Cloud Times Article Distorts Scripture to Falsely Justify Refugee Resettlement," *Minnesota Sun*, September 17, 2018, accessed September 30, 2018, http://theminnesotasun.com/2018/09/17/evangelical-leader-st-cloud-times-article-distorts-scripture-to-falsely-justify-refugee-resettlement/.

433. Ibid.

434. Ibid.

435. Ashoka Fellow David Lubell, *Ashoka.org*, accessed December 5, 2018, https://www.ashoka.org/en-US/fellow/david-lubell.

436. Ashoka Fellow, *op. cit.*

437. Brian K. Ray, "Building the New American Community: Newcomer Integration and Inclusion Experiences in Non-Traditional Gateway Cities," *Migration Policy Institute*, 2004, accessed May 12, 2015, http://www.ncsl.org/Portals/1/documents/immig/BNAC_Report1204.pdf.

438. *Ibid*, ii.

439. Ashoka Fellow, *op. cit.*

440. Ibid.

441. Don Haney, "Backers drop drive to recall Fargo city commissioner," *KFGO*, May 12, 2017, accessed August 17, 2018, https://kfgo.com/news/articles/2017/may/12/backers-drop-petition-to-recall-fargo-city-commission/.

442. "Welcoming America," *Foundation Search*, August 16, 2018.

443. Stephen Dinan, "House votes in favor of illegal immigrant voting," *The Washington Times*, March 8, 2019, accessed March 8, 2019, https://www.washingtontimes.com/news/2019/mar/8/house-votes-favor-illegal-immigrant-voting/.

444. J. Christian Adams, "H.R. 1: Democrats Act to Strip State Powers Over Elections," *PJ Media*, January 10, 2019, accessed March 8, 2019, https://pjmedia.com/jchristianadams/h-r-1-democrats-act-to-strip-state-powers-over-elections/.

445. Ashley May, "Antifa protesters chant outside Fox's Tucker Carlson's home, break door," *USA Today*, November 6, 2018, accessed November 10, 2018, https://www.usatoday.com/story/news/politics/2018/11/08/mob-tucker-carlsons-home-antifa-break-door-chant-fox-host/1927868002/.

446. Allyson Chiu, "'They were threatening me and my family': Tucker Carlson's home targeted by protesters," *Washington Post*, November 8, 2018, accessed November 10, 2018, https://www.washingtonpost.com/nation/2018/11/08/they-were-threatening-me-my-family-tucker-carlsons-home-targeted-by-protesters/?utm_term=.fd750a195480.

INDEX

N

O

P

T

U

United Arab Emirates · 40
United Nations (UN) · 22, 33, 34, 35,
36, 37, 38, 39, 40, 41, 42, 44, 76,
101, 117, 119, 125
United Nations International
Children's Emergency Fund
(UNICEF) · 22
United States Council of Muslim
Organizations (USCMO) · 106, 107,
108, 109, 110
United Technologies · 88
United Way, The · 84, 88
USAID Foreign Assistance · 68
USSR (Union of Soviet Socialist
Republics) · 34, 35, 57, 146

V

Van Gogh, Theo · 11
Vancouver Plan of Action · 35
Vancouver, British Columbia · 35
Vanguard Charitable Foundation · 79
Vanguard Fund · 75
Variance Ventures · 101
Vera Institute of Justice · 14
Vietnam War · 18, 19, 122
Vignarajah, Krishanti O'Mara · 79
Virginia Council of Churches · 72
Volunteer Agencies (VOLAGs) · 11,
44, 59, 63, 66, 67, 68, 69, 70, 73,
75, 77, 78, 81, 82, 83, 84, 86, 87,
91, 92, 93, 94, 95, 96, 99

W

Wahhaj, Siraj · 108
Walz, Gov. Tim · 47

Welch's Grape Juice · 77
Welcoming America · 83, 92, 94, 95,
126, 127, 128, 129, 130, 131
Werner, Tom · 101
Western Union · 82
White, Harry Dexter · 34
Wilson, Pete · 94
Wilson-Fish · 91, 94, 95
Winkler, Jim · 75
Woman, Infants, and Children (WIC)
Special Supplemental Nutrition
Assistance · 65
Woods, Laure · 102
World Bank · 38
World Council of Churches · 72
World Relief Corporation of the
National Association of
Evangelicals (WRC) · 66, 68, 78, 79
World Trade Center bombing (1993)
· 108

Y

Yalta Conference · 34
Yemen · 61
Yiannopoulos, Milo · 134
Young, Quentin · 75
Youth Co-Op, Inc. · 81

Z

Zakat Foundation of America · 109

www.ingramcontent.com/pod-product-compliance
Lightning Source LLC
Chambersburg PA
CBHW020317290526
45785CB00007B/2822